DEFYING "THE PLAN"

DEFYING "THE PLAN"

Intimate Politics among Palestinian Women in Israel

—ᴍ—

KIM JEZABEL ZINNGREBE

INDIANA UNIVERSITY PRESS

This book is a publication of

Indiana University Press
Office of Scholarly Publishing
Herman B Wells Library 350
1320 East 10th Street
Bloomington, Indiana 47405 USA

iupress.org

Manufactured in the United States of America

First printing 2022

Cataloging information is available from the Library of Congress.

ISBN 978-0-253-06249-9 (hardback)
ISBN 978-0-253-06250-5 (paperback)
ISBN 978-0-253-06251-2 (e-book)

To Lilith, Veit, and Lovis

CONTENTS

ACKNOWLEDGMENTS

A GREAT NUMBER OF PEOPLE have inspired and supported the research and writing of this book—a process that in many ways started almost a decade ago. Since then, the manuscript has undergone many changes as I moved back and forth between Palestine, the United Kingdom, and Germany.

First and foremost, my gratitude goes to all the Palestinian women and men who supported this research and without whose participation, self-evidently, this book would never have been realized. Upon reflection, I have the privilege of being able to say that my fieldwork, from beginning to end, felt like one long, thrilling conversation with (mostly) women who were not only a pleasure to talk with but who, ultimately, opened up their personal lives and homes to me and who supported me and my research by sparing me their valuable time and thoughts. Even though you are far too many to be mentioned by name and many of you prefer not to have your names made public, please know that I appreciate that your sincere support is what drove this book from its initial development from a brief research idea discussed in an nongovernmental organization office in Haifa up until its final write-up as a book manuscript in a small mountain village near Frankfurt. The stories, support, and critical commentaries of my research participants constitute the very fabric of this book, and I am satisfied if I have managed to capture at least a part of the intimate and powerful politics of their daily lives as indigenous women living under Israeli occupation.

Fellow researchers, friends, supervisors, PhD examiners, and anonymous readers have read drafts and given their astute advice over the years—for that I am immensely grateful!

My PhD supervisors at SOAS University of London, were invaluable in preparing me for this book project. At the risk of exaggerating, I want to thank Ruba Salih for being the best supervisor I could have asked for. I hope her remarkable capacity for consistent support, constructive criticism, and motivation is reflected in this book. Her wit and sensitivity made all the stages of my journey as a young researcher a true pleasure. Laleh Khalili and Yair Wallach provided insightful and critical feedback throughout the development of my work, and I thank them for their encouragement and guidance during the years that led to the completion of my doctorate in 2017.

Parts of this book appeared in earlier publications. An earlier version of chapter 1 appeared in 2019 in volume 9 of the journal *Settler Colonial Studies*. A number of ideas and arguments made in chapter 1 and chapter 4 appeared in volume 112 of the journal *Feminist Review* in 2016. Some material of those chapters also appeared in 2015 in the volume *Contentious Politics in the Middle East* edited by Fawaz Gerges. Many thanks go to the editors and anonymous reviewers of these publications.

The encouragement and assistance of my dear friends Mary Haddad and Rahma Al-Sana were invaluable during my fieldwork, and I am very grateful to them for introducing me to their friends and relatives and for hosting and feeding me for months. I am also indebted to Minem Marouf not only for being a big-hearted and much-cherished friend, but also for always being available and keen to help whenever I bothered him with yet another question about life in Palestine (or life more generally). I thank Magdalena Suerbaum for her unrelenting engagement with and countless discussions about my research throughout the years, but, above all, for our extraordinary friendship.

My research benefited greatly from the conversations with my inspiring and brilliant PhD cohort at the Centre for Gender Studies at SOAS. I am particularly grateful to Nydia Swaby, Hila Amit, Akanksha Mehta, and Sabiha Allouche for continually sending me productive vibes of feminist solidarity from both near and afar and making me feel that my research was of importance and value. I would also like to thank Gina Heathcote and Nadje Al-Ali at the Centre for Gender Studies for their continuous support of both my research and me personally throughout the different stages of my PhD.

The research for this book was made possible by Evangelisches Studienwerk Villigst, which not only funded my PhD program and fieldwork but also demonstrated to me time and again that religious institutions *can* support and encourage critical political research. I have always felt embraced, fortunate, and completely contented among my fellow scholarship holders. Much to my initial surprise, it was within their circle that I had some of the most captivating and radical conversations about politics, sex, and religion.

At Indiana University Press, I wholeheartedly thank Jennika Baines for her unfailing enthusiasm for my book and her enduring flow of encouragement from the beginning. I also thank Sophia Hebert for her continuous support throughout the final stages and her kind understanding whenever I struggled to make a deadline. Moreover, I thank the immensely talented Raya Manaa for providing one of her gripping photographs for the book cover—no other image could be more suitable.

Finally, I thank my much beloved family, my partner, my three children, and my dogs, without whom this book would have been published years ago, but without whom my life would be rather dull. Their love means everything to me. Ultimately, my gratitude goes to everyone who looked after my kids so that I could complete writing this book (during a pandemic).

NOTE ON TRANSLITERATION AND TRANSLATION

IN THIS BOOK I LARGELY follow the system of Arabic transliteration as outlined in the guidelines of the *International Journal of Middle East Studies* (*IJMES*), except for words, names, and places that have standardized spellings in English like "Deir Yassin" or "Bedouin," I use Palestinian-Arabic names of places like "al-Naqab" (rather than "the Negev") and "Bi'r as-Sab'" (rather than "Beersheva") because of the political importance of displaying place names in their original form in the context of the Palestinian displacement. Diacritics are used only to mark the 'ayn and the *hamza* (except for initial hamza, which is dropped). Diverging from IJMES standard and in an attempt to better capture pronunciation, I have transcribed words in Al-Naqab Bedouin local dialect as I encountered them during my fieldwork. For Hebrew, I follow the Library of Congress transliteration system. In both languages, I privilege the colloquial over the literary spelling. All translations in the book are my own, except when specifically stated otherwise.

DEFYING "THE PLAN"

INTRODUCTION

"MY HOMELAND IS MY MOTHER'S WOMB": THE STORY OF THE RESEARCH

Even though this research has undergone considerable developments throughout the last years, its point of origin can be traced back to the afternoon of Wednesday, September 8, 2011. Back then, I—"the new German intern from London"—was waiting in a small, Spartan office of a Palestinian[1] feminist organization for my new boss, Huda,[2] a renowned feminist activist, founder, and director of the organization, to finish a telephone call so that I could find out about my upcoming work tasks. As Huda was known among her staff as "a real busy bee" and difficult to get hold of, I knew that it was likely that I would have to wait for a while. I made myself comfortable surveying the office decorations: a handful of cards and stickers in Hebrew, Arabic, and English were scattered over a small part of the wall. I could make out only one of the Hebrew stickers, which read "*saḥar be-beitsiot hu saḥar be-evarim*" (egg trade is organ trade). Pacing back and forth across the room, while babbling bouncily on her telephone in fluent Hebrew and playing with one of her big signature earrings, Huda winked at me from time to time to assure me that she was doing her best to finish the call as soon as possible. After the long-anticipated *lehitraot* (goodbye), I expected us to toss some broad ideas around together, considering that I was completely new to the subject of Palestinian women's rights in Israel.

Instead, Huda surprised me with a concrete proposal. "I think you should write a paper about citizenship," she said forthrightly, as if she had already made up her mind about it. I couldn't help but look off guard as her curious, smirking eyes searched my face for a reaction. "Citizenship?" I enquired. "Yes, *our* citizenship here in Israel," Huda responded. "I thought a lot about this with the demonstrations going on in Tel Aviv, you know. Where are *we*? Where are the Arabs? Shouldn't we be among the first to protest against social inequality?" Knowing Huda a little by now, I was sure that she already had some answers to these questions in mind. Nevertheless, it was clear that she was keen on hearing my opinion, as she continued, "You have studied the politics of this region; I'm sure you could make a very good contribution to our organization with a special report on this topic, no?"

My initial reactions to Huda's suggested research were mixed. I was struck by her enthusiasm and felt a little flattered by her compliments but at the outset, "citizenship" felt somewhat theoretical, almost technical, to me as a research topic. I was not really keen on researching anything that I considered too "political-science-y" so shortly after a rather disenchanting experience of studying the politics of the region at Oxford. Truth be told, I also felt ill-equipped, and embarrassed to admit that despite holding a degree in Middle Eastern studies, I really knew *nothing* about Palestinian women's actual lives in Israel. Therefore, it did not feel appropriate for me to "make sense" of their citizenship experiences. But Huda is a person to whom it is rather difficult to say "no," and so we agreed that I would work on questionnaires, interview feminist activists, and accompany social workers to what Huda and other members of staff of the organization referred to as "the field" (Palestinian villages in the northern Galilee). This way, I could also get to know Palestinians in rural areas, including women from poor socioeconomic backgrounds. Even though I was not aware of it at the time, I was in the midst of preparing my preliminary PhD research.

Palestinian women's active participation in both formal and informal conversations with me all over the country quickly came to be the main driving force behind my exploration. Women's associations with citizenship were frequently expressed in short phrases such as "simply a paper," "a lie," or "a painful reminder," and the conversations that followed expanded on the complex and often contradictory ways in which the women experienced being citizens and life in a settler colonialist state more generally. Even though their narratives were diverse, they shared expressions of "a lack of belonging" to the state and the perception of citizenship as a "hurtful reminder" of the *nakba*: the loss of family members, homes, land, and national identity, which, that was clear, was very much ongoing for them.[3]

What stood out from the beginning was the fact that, contrary to my initial perception, our discussions were far from theoretical or political in the conventional sense. Instead, our conversations quickly turned personal, often emotional, and frequently centered on intimate experiences casting the body as the key medium through which Palestinian women experienced daily life as indigenous women in a settler colonial state. Soon the stories that I encountered revealed clearly that, despite of its enormous impact on their daily and intimate lives, the women's experiences could not be explained by looking at citizenship alone. Strikingly, many women described a notion, which one of them aptly referred to as "the plan" of Palestinian women's lives in Israel: a plan that functions as a product of the interplay between settler colonialism and patriarchal forms of oppression and their intrinsic and reciprocal racial, class, and gender orders (Connell 2009, 127); and, in consequence, a plan that prescribes the ways in which Palestinian women are expected to lead their personal lives in Israel.

The research shift from citizenship to women's intimate politics was far from straightforward, mostly because of my initial struggles with the idea of writing about women's intimate lives. My hesitancy was mainly rooted in the fear of sensationalizing or exoticizing women, who had not only shared their personal stories with me but who had also opened up their homes and daily lives to me. Notwithstanding, the more I listened to my interviews again and revisited my field notes, the clearer it became that daily intimacies such as relationships, dress, the body, child bearing and rearing, sex, and marriage are inextricably bound up in—if not pivotal to—the question of what characterizes Palestinian women's lives in Israel. Notably, strategic importance was also ascribed to women's intimate politics by multiple players, including the Zionist state, family members, religious authorities, political leaders and (feminist) activists. It became unmistakable that if I were to continue, I could not *not* explore the relationship between Palestinian women's intimate politics—their bodies, sexuality, and love lives—and Zionist settler colonialism, Palestinian nationalism, land, and feminisms.

Deeply anchored and widely spread assumptions and expectations about Palestinian women's intimate politics have meant that a large number of women feel displaced, marginalized, discriminated against, or underrepresented by not only the State of Israel but also by political bodies and movements within Palestinian civil society, including the women's movement at times. During one of my talks with Huda, she expressed this common sentiment succinctly in Frantz Fanonian terms:

> It's like putting on a mask for each identity. When I'm demonstrating in Tel Aviv, I'm "Arab," on Land Day I have to be "nationalist," when I demonstrate for women, I'm a "feminist." I don't want to be in a place where I'm perceived as only one identity. Really, there is nothing that I can say about "this is what or who I belong to" and that's it. I belong to the people I love. If I have a homeland, my homeland is my mother's womb. I don't want to sound dramatic, but that's the only thing, the only place, that I can say that I truly belong to.

Rereading this conversation today, these lines stand out for me as they not only highlight the central role that intimacy plays in the political exclusion and marginalization of Palestinian women in Israel but also women's utilization of intimacy as a key medium through which to counter their subordination. Palestinian women's bodies—particularly their wombs with the exclusive ability to reproduce—are a strategic site of the struggle for power between Zionist and Palestinian forces. Palestinian women's bodies are the linchpin of women's intimate politics and the place into which both Zionist segregation and patriarchal control begin to launch. It is important to note that Palestinian women's bodies are also a key site for women's acts of defiance. By claiming her mother's womb as her homeland and the only place she "truly belongs," Huda effectively defies *the plan* on multiple levels. In the face of Zionist displacement, she reclaims a sense of belonging to a place that she cannot be dispossessed of. In addition, by claiming that her mother's womb is her only homeland, she flouts nationalist constructions of the homeland as a fixed territory.

Moreover, she defies the nationalist discourse of "land before honor," which in many parts of Palestinian society continues to prioritize national liberation over women's liberation. Huda thereby claims women's ownership over their bodies, as well as women's right to redraft their own notions of "home," "belonging," and "return." Huda's rhetoric defies nationalist and settler colonial discourses and practices that continue to conflate indigenous women's bodies and indigenous land by inverting and appropriating them on her own terms. By saying "I belong to the people I love," she emphasizes the power of affect and underscores the fact that love is indeed a political force to be reckoned with. At the heart of this book lies the argument that in a settler colonial context in which specific intimate politics are explicitly stigmatized, prohibited, and forcibly dissolved, while others are encouraged, indigenous women's quotidian reclamations over their intimate lives—their intimate politics—defy this plan and thereby destabilize and challenge both Zionist and patriarchal power and social orders.

PALESTINIAN WOMEN IN ISRAEL

Zionist Settler Colonialism

Any exploration of Palestinian women's lives in Israel today must consider Zionist settler colonialism as the framework in which their lives are lived every day. Settler colonialism is theorized here as a distinct type of colonialism that functions as an ongoing system of power—"a structure rather than an event," as the late anthropologist Patrick Wolfe reminds us (1994, 96)—via which a settler society aims to invade and settle on populated land. On the basis of its "logic of elimination" (Wolfe 2006, 390), settler colonialism entails the replacement of an indigenous population with an invasive settler society that normalizes its continuous occupation, expropriation, and exploitation of indigenous peoples, land, and resources. Resorting to Daiva Stasiulis and Nira Yuval-Davis, my research conceptualizes settler societies as "societies in which Europeans have settled, where their descendants have remained politically dominant over indigenous peoples, and where a heterogeneous society has developed in class, ethnic and racial terms" (Stasiulis and Davis 1995, 3).

Since the *Settler Colonial Studies* pioneering special issue "Past Is Present: Settler Colonialism in Palestine" was published in 2012,[4] an ever-growing body of scholarship has been investigating how Zionist settler colonialism has emerged in Palestine since the late nineteenth century as well as the manifold ways in which it manifests itself today. More recently, Yara Hawari, Sharri Plonski, and Elian Weizman have carried forward the study of the concrete contemporary forms of Zionist settler colonialism in their special issue "Settlers and Citizens: A Critical View of Israeli Society" (2018). With a particular focus on the everyday life, the articles of this issue shed light on how "the agents of settler colonial systems and states work endlessly to evolve and entrench themselves through both productive and coercive processes, in order to further sustain their dominance over the territory, capital, institutions and people, and at the same time eliminate even the memory of that which existed before them" (2018, 2). Such studies have also emphasized the interlocking nature of the forms of oppression produced by settler colonialism, such as racism, white supremacy, heteropatriarchy, militarism, and capitalism.

But what is particular about *Zionist* settler colonialism? Because the term *Zionism* captures a plethora of ideological strands, it is important to point out that Zionism will be referred to in this book as a movement for Jewish national self-determination in the form of a Jewish nation-state in *Eretz Israel* (the Land of Israel), which covers the areas of Mandatory Palestine along with southern Lebanon and Jordan.[5] In context of Palestinian citizens in Israel, a number of Zionist ideological discourses are important for the justification and legitimization of settler colonial practices that continue to take place at present. These discourses include the myth of *terra nullius* (barren or sparsely populated lands) for the *kibush ha-adamah* (conquest of the land) (Stasiulis and Yuval-Davis 1995). First uttered by Zionist Israel Zangwill in 1901, a Zionist narrative that became one of the most predominant was that, before the arrival of Jewish settlers, Palestine had essentially been a "land without people, for a people without land" (Graham-Brown 1990). This classic settler colonial construct of "the disappearing indigene" became increasingly important as the efforts of the *Yishuv* (the Jewish community in Palestine before the creation of the State of Israel) to conquer the land and labor market in Palestine intensified during the 1920s. Subsequently, Palestinians were targeted—and, as a consequence, racialized—along the lines of *where* they were rather than *who* they were (Wolfe 2002, 51). A deliberately widespread belief in an inferior Arab human quality fueled Zionist notions of the local population as merely another part of the landscape to be tamed. The logic of elimination of the indigenous population was integral to the Zionist settlers' paired goal of maximum land control and the eventual working of this land through self-sufficient *avodah ivrit* (Hebrew labor) or "conquest of labor."

Between 1947 and 1949, in an action known as the *nakba* (catastrophe), out of the one million Palestinians who formerly lived in what became the State of Israel (78 percent of the British Mandate), Zionist forces killed 15,000 people and forced more than 750,000 to abandon their homes. A minority of 160,000 Palestinians remained in their homeland, where many of them were forcibly displaced within the country. They were eventually assigned Israeli citizenship by the new state but their identification cards indicated their nationality as their religious affiliation and not their national one. Importantly, according to the identification cards, there were no Palestinians or atheists among Israel's citizens. In the legal and official jargon of the state, they appeared as *bney ha-miutim* (members of the minorities; note plural: as if there were other minorities apart from the Palestinians) (Pappé 2011, 24).

The alienation and marginalization of Palestinian citizens in Israel who are connected to a nation that stretches across multiple states yet remain "trapped within their homeland" has led to their special depiction as a "trapped minority" (Rabinowitz 2001, 64–85). The pivotal factor that forged the relationship between Palestinian citizens and the State of Israel, it is argued here, has been the usurpation of Palestinians and their alienation from their land. The paradoxical status of being both citizens in a formally liberal state and subjects under colonial rule (Robinson 2013, 3) persists today as Israel's land regime continues the expropriation of Palestinian land. Land allocation policies designed by the Israel Land Administration, in which the Jewish National Fund maintains a constitutional majority, consistently ignore the needs and historical rights of Palestinian communities. Although Palestinians comprise 20 percent of Israel's population today, numbering almost 1.7 million people—including Muslims (82 percent), Christians (9.5 percent), and Druze Palestinians (8.5 percent)—they own a mere 3.5 percent of available land.[6]

Even though the status of Palestinian citizens of Israel is that of a national, ethnic, linguistic, and religious minority according to international human rights law, the Palestinian minority is neither officially recognized as such in Israel's Declaration of Independence nor its Basic Laws. The absence of a written constitution that explicitly guarantees the right to equality for Palestinian citizens and Israel's continuing preferential treatment of Jews based on its self-proclamation as a Jewish democracy allows the government to carry out an arbitrary policy of "reasonable discrimination" against Palestinian citizens (Jabareen 2004).

A significant assault on the minority's rights is embodied in the Nationality and Entry Law, which was passed by the Knesset in 2003. Initially claimed to be a temporary measure, it has been renewed ever since. The law prohibits the granting of any residency or citizenship status to Palestinians from the 1967 Occupied Palestinian Territories who are married to Israeli citizens.[7] Officially intended to prevent Palestinians from abusing Israeli citizenship in order to support terrorist attacks on Israel, the law aims to preserve a clear Jewish majority by prohibiting Palestinian spouses from citizenship and permanent or temporary residency status in Israel, essentially obstructing family unification. To the same effect, the so-called loyalty oath bill, which successfully passed in 2010 after being initiated by right-wing foreign minister Avigdor Lieberman, obliges non-Jewish candidates for citizenship to swear loyalty to a "Jewish and democratic" state. Overall, these legislative measures prevent the return of Palestinians and maintain the superior role of Jewish nationality over Israeli citizenship as a status that defines the relationship between the state and individuals living in it.

Citizenship in a Jewish Democracy

Israel's self-definition as a "Jewish and democratic state" and the ongoing efforts made by Israeli state and society to maintain a Jewish superiority in the country contribute to a sociopolitical setting in which citizenship depends on contradictory forces of inequality defined by categories such as gender, religion, race, and class.[8] There is an intrinsic distinction between citizenship and nationality, an issue confused by the fact that in English the two terms are sometimes used interchangeably. In Israel, *leum* (nationality) and *ezraḥut* (citizenship) are two separate, distinct statuses, conveying different rights and responsibilities (Tekiner 1988, 70). Accordingly, as "non-Jews," Palestinians in Israel can be citizens but never nationals and are thus denied the rights and privileges enjoyed by those who, for instance, qualify for Israeli citizenship under the 1950 Law of Return (Tilley 2005, 147). This notion of nation contributes to maintaining the separation between citizens who belong to the Jewish people and those who do not. It also reinforces the dichotomy between the state as a political framework for all its citizens and the state as the particularistic nation-state of the Jewish people (Kretzer 1990, 44). In other words, "There is a fundamental disjuncture between nation and state: the Israeli state is defined as Jewish, Palestinians are not" (Kanaaneh and Nusair 2010, 2).

Critiquing the depiction of Israel as a liberal democracy, the conception of Israel as an ethnic democracy was first introduced in 1997 by Israeli sociologist Samuel Smooha, who considered the nature of the Israeli state as "a system that combines the extension of civil and political rights to individuals and some collective rights to minorities, with institutionalization of majority control over the state" (1997, 199). Driven by ethnic nationalism, the state is identified with a core ethnic nation rather than with its citizens. At its heart, this model puts forward the idea that Israeli citizenship functions according to two contradictory principles—a democratic and an ethnic principle—operating simultaneously. While the Palestinian minority is provided with citizenship and voting rights, it remains in effect excluded from the national power structure (Smooha 1997, 200).

One serious flaw of the ethnic democracy paradigm is that Israel proper qualifies as a democracy simply on the basis of providing universal voting rights, a multiparty system, fair elections, peaceful change of governments, civil rights, free speech, civilian authority over the army, and popular/elite support for democratic institutions (Smooha 1997, 205). Israeli and Palestinian revisionist and new sociologists, who regarded those elements as democratic features rather than structures, initially were critical of the model of ethnic democracy (Ghanem, Rouhana, and Yiftachel 1998, 254). Thus, whereas Smooha had pointed out the three weaknesses of Israeli democracy—the continuous application of emergency regulations that provide state authorities with excessive power to suspend civil and political rights, insufficient protection of minorities in the absence of a written constitution, and the focused nature of political intolerance (Smooha 1997, 205)—the revisionist response stressed the impossibility of a "structural, state sanctioned, and long-term inequality of ethnic rights" coexisting with democratic rule (Ghanem et al. 1998, 254).

Ultimately, Ghanem et al. (1998) proposed the concept "ethnocracy" as a critical replacement model to analyze the structural forces marginalizing and discriminating against Palestinian citizens (See also Yiftachel 1997, 2006.) The concept "ethnocracy" captures Israel's political structure as neither democratic nor authoritarian, but appropriated by one ethnic group and its diasporas, relegating other groups to a secondary type of citizenship. This argument is just as ethnocentric as the ethnic democracy model, and it also reproduces the very conceptual binaries the revisionists had initially criticized, the most important being that of "superior Jews versus inferior Arabs." After questioning the credibility of including two contradictory principles of political organization implied in "ethnic democracy," Ghanem et al. ultimately replace one binary with other binaries such as ethnos (selective association by origin) versus demos (inclusive association by residence or citizenship) and features versus structures, failing to account for the fluid ways in which especially the latter binary pair are intertwined.

Nevertheless, there are some valuable points that can be taken from the revisionists' critical response to ethnic democracy. For instance, it points out the problematic nature of relating to post-1967 Israel as a solid unit of analysis when the state ruptures territorial and political boundaries (Ghanem et al. 1998) via the ongoing expansion of Jewish settlements into the Occupied Palestinian Territories and the ongoing involvement of Jewish diaspora organizations in Israel's sovereign governance. The conceptual aberration that results from the impracticality of defining the borders of Israel's political body emphasizes the necessity for a theoretical approach to citizenship that thinks outside the clearly demarcated Western nation-state paradigm.

Notably, Gershon Shafir and Yoav Peled have taken ethnocracy a step further by contextualizing their discussions of Zionist policies in a historical setting of settler colonialism (Shafir and Peled 2002, 1). For some reason, in regard to Palestinian citizens in Israel, this contextualization is applied only up until the end of the military administration in 1966, when it is replaced with an ethnic-based description of Israel's exclusionary policies toward Palestinians who live within it (2002, 125). The lack of explanation for this conceptual shift is problematic in that it brushes aside the underlying racialized structures of citizenship that are rooted in Israel's settler colonialism post-1966. This lack is highlighted further by the fact that the usually neo-institutionalist approach that is employed here theorizes citizenship as more than a mere bundle of rights but rather as an entire mode of incorporation of individuals and groups (or lack thereof) into Israeli society and politics (Shafir and Peled 2002, 11). Shafir and Peled claim that further liberalization of Israel's state and market (which they consider an already ongoing process and somewhat a natural result of globalization) will ultimately translate into an acceleration of sociopolitical incorporation of various ethnic groups, eventually leading to Israel's transformation into a liberal democracy. Taking into account how entangled liberalization and settler colonial processes in Israel are at present, this claim appears implausible when it comes to the Palestinian population.

The extent to which Western liberal theories can explain and capture the lived realities of Palestinian citizens in Israel is doubtful in light of their premise

of the individual as a free agent and the fundamental bearer of rights and privileges (Rabinowitz 2001; Rabinowitz and Abu-Baker 2005), but also in light of
the fact that Israel does not qualify as a secular democracy. The promise of a
democratic regime has been criticized by several scholars as a "fundamental
misunderstanding of Israel's citizenship regime, both historically and contem-
porarily, especially as it relates to Palestinian citizens" (Abdo 2011, 15). Taken as
a whole, ethnocentric scholarship, despite its critique of Israel's governmental
nature, raises a series of theoretical and methodological questions. First, the
frequent bracketing together of Mizrahis, Ethiopians, and Ashkenazis as one,
unified "Jewish" ethnicity is problematic, particularly as it is constructed in
opposition to an Arab ethnicity. Second, by focusing on the ethnic elements
of citizenship, scholarship of the type fails to account for other fundamental
categories such as race, gender, and class. Overall, and finally, by being largely
ahistorical, such theorizations of Israel's democracy lack the imperative consideration of a political economy in Israel that has been produced by the state's
settler colonial policies of occupation, confiscation, and expropriation.

Israel was established as a Jewish state and a homeland of the Jewish people.
As such, membership of the Jewish community implies not only a complex
and diverse ethnic category, but also a religious one. In sharp contrast to
many Western liberal democracies, Israel does not separate between state and
religion but, in fact, firmly embeds Orthodox Jewish religious principles and
political groups within its governmental structures.[9] The term "Jewish state"
connotes that the relationship between an individual and the State of Israel is
determined by the individual's belonging to the *Jewish people* (regardless of citizenship or residency) rather than by her or his belonging to the state's *citizenry*
(Rouhana and Ghanem 1998, 322). This relationship has been enabled by the so-
called status quo arrangement between the government and Orthodox Jewish
parties agreed long before the establishment of the state in an effort to find a
compromise between the secular visions of the Zionist movement and critical
Orthodox religious leaders whose support the settlers significantly relied on.

Various meanings attach to *Jewish* in this context, many of which continue
to be the subject of controversial debates and causes of conflict among Jewish
Israelis today, particularly so between secular and religious Israelis.[10] Such
meanings include a state with a large Jewish majority, a state in which the Jewish people exercise political self-determination, and a state inspired by *halaḥah*
(Jewish religious law). A key aspect of the role of *halaḥah*, however, is that it
not only inspires Israeli state structures as a symbolic part of it, but also constitutes a fundamental and institutionalized decision-making power in determining citizens' rights in Israel by their official religious affiliation and gender,

with non-Orthodox Jews, "partial" Jews, and Jewish women receiving only a more limited package of rights and capabilities than, say, Orthodox Jewish men receive (Yiftachel 2006, 85).

Instead of addressing the state as a national minority, Palestinians in Israel can relate to Israel only as subdivided groups. The state's maintenance and imposition of legal-political categorization on various denominations and ethnic-religious groups such as Muslims, Christians (consisting of nine religious denominations), Circassians, Druze, and Bedouin made it possible to fragment Palestine's indigenous population and thereby increase the state's power over them. This is an important precondition for the state in order to continue its project of Judaization—a strategy driven by the Zionist premise that Israel should belong to the Jewish people only; one that is carried out by various policies that aim to extend Jewish political hegemony and demographic takeover of areas with an extant, predominantly Palestinian population such as the Galilee and al-Naqab (the Negev).

As a result of its fundamental patriarchal nature, the central role of institutionalized religion within the state's structures severely affects Palestinian women's everyday lives. The effect is most apparent in the existence of two overlapping and sometimes competing family court systems, civil and religious, which not uncommonly act to the detriment of indigenous women. Issues of personal status—which refers to women's rights as related to family law and can include divorce law, child custody, alimony, inheritance, and assets—remain under the strict jurisdiction of religious courts and have historical sectarian roots dating back to early Islam and the Ottoman Empire. As pointed out by social historian Ido Shahar in her investigation of indigenous law in *shari'a* courts, "the space of these 'indigenous' courts in Israel is double-faced and paradoxical: It constitutes a site of state intervention and control and, simultaneously, a site of agency, autonomy, and opposition" (2015, 84).

Much like their British Mandatory predecessor and unlike other states in the Middle East, rather than reforming the Ottoman Muslim family code, Israeli authorities chose to uphold it in its entirety (Brownson 2019, 57). They did so largely out of a colonial concern about arousing the animosity of indigenous communities in Palestine and a desire to have a way to assume the management of religious communities, particularly as regards the sensitive subject of personal status, even before the creation of the State of Israel. In her recently published investigation of Palestinian women's agency in *shar'ia* courts during the British Mandate, historian Elizabeth Brownson has shed light on how a hands-off approach to family law was also rooted in a colonial lack of interest in any actual improvement in the legal status of indigenous women (Brownson

2019, 5). In an effort to preserve the status quo, the British continued a system like the Ottoman "millet," which granted legal autonomy in matters of personal status to the various religious communities.

The millet system had already proven a perfect fit for the colonial rule of Palestine, and the British adopted it, particularly its reformative Ottoman Law of Family Rights, in a very selective manner: In 1917 the Ottoman Empire had aspired to turn the law into a general family law that would apply to all the subjects of the empire, both Muslim and non-Muslim (Shahar 2015, 87). The British did adopt the Ottoman Law of Family Rights in 1919, but they did so by employing it as a code that bound *shar'ia* courts and that would apply only to Muslims. Brownson finds that, overall, "there was more continuity between the two periods (Ottoman Empire and British Mandate) because neither party that could have effected meaningful reform was interested in doing so" (2019, 3). Nevertheless, the stagnation of family law and its patriarchal bias through a lack of reform should not be mistaken for a lack of women's agency. In fact, Brownson's (2019) historical investigation identifies a variety of ways and creative strategies by which Palestinian Muslim women have maneuvered within *shar'ia* courts in order to benefit within a system that primarily privileges and is dominated by men, particularly so in the areas of maintenance claims, divorce, and child custody.

When the *shar'ia* courts (in Nazareth and Acre) were revived by the Israeli Ministry of Religion as early as August 1948, Israel continued to implement the Ottoman laws that were previously approved by the British mandatory government. The revival and indeed augmenting of religious courts not only assisted Israel in perpetuating the colonial strategy of divide-and-rule in order to establish and maintain control over the Palestinian minority, it also facilitated the indispensable status quo between those members of the *Yishuv* who envisaged the State of Israel first and foremost as a *Jewish* state, and those who wanted it to operate as a *democracy*.

Jewishness as a precondition of Israeli democracy (Yiftachel 2006, 94) and the contradiction inherent in a democracy that openly declares itself an ethnoreligious state with a clear preference of Jews over non-Jews (Rouhana and Ghanem 1998, 322) is further revealed in the light of some basic pillars of what constitutes a "democracy": (1) equal and inclusive citizenship and civil rights; (2) popular sovereignty and universal suffrage; (3) protection of minorities; and (4) periodic fair and free elections. The extent to which the state prioritized its Jewishness over its democratic character is demonstrated by legislation such as the 1985 Knesset Amendment to a Basic Law that prohibits a political party or list to run if it explicitly or implicitly denies the Jewishness or democracy of the State of Israel.[11] Although Israel is not unique in being a democracy with an emphasis on ethnicity and *jus sanguinis*, its peculiarity lies in the legal and social institutionalization of Jewish religious, cultural, and political dominance.[12] Across the whole spectrum of the population that currently lives in Israel—Ashkenazim, Mizrahim, Sephardim, Haredim (Jewish Orthodox), and Ethiopian Jews, Palestinians, migrant workers, African refugees—one can observe an allocation of different levels of "Israeliness" that is based on membership in the (Orthodox) Jewish community as the principal qualification for the allocation of democratic rights.

Hampering any accounting for a Jewish democracy further, Israel operates as a political body without defined borders, which translates into Israel's lack of a defined demos, and arguably undermines one of the basic requirements of a democracy (Yiftachel 2006, 97). As a territorial and demographic unit, the state regularly ruptures its borders by illegal colonial Jewish settlement in the Occupied Territories, the persistent political involvement of the Jewish diasporas in its politics, the uncertain future of Palestinian refugees, and the question of how to deal with a significant influx of non-Jewish foreign workers and African refugees. As a political body, the boundaries of the state remain blurry as it constitutes an organized community under a central government accompanied by state institutions such as the executive branch and administrative bureaucracy, legislative power vested in the Knesset, a judiciary branch that includes religious, military, and civil courts, religious organizations (including the Chief Rabbinate of Israel), and the military. To that point, the Jewish National Fund, the Zionist Federation, and the Jewish Agency for Israel continue to hold significant executive power in Israel based on covenants struck with the Israeli government. These bodies perceive themselves as funding, serving, and representing "World Jewry" and are not accountable to Israeli citizens, thereby crucially infringing on democratic principles.

Palestinian Citizens in Israel

Drawing on the insights into Israel's citizenship regime by critical social science scholars Shira Robinson (2013) and Shourideh Molavi (2014), the point of departure for my research is the seemingly paradoxical argument that Israel's provision or imposition of citizenship on Palestinians and their "inclusion" within the Israeli citizenship regime constitute the very medium through which they are kept under strict control and, in fact, remain excluded from any real political power. Part and parcel of this "exclusive inclusion" (Molavi 2014, 22) is the aim to complete the Zionist project by preventing Palestinians from returning to their homes, regardless of where they are. Within the 1948 borders, the Zionist tactics to achieve this goal include the active recruitment of Palestinians as "Arab-Israelis" into the state's public culture "in order to reassure Jewish labor leaders, school principals, commanders, and civil servants that they had internalized their defeat, and that they were grateful for it as well" (Robinson 2013, 8). Ultimately, as Molavi neatly encapsulates, "It is through Israeli citizenship that Arabs are deemed stateless" (Molavi 2014, 7). Therefore, not only is settler colonialism inherent in Israel's citizenship regime, but citizenship provided to Palestinians functions as a central component of Israeli settler colonialism.

This book considers the historical emergence of the concept of citizenship and its aim of social equality as an idea that has always developed in close proximity to a concept of race that essentially served to restore inequality (Wolfe 2005). Moreover, Israel's coexisting structures of colonial rule and liberal citizenship can be understood only when linking the history of Western liberalism as a crucial force of exclusion and fuel of imperial conquests with Palestine (Robinson 2013). Israel has "sliding scales of citizenship" that are gendered, racialized, and classed and that therefore rely on corporal power hierarchies. Scales of citizenship allow the state to maintain its preferred racist social order and to pursue new strategies to eliminate indigenous presence (Wolfe 1994, 96). Strict and oppressive military rule helped to restrict the resistance and contestation of power by Palestinians in Israel until 1966 while containing the contradictions of liberal settler sovereignty. Even though the outward manifestations of this regime were abolished largely because of the attendant political costs, their legal basis remains intact (Robinson 2013, 10).

The logic of elimination continues to be realized today through various strategies such as violence, land dispossession, spatial expulsion and confinement, various forms of (forced) assimilation, and a representational discourse for which Patrick Wolfe coined the term "repressive authenticity" (Wolfe 1994, 110). One of the strategies that stands out in particular in this context is the persistent assimilationist drive of Israeli citizenship, which functions to recruit Palestinian citizens to the state while preserving Jewish citizenship privileges. Israel's settler colonialist structures are also largely sustained by its ongoing military occupation of Palestinian territories outside the 1948 armistice line and the connected comprehensive military-industrial complex that serves as a crucial decision-making mechanism for the question of who belongs to the nation and who does not. A major role is assigned to citizens' military service in the Israeli Defense Force, which functions as a Jewish national identity melting pot whose priority is the production of obedient and loyal nationals rather than citizens.

The widespread treatment of Palestinians as unwanted and unwelcome in Israel, if not as the "inner enemy," has remained a potent part of Zionist discourses that permeate the Israeli establishment and society and are expressed in various ways of marginalization and neglect. The Israeli government (except under Yitzhak Rabin) does not allocate any subsidies or development incentives to Palestinian towns and reserves welfare benefits and state-subsidized mortgages for *olim* (new immigrants) and army veterans (Rabinowitz and Abu-Baker 2005, 7). Within the Israeli economy, too, Palestinians are considered unwanted guests excluded from essential spheres such as banking, import and export franchises, and advanced technology. Moreover, the government strictly controls school curricula since 1948 in order to weaken the spread of knowledge about Palestinian history and language in an attempt to fortify its power over memory and the production of history and thereby produce submissive citizens with no sense of political identity. A further disparity is that Palestinians are significantly more likely than Jewish Israelis to end up being charged with a crime when detained by the police. Decisions made at all levels of the law enforcement system—police investigation, state prosecution, and judgments handed down by the judiciary itself—consistently indicate a disproportionally harsh treatment of Palestinians. Moreover, the Israeli Ministry of Justice's Police Investigation Unit (colloquially known as *Mahash*) consistently investigates cases of police brutality against Palestinians only superficially, whitewashes some of them, or fails to investigate them at all.[13]

Despite such circumstances, many Palestinian citizens today continue to rise up, contest, and reach out, particularly among the generation that was born in the last quarter of the twentieth century, the grandchildren of the survivor generation who lived through the *nakba* and the children of those born under the military regime. Dan Rabinowitz and Khawla Abu-Baker refer to this group as a new sociological generation, the "Stand-Tall Generation" who strive to "display a new assertive voice, abrasive style, and unequivocal substantive clarity. They have unmitigated determination, confidence, and a sense of entitlement the likes of which had only seldom been articulated previously by Palestinians addressing the Israeli mainstream" (2005, 3). This cohort shares with its political predecessors of the mid-1990s not only a call for Israel to redefine itself as "a state for all of its citizens" but also the challenge of finding a political place and role alongside Palestinians outside Israel. More outspoken than their predecessors, they are no longer interested in being marginal hangers-on of the Zionist project who are allowed to participate in, but not to challenge, the fundamentals of the State of Israel; and they question more publicly than ever the false prospect of ever becoming equal citizens in Israel. They seek to realize their interests through the use of complex and contradictory maneuvers and strategies around the Israeli system of restrictions as they consider citizenship not just a personal affair anymore but a collective entitlement that can be used to aspire to deep historic justice and meaningful incorporation into a transformed Israel.

The Israeli state and media frequently deploy a modernization rhetoric to the Palestinian society, often referred to condescendingly as the *migzar ha-aravi* (the Arab sector). The status of Palestinian women within Palestinian society plays a central role in this discourse by serving the purpose of societal boundary making against Palestinians as "the Other," often in an attempt to legitimize differential treatment and discriminatory policies toward Palestinian citizens. Israeli Orientalist rhetoric and practices that depict Palestinians as socially and culturally backward, traditional, tribal, and sexist are part and parcel of an effort to distinguish Jewish Israelis from Palestinians and thereby strengthen Israel's own struggle to secure its modernity (Kanaaneh 2002). Israeli media interest in Palestinian women, which tends to increase during election campaigns, largely concentrates on the oppression of women within the field of sexual violence, Arab culture, and the Arab family. But despite their marginalization by both the Israeli state and Palestinian society, Palestinian women cannot be considered silent victims of their status: They are not mere recipients of oppression but also agents of self-determination. Whereas some observers emphasize the recently gained momentum of Palestinian women's agency and activism as they assume "more visible public presence" (Abdo 2011, 46), in many ways they have been able to create and utilize various options available to them in order to struggle for their interests and those of their community since before 1948.

Palestinian women in Israel are far from being a homogeneous group of equally oppressed women. They belong to and identify with various religious, secular, ethnic, sexual, and cultural orientations, they differ in class and educational backgrounds, and they live in a variety of locations ranging from Palestinian recognized and unrecognized villages to "mixed cities."[14] Their membership in one or more distinct subgroups, often marked by patently patriarchal structures, exposes them to what has been dubbed "compound discrimination" in civil society circles.[15] Multiple forms of differential treatment converge in an environment in which the status of women serves the purpose of collective (self-)identification and the marking of societal boundaries. Many Palestinian woman's-rights activists in Israel understand their movement as an intersectional struggle for both women's and national liberation. The relationship of Palestinian women to the Israeli state and Palestinian society is further complicated in that two distinct gender orders are brought into contact: that of Israel and that of Palestinian communities. The two orders frequently conflict and reinforce their power over women, often violently and disruptively. Palestinian patriarchy, for instance, is reinforced under the stresses of Israeli occupation. This process takes place in an overall environment in which the status of women, in both societies, serves to mark collective identity boundaries and to express masculinist notions of power, especially during times of intensified conflict. Palestinian women's narratives about citizenship have always involved descriptions of a racialized and gendered citizenship that they describe as "imposed" or "forced" on them by the state. These experiences of citizenship are marked daily by severe power struggles over political, social, and cultural superiority, historical memory, and, above all, land.

Despite the fact that Israel has some of the most progressive and forward-thinking legislation and policies with regard to some marginalized groups, including women, Palestinian women citizens do not receive the full benefit of such protections and, instead, are discriminated against on a number of levels through laws, government policies, and social norms and customs. Ordinary domestic law that protects women's equality, such as the Women's Equal Rights Law of 1951 (which prohibits all forms of discrimination against women) or the 1993 and 2000 amendments to the Government Companies Law 1975, are not effectively implemented as regards Palestinian women. Another case in point is the legal status and implementation of the UN Convention Prohibiting All Forms of Discrimination against Women (CEDAW). Signed and ratified by Israel in 1991, the state has refrained from formally incorporating it into Israeli domestic law, which renders the convention's provisions nonbinding on the courts. Upon ratification, Israel has entered substantive and procedural reservations about the convention; most notably, article 7(b), which concerns the appointment of women to serve as judges of religious courts, and article 16, which concerns personal status.

Even though there are specific legislative equality measures to guarantee fair representation of women in general and of Palestinian women in the civil service and on boards of directors of government companies, the state does not recognize Palestinian women citizens as a distinct protected subgroup. Instead, Palestinian women face the severest consequences of Israel's differential treatment of its citizens in several areas, such as the protection against violence, political underrepresentation and participation, employment, education, health, issues relating to personal status and social and economic benefits. Nevertheless, Palestinian women have experienced major shifts over the last two decades, including an exceptional increase in the level of education, as they have increasingly engaged in many fields of work dominated by men, such as law and medicine. But despite the government's public promotion of Palestinian women's employment rates in the Israeli labor market, the educational shift has failed to translate into an increase in their rate of participation in the labor force (22.5 percent), as most of them remain strictly employed in the areas of education, personal services, and health services, where they frequently suffer a wage gap (Daoud 2012). Their experiences stand in sharp contrast to Jewish women in Israel, who have one of the world's leading participation rates in the labor market (71 percent; King et al. 2009). Four in five Palestinian women continue to fulfill a traditional domestic role mostly because of social and logistic barriers (e.g., lack of mobility, public transportation, opportunities, and support). Most notable, Palestinian women are badly affected in health matters, particularly incidences of chronic diseases such as heart diseases and diabetes, and more than half of Palestinian women in Israel continue to live under the poverty line today, in contrast with 12 percent of Jewish women (Muhammad et al. 2012).

The framework for these experiences—Israel's settler colonial structures and the foundations of its various kinds of "citizenship"—long preceded the establishment of the state. The lives of Palestinian women in Israel can be understood only within the context of the forces of change and continuity that have shaped their experiences in the past and present. Since the early twentieth century, these women have individually and collectively experienced successive waves of crisis and turmoil under the crumbling Ottoman Empire, the British mandate, and Zionist occupation, such as the Wailing Wall incident of 1929, the violent upheavals of 1933, the general strike and great revolt 1936–39, the war of 1948, the *nakba*, the 1967 war, the two intifadas, and the Oslo accords, to name but a few. The external impact of these events went hand in hand with tremendous socioeconomic and cultural change, as tradition and innovation coexisted in an often uneasy amalgam and contributed to an ongoing process of redefinition of Palestinian society and culture. Such complex experiences have included, for instance, the conditional integration of Palestinians in Israel into Zionist state institutions, spaces in which Palestinian citizens found themselves simultaneously included and excluded, strengthened and weakened, as an overall unwelcomed and threatened minority. In an effort of self-preservation, Palestinian society looked increasingly inward and became more restrictive toward women and women's movements, particularly so after the war of 1948 (Daoud 2009, 6).

Today, Palestinian women's intimate politics continue to constitute a pivotal site for the power struggle between colonizer and colonized. Their experiences and narratives of citizenship are miscellaneous, complex, and often ambivalent. Most important, they are inherently political because they unsettle many of the deep-seeded discourses of power that entrench the vested interests of the settler colonial state and society. The aim of this book is to read their experiences through the lens of intimate politics, which reveals that the main function of citizenship is not to protect Palestinian women, but to sustain their marginalization within and, at times, exclusion from the Israeli body politic.

WHY INTIMATE POLITICS MATTER

The realization that intimate politics would play a central role in this research took place during the early stages of my fieldwork, when an increasing number of women and a handful of men began to share very personal stories about romantic and sexual relationships, family life, and everyday corporeality with me. My realization made it imperative to look into the meanings of people's daily intimate politics. How could our discussions, which started off about issues of citizenship, so quickly move on to topics like menstruation, dress choices, sex, violence, tattoos, and family formation? The more I started to take part in women's daily lives, the more it manifested that it is, in fact, through the imposition of Israeli citizenship that the physical and emotional displacement and dispossession of the *nakba* can continue almost unimpeded. Palestinian women's political marginalization in the country is maintained through *exclusionary inclusion*, which severely affects the realm of intimacy as specific intimate politics are encouraged, some are tolerated, and others are prohibited by the state and society. And so, rather than looking for an answer to Huda's question "Where are we?" in nongovernmental organizations (NGOs), municipalities, or even the Knesset, I began to look for one in cafés, offices, tattoo studios, bars, hair salons, university campuses, and women's homes.

From a feminist perspective, investigating intimacy is integral as an analytic concept that "interrogates and transgresses established understandings of private and public domains" (Zengin and Sehlikoglu 2016, 140). The feminist slogan "the personal is political" is of special relevance to the Palestinian context, in which the struggle for survival and a sense of ordinary life experienced through quotidian practices takes on a particular political significance. For more than a decade, a shift in the scholarly focus from conventional to the informal, everyday politics of Palestinian women and men has taken place (Richter-Devroe 2018; Junka 2006; Salih 2017; Khalili 2015). Nevertheless, much of Palestinian women's informal politics remains unrecognized, and the bulk of existing scholarly work concentrates on Palestinians outside the

1948 borders. By shedding light on daily intimate politics among Palestinian women inside Israel, this book intends to contribute to the recognition of their informal politics and their everyday struggles for normality and happiness for themselves and their loved ones.

Intimate politics matter not only in bottom-up experiences and narratives but also in understanding how Israel's intimate state power operates through everyday encounters and discourses. Intimacy here not only constitutes a crucial site of the struggle between settler and colonized but, moreover, plays a fundamental role in the very production of the two categories and the process of their sustainment.[16] The state's precept about which forms of intimacy are considered legitimate, for instance, in marriage, family relations, domestic arrangements, or sexual relations, takes place through its interference in its citizens' intimate lives (Parla 2001; Kandiyoti 1991; Aretxaga 2003; Stoler 2001). This is particularly relevant to settler colonial state power, which has always been preoccupied with indigenous intimate lives, and especially so in case of indigenous women's bodies and sexuality (Stoler 2002; Smith 2003; Shalhoub-Kevorkian 2015). Women's struggles in regard to mixed relationships, alternative family formation, sexual liberation, and menstrual products, as well as the hypersexualization of black women and racial segregation, which start in the womb and continue through to nurseries, schools, universities, work offices, and graveyards, are not merely revealing illustrations of how settler colonial privileges and deprivations are unequally distributed within intimate realms as a nexus of race and gender, they are, in fact, the everyday grounds of contestation (Stoler 2001, 894) and the realms in which constructs of race and gender are put to the test again and again.

It is important to note that there is no scholarly consensus on "what counts as the intimate and why it matters" (Stoler 2006, 3). To an extent, this ambiguity makes discourses and practices of intimacy all the more important as a means of mediating between settler and colonized and their spaces. The fact that the definitions of those categories are never stable but blurred and constantly re-negotiated may not necessarily indicate a Zionist settler colonialism in distress but, rather, one in active realignment. Naturally, the ambiguous borders of the intimate lend themselves to political regimes that are, in a pinch, aiming to repeatedly safeguard their categories of race and gender. In "Why Revisit Intimacy?," an introductory chapter to a special issue of the *Cambridge Journal of Anthropology* dedicated to the subject of intimacy, Asli Zengin and Sertaç Sehlikoglu foreground the central role of intimacy in the formation of selves and subjectivities as well as in collective communities, publics, and socialities (2015, 20). It is noteworthy that the authors emphasize the ability of intimacy to create not only boundaries and borders but also flows and transitions between bodies, selves, and groups, thereby allowing the emergence of new bonds and attachments and the creation of new meanings (Stoler 2008). Moreover, as Sehlikoglu notes in a separate article about the Islamicate Culture of *mahremiyet* (intimacy, privacy) in Istanbul, it is through intimacy that the very boundaries and borders of the gendered (and, as will be argued here, racialized) female body, female heterosexuality, and femininity are "built and rebuilt, made and remade in everyday life" (2016, 145).

A conversation between the renewed scholarly attention to intimacy in the Middle East (Zengin and Sehlikoglu 2016; Georgis 2013; El Feki 2013; Mahdavi 2009; Najmadi 2005 Ozyegin 2015; Peirce 2010; Pursely 2012) and settler colonial studies not only allows us to examine and analyze the intimate as a strategic site of settler colonial governance and the indigenous everyday experience of settler colonial citizenship but, furthermore, engenders an analytical framework that is capable of adapting to the progressive reformation of settler colonial strategies that aim to "destroy in order to replace" by invading, interfering, and controlling indigenous bodies and spaces through, for instance, strategies of assimilation (Wolfe 2006, 397) and self-indigenization (Veracini 2010b, 21).

The importance of analytical adaptability has been emphasized by scholars in queer decolonial studies, who, for years, have pointed out how sexuality constitutes a central site of Zionist invasion, where Palestinian queer people are coopted as "Israel-ized" agents under the homonationalist banner of the Israeli LGBT movement (AlQaisiya, Hilal, and Maikey 2016). The presentation of Israel as "progressive and gay loving" (Morgensen 2011) serves the naturalization of the settler colonial regime, its ongoing occupation, and the logic of native exclusion and elimination. What has changed, however, is the Zionist discourse about whose bodies are worth saving and protecting, and the settler state and society are presented as the only providers of a safe haven. In this context, Palestinian queers are frequently presented as victims of their own homophobic and backward communities (AlQaisiya et al. 2016, 132) who are rescued by Israeli modern sexuality (Morgensen 2011), which simultaneously denies their own Palestinian queer movement.

FIELDWORK AND SITUATING THE RESEARCHER

The research presented in this book is based on fieldwork conducted both on and off the ground during the past decade. I undertook ninety interviews with eighty-two Palestinian women and eight Palestinian men during the periods

September 2011 to March 2012 and September 2013 to March 2014, when I stayed and traveled widely throughout Palestine and Israel. Off the ground, some parts of my research continued throughout the writing process up until June 2017. Because of the sensitive nature of my research questions and the primary goal of exploring individual practices, personal experiences, and subjective meanings attached to intimate politics by Palestinian women in Israel, I drew exclusively on qualitative research methods consisting of half-structured interviews, focus groups, and participant observation. The aim in doing so was never to collect facts or identify trends but to produce and present a comprehensive collection, description, and interpretation of the various forms of intimate politics that I encountered during my fieldwork.

The great majority of my research participants were resident from all over the 1948 territory (within the borders of the State of Israel as it was officially founded in 1948) and included the cities of Haifa, Tel Aviv–Jaffa, Jerusalem, Bi'r as-Sab (Be'er Sheva), Rahat, Lyd, and Ramle, the recognized Bedouin townships of Laqiya and Tel al-Sabi (Tel Sheva), and the Palestinian villages of Jish, Arrabe, Kafr Kanna, Kafr Manda, Kafr Yassif, Kafr Qasim, Tira, Taybeh, Nahef, Kafr Bir'im, Al-Muthalath, and Kisra-Sumei—all in the northern Galilee. At the time the interviews took place, two of the women were resident in Canada and three lived and worked in the United States. Of the men, two were resident in Germany and Holland. All the interviews outside Israel were conducted via Skype or telephone. I also carried out two spontaneous focus groups: One with six women from the unrecognized Bedouin village of Wadi el-Khalil in al-Naqab and one with a group of five women who came together in a bridal store in Lyd to discuss their experiences of citizenship in Israel at the suggestion of a woman I had interviewed previously.

During the very early stages of my research, I drew on the snowball method in order to identify and reach out to potential interview partners through my contacts with various NGOs and individuals whom I got to know during my work with a Palestinian feminist organization in Haifa.[17] Therefore, in the beginning, the majority of my personal contacts were feminist and women's rights activists working within the frameworks of Palestinian and Jewish-Palestinian women's organizations operating in the Galilee and the Bi'r as-Sab region. The reason for my initial regional focus on the north was the fact that most of the Palestinian population in Israel reside there. The two cities of Nazareth and Haifa are of particular importance in this context, as they are two localities where a large number of Palestinian women started to organize themselves in Israel. Although the rural areas, which are home to about 70 percent of Israel's Palestinian community, have not witnessed similar levels of women's activism, there are some notable rural women's organizations, such as the religious feminist organization *Nissa Wa-Afaq* (Women and Horizons), in the village of Kafr Qari, and the Arab women's organization *Al-Zahraa*, established in Sakhnin, a town with the infrastructure of a small, underdeveloped village. Similarly, the majority of Bedouin feminists in the south reside in villages that are not officially recognized by Israel and, thus, often lack basic infrastructure and facilities.

While NGO networks served as a reliable starting point to organize my interviews, I increasingly strove to include women in my research whose narratives had frequently been marginalized from mainstream discourses. I started to extend my contacts to include not only the feminists, with whom I was already familiar (mostly secular, highly educated, middle-class Palestinian women living in urban areas), but also women from other religious, geographic, educational, and professional backgrounds. In doing so, I entered into deeper conversations with women from Druze communities in the north, women with disabilities, black Bedouin women, women residents of unrecognized villages, women entrepreneurs, one professional football player, one intersexual woman, women who chose to live abroad, and academics. Notably, in an effort not to treat Palestinian women as segments made up of constructed categories rooted in colonialism, I did not look for women belonging to any of those categories specifically but decided at some point to simply "go with the flow" of referral sampling through personal contacts rather than organizations. At the same time, in order to gain a deeper understanding of the patterns that emerged throughout my data collection, I decided to also organize interviews around the edges of my target groups, for instance, with Palestinian women who did not carry Israeli citizenship, women who rejected the label "feminist," and a number of Palestinian men.

Participant observation enabled me to gain a close—and often intimate—familiarity with some of my research participants' daily personal and work environments, as well as their daily routines and intimate politics. I lived with research participants in Laqiya, Jish, and Jerusalem for days and sometimes weeks at a time. Doing so allowed me to participate in their daily lives, which included accompanying them to their workplaces and to the university, attending lectures and talks with them, socializing on campus (particularly at Ben Gurion University), and also spending time at home, visiting friends together, going shopping, going to parties or public film screenings, visiting exhibitions and museums, going out for dinner, drinks, or dancing. Traveling together turned out to be a valuable way of deepening existing acquaintances and making new ones, especially when visiting the West Bank together. I participated in numerous women's organizations' meetings, classes, and seminars and thereby managed to gain crucial contact with members of the so-called Palestinian Feminist Forum, a young nationwide network of Palestinian feminists in Israel. As "the Forum," as it was commonly referred to, has no physical space or location, it was difficult to track down and gain access to online discussion forums and newsletters and the like. The Forum is particularly worthy of research, as, unlike the about-dozen Palestinian women's rights organizations that currently exist in Israel, it does not function as an NGO, and yet it is where I have encountered some significant expressions of a reproduction of power hierarchies along the lines of class, race, and religion/secularism.

The research for this book drew on various methods that I selected as I found them suitable. The settings of my interviews sometimes varied with the personal preferences of the individual interview partner (some women preferred a neutral place to talk and others preferred a homely or at least familiar environment) and sometimes with practical realities (e.g., Skype interviews with women who live abroad).

Within the Bedouin community, it was impossible to simply go "in and out" of the community for an interview, and it would have had a considerable negative and limiting impact on the quality and depth of our conversations. Instead, I spent several weeks introducing myself to and spending time with various families, who showed me around their homes and villages while sharing much of their family history. This arrangement allowed me, for example, to work out the life history of a renowned Bedouin women's rights activist, the daughter of a sheikh. Her story allowed me to find out much about storytelling as a way of resistance, the attribution of meanings, and the role of gendered memory. It helped tremendously in historically contextualizing not only Bedouin women's relation to the State of Israel but, more important, the role of women's storytelling in creating meanings that often dissent from the meanings presented by hegemonic histories. I believe that my exploration of the tribe's family history, my living with them, and my having both casual daily and in-depth conversations with them rather than interviewing them helped to allow our conversations to reach a very deep and personal level. In contrast, other women, mainly working women in Haifa, Tel Aviv, and Jerusalem, had very busy schedules and, therefore, preferred for me to conduct semistructured interviews with them at specific times and places. We usually met in local cafés or bars, or, if they preferred, at their work or homes. Of course, having interviews in such ways did not mean that the conversations were in any way less deep.

Both in the field and at my desk, I strove to conduct my conversations openly and without any deception. I informed everyone involved in my research straightforwardly about my work, answering all their questions about it, proceeding only with their voluntary consent, and doing my best to consider all their concerns and requests. Confidentiality rather than anonymity—which would entail that nobody, not even the researcher, can identify who provided the data (O'Reilly 2005, 65)—was ensured throughout the gathering of information through interviews, focus groups, and participant observation.

Being in touch did not simply end whenever I exited the physical field, as I remained in continual conversation with several individuals via telephone, email, Skype, and various social media channels such as Facebook, Instagram, and WhatsApp. In many ways, I contend that these channels, particularly in the research context of this book, have changed the manner in which we ought to (re)define the field and fieldwork. Such a change would not make physical encounters and observations any less important or valuable, but I fathom that social media needs to be considered closely and carefully when demarcating boundaries of the field and fieldwork, as they have become more challenging to define with the vast spread of digital communication technology; and, also important, more difficult to identify the location of the researcher.

The research process was further complicated by the fact that much of anthropological analysis takes place while writing, something that, as a trained historian, I fully grasped only when I was in the midst of it. I rewrote the present ethnography entirely at least three times, moving from striving to disentangling the many apparent contradictions that I encountered in accepting them and making sense of them. Even though the process sounds straightforward with hindsight, I found myself in what I called a messy place of constantly moving back and forth between the field, the desk, and various channels and places between, ending up with various big piles of themes and narratives that refused to be squeezed into neat, equal-sized chapters.

As relationships in general have changed as a result of new means of communication technology, so have those between researcher and research participant, opening up a whole series of questions about how we conduct not only our research projects in our methods but also how we conduct ourselves as researchers, people who come to explore other peoples' personal lives and to collect their stories. Primarily thanks to these new channels of communication, I continue to be in conversation with numerous research participants up until today, although, I am, of course, no longer taking part in their daily lives, which have moved on in many ways that I'm unable to follow up on or comprehend from afar.

This book has grown out of my personal dissatisfaction with the education that I received throughout my academic journey in Western Europe and the frustrations that emerged as a result. In the face of the objectification of knowledge that continues to prevail in the mainstream white and masculinist academia in the West, I concur with the importance that Cree-Métis scholar Kim Anderson assigns to what she calls "an Aboriginal method of contextual- izing knowledge" (2000, 21). Such a method, put forward by many indigenous women scholars, is based on the idea that writers should identify themselves in order to contextualize the knowledge that they present (Monture-Angus 1995, 45). As pointed out by Donna Haraway (1988) and Sandra Harding (1991), all knowledge is marked by the context in which it is produced and, therefore, knowledges are always situated.

Taking account of my position and the specific and partial knowledge pro- duced from it was an objective that accompanied me continuously throughout the past decade. The contextualization of the knowledge presented here is re- quired, because the authority of this book is based on my person: my interpreta- tion, my relationships with the interviewees, the conversations that I led, and, important to note, the privileges that accompanied me throughout the journey of researching and writing. In other words, a different researcher could have spoken to the same women whom I spoke to and produced a totally different book. The process of analysis in this book was certainly affected by the course and messiness of my own life throughout the last ten years as I turned from an unchained PhD candidate in London into a mother of three working as history lecturer and birth doula based in Frankfurt.

One of my objectives was to remain conscious of issues relating to the inher- ent personal and group disparities between researcher and participant in terms of wealth, power, and legal status: the differences in material inequalities and opportunities and the rights enjoyed by myself and by my research partner (Gilbert 1994). My privileges included my being a white, middle-class, German woman holding a research scholarship provided by the German Protestant Church. The combination proved beneficial on several levels: First, even though I had to keep a close eye on my expenses during my PhD (especially while I was in London or Tel Aviv), I did not suffer from any existential financial wor- ries thanks to my scholarships, my teaching jobs, and my parents' willingness to cover my tuition fees for two years. Second, carrying a German passport, a Hebrew second name, and a viable knowledge of Hebrew certainly helped in entering and exiting the field safely and whenever I wanted. This situation became increasingly difficult, however, as the number of Jewish Israeli friends I could mention as contacts at the border crossing decreased the longer I stayed. Also, my research topic, my frequent travels to the West Bank, and the fact that some of my friends and acquaintances included Palestinian political activists who were exiled or imprisoned eventually raised suspicion among the border police officers who, I presume, found out about my acquaintances by checking my personal background at some stage.

Ultimately, talking to Palestinian women about their intimate politics in Israel is a sensitive issue that may be regarded as inherently unethical in that it involves intruding into women's daily and private lives by speaking about topics that are likely to stir up painful memories and to remind them of ongoing traumatic experiences. Something that stuck with me is Julie Peteet's understanding of the role of the anthropologist in the colonial present, which she describes as twofold in her enthralling ethnographic work *Space and Mobility in Palestine*: "First, to compile an ethnographic archive of ordinary everyday life under a settler colonial occupation and, in doing so, to challenge the official story, which has long silenced and marginalized a Palestinian narrative; and second, to provide theoretical analysis of how contemporary forms of colonial power operate through fast-changing spatial parameters that intertwine with ever-changing rules, at once unpredictable and comprehended viscerally in a violence-saturated environment" (Peteet 2017, 30). As I sit at my desk trying to finish this book in early 2022 as Palestinians in Sheikh Jarrah, Gaza and many friends in the al-Naqab face renewed settler colonial brutality, the exigency of such an endeavor could not be any greater and I am content if I have managed to contribute to it in any way.

STRUCTURE OF THE BOOK

Divided into six core chapters, this book begins with two chapters that are dedicated to defining the plan, considering the wider, intersectional context in which Palestinian women's intimate politics are negotiated, and is followed by four chapters that explore the intimate relationship and struggle between Zionist settler colonialism and Palestinian women's intimate relationships as well as their bodies and sexual and feminist politics.

The first chapter outlines how citizenship in a settler colonial state functions as a key mechanism of exclusionary inclusion as a means through which the Zionist state advances its logic of elimination and self-indigenization, for instance, through strategies of assimilation. It shows that at the heart of the plan designed by the state for indigenous Palestinian women lies the expectation for them to disappear and simultaneously remain identifiable as readable bodies. The analysis of citizenship as a gendered and racialized corporeal experience presented here reveals how Palestinian women's bodies—conceptualized as both object and agent—constitute a key site of the struggle between settler and colonized. An important aspect of the chapter is its highlighting of some of the ways in which Palestinian women's bodies are Othered and marked by difference in everyday life in order to display which bodies in Israel are in place and which out of place according to Zionist logic.

The second chapter further suggests and outlines the plan as a more fruitful way to conceptualize the context of Palestinian women's lives in Israel, in contrast with the commonly used notion of "two layers of oppression" (national and women's oppression). It elaborates on the plan as the product of a complex interplay of interlocking systems of domination intrinsic to patriarchy, such as settler colonialism, classicism, racism, and ableism. It thus builds on chapter 1's briefer investigation of the Zionist state by deconstructing what has frequently been referred to as patriarchal Palestinian society. By taking a more nuanced look at Palestinian society, chapter 2 draws a more complex and coherent picture that includes the experiences of many women who have remained by and large excluded from existing discourses and accounts of Palestinian women, such as black Palestinian women, women with disabilities, unmarried and divorced women, Bedouin women, and lesbian, gay, transgender, queer/questioning, and intersex (LGBTQI) women.

The book then moves on from discussions of Palestinian women's bodies in terms of embodiment to explorations of their bodies as active agents. To that end, the third chapter brings into question the ways in which Palestinian women's bodies defy the plan in practice. Thereby, it interrogates, in detail, some of the stories and experiences of women who refuse allowing their bodies to be read and controlled by others. By focusing on three examples—the politics of menstruation, tattoos, and dress—the chapter offers insights into how Palestinian women defy social norms and taboos through their bodies both in public and provocative and in subtle and discreet ways. Intimate politics in this context are about how women use their bodies as an important means and medium to (re)define borders ("border skirmishing") between the Self, the Other, society, and nation. The chapter demonstrates that Palestinian women frequently use their bodies to (re)tell their own stories, which include elements of family history, national belonging, and (feminist and religious) identity. Moreover, as settler colonialism is a spatial project, women's bodies are used to access spaces and other resources that are reserved for the somatic (Jewish) norm.

The book turns to an apparent incongruity between public and private discourses about sex in its fourth chapter: On the one hand, there is a movement of women who work hard in order to improve the access to sex education, as well as a general increase in communication about sex within Palestinian society. Talk about sex mainly takes place within the framework of sexual education programs led by various feminist NGOs and includes issues of sexual violence and health, and also sex advice for couples. These initiatives, as the women activists emphasize, are all the more important in light of Israel's "modern sexuality," which neglects the sexual education of Palestinians through educational segregation while the state also fails to provide adequate protection against sexual violence to Palestinian women. On the other hand, even though public discussions about sex and sexuality are on the rise, personal sexual experiences, including sex practices, the loss of virginity, experiences of sexual harassment and abuse, are strictly kept silent even among the most outspoken women's rights activists and feminists. The main reason behind this reticence, the chapter claims, is the interplay of patriarchal settler colonial and traditional regimes. This mutual reinforcement of oppressive power structures makes the price to pay for speaking out openly about their personal sex lives simply too high for some Palestinian women and especially for those who cannot count on the support of their families in the event of social scandals.

The fifth chapter is an investigation of Palestinian women's affective, romantic, and love relations that defy the plan. It looks at how Zionist state control over and direct encroachment in Palestinian intimate relationships and family life remains crucial for the preservation of the Jewishness of the state. Formal and informal methods of surveillance and regulation include the withholding of citizenship for intimate partners, the prevention of family unification, the overlapping of religious and civil courts in adjudicating family law, and the difficulty for Palestinians to access alternative ways of family formation such as adoption. Both Palestinian and Israeli society adhere to traditional social orders when it comes to serious, long-term intimate relations and family life, as they prefer a model of "sexual normalcy," which in both societies implies heterosexuality and sticking to "one's own" in terms of religious, class, racial, and ethnic memberships. The chapter explores the stories of women who have—out of love—resisted this control in order to form alternative families, to be in mixed relationships and marriages, to remain single, or to get divorced.

The final chapter of the book explores individual personal narratives of feminism rather than the official discourses that are produced by organizations. Nevertheless, it is important to understand the context in which these narratives emerge. While the Palestinian women's movement outside Israel is inextricably embedded within the wider Palestinian national movement, the situation in Israel is more complicated. In Israel, narratives of feminism take place within the borders of a settler colonial state into which the women were born and grew up in. As a result, many women were exposed to and have become very familiar with Western feminist thought as it is embraced by Israeli academia, public discourses, and Jewish Israeli feminist organizations. Despite such exposure, Palestinian women have for a long time produced their own *Palestinian* feminist thought that entails constructions of a feminist identity that is often linked to notions of "naturalness" and the idea of being "born a feminist." This sentiment is exclusively spread among middle- and upper-class women who actively participate in and contribute to organized feminist discourses. Women who remain marginalized from these discourses (and the organizations that bring them forth), such as religious, black, and poor women, frequently criticize or reject feminism as a result of their own experiences of being excluded and patronized by self-identified feminists. It is important to recognize that women across the divides of class, race, and religious membership frequently articulate a Palestinian national subjectivity that functions as a driving force for their intimate politics, one that carves out an imagining of Palestinian women as liberated and freely acting agents with the right to write their own plans on all levels. Even though, during our conversations, the women proudly identified as Palestinian, their disappointment with the national movement was apparent at all times and was most clearly expressed in their rejection of nationalism and all the negative connotations they bestowed on nationalism. I found that the central agenda of Palestinian feminists—according to their personal narratives—is not so much to make space for women within the movement of national liberation but, instead, to create a national subjectivity of their own accord—a movement that is, by its very nature, feminist.

To conclude, I revisit "the field" for a Bedouin friend's wedding, where I reflect on my insights into the role of intimate politics in the workings and transgression of Zionist settler colonialism. My concluding insights underscore how intimate practices that defy the plan should be regarded as political, as they constitute the daily contested ground not only for settler colonialism but also for indigenous people. Bodily politics, physical and emotional desires, and, above all, love are what arguably constitute the very fabric and, arguably, purpose of life. While not all acts that defy the plan are intended by women to resist patriarchy or settler colonialism, they serve the purpose of Palestinian women's self-determination and, thereby, undermine the legitimacy and functioning of the plan. By exiting the normative path and constituting significant deviations from the plan, intimate politics are potentially transformative, especially when repeated collectively, opening up new opportunities for Palestinian women in Israel as a whole.

NOTES

1. The choice to use the term "Palestinian" or "Arab Palestinian" women rather than "Israeli Arab" or "Arab Israeli" women is a political one that

acknowledges the fact that Palestinians are an indigenous population in their historical homeland Palestine. It also counters hegemonic Zionist discourses, which, by not referring to Palestinians as "Palestinians" (but instead "Arab-Israelis" or "Israeli Arabs"), continue to detach Palestinian citizens in Israel from the Palestinian national collective and their historical entitlement to the land of Palestine.

2. In order to maintain and protect the identities of my research participants, pseudonyms are used throughout the book.

3. The *Nakba* Day (Day of the Catastrophe) marks the day after the anniversary of Israel's "Day of Independence" on May 15, 1948, when hundreds of thousands of Palestinians fled their homes or were forcibly displaced.

4. Salamanca, J. O., M. Qato, K. Rabie, and S. Samour, eds. 2012. "Past Is Present: Settler Colonialism in Palestine." *Settler Colonial Studies* 2, no. 1.

5. Although Zionism's modern adherents mainly understand it as a movement for Jewish national self-determination in the form of a Jewish nation-state in Eretz Israel, it is important to note that there were also Zionist thinkers who critiqued this state-centric, militaristic, and xenophobic reading of Zionism, such as Martin Buber, Judah Leon Magnes, and Ernst Simon. When referring to Zionism in this book, I am pointing to the settler colonialist movement and political project that aims to dispossess and displace the indigenous people of Palestine by force.

6. "Land and Housing Rights—Palestinian Citizens of Israel," UN CESCR Information Sheet No. 3 (Shfaram, Isr.: Adalah, 2003), https://www.adalah.org /uploads/oldfiles/eng/intladvocacy/CESCR-land.pdf.

7. This law was amended in 2007 to include citizens of the "enemy states" Iran, Iraq, Syria, Lebanon, and others.

8. In 1948 Israel declared itself a "Jewish state" in its Declaration of Independence; in 1992 *democratic* was officially added in the amendment to the Basic Laws.

9. Declaration of the Establishment of State of Israel, May 15, 1948, Israel Ministry of Foreign Affairs, http://www.mfa.gov.il/mfa/foreignpolicy/peace /guide/pages/declaration%20of%20establishment%20of%20state%20of%20 israel.aspx.

10. It is important to note here that Israelis commonly use the term *secular* when referring to a nonreligious person rather than to the condition of separation between the state and religion.

11. Jewishness remains, however, undefined.

12. Alan Dowty (1999) mentions other states such as Germany or Russia, which still maintain that ancestral links should grant the right of return.

13. *Mahash: The Green Light for Police Brutality in Israel*, September 2014 Report (Shfaram, Isr.: Adalah). https://www.adalah.org/uploads/oldfiles/Public /files/English/Newsletter/Sep-2014/Adalah-Mahash-Data-Report-Sep-2014.pdf.

14. Though disputed among academics, in Israel "mixed city" usually refers to cities such as Akko, Haifa, Jaffa, Lod, and Ramle where large communities of both Jewish and Palestinian citizens reside.

15. Adalah, "Exclusion of Arab Citizens of Israel from Civil Service Jobs, Municipalities in the Mixed Cities and in the Private Sector," press release, June 26, 2011, https://www.adalah.org/uploads/oldfiles/eng/pressreleases /pr.php?file=26-2_06_11.

16. See, for example, "Ann Stoler Discusses Her 'Carnal Knowledge and Imperial Power' Book (2002) in Riprap Interview," accessed May 15, 2021, https://www.youtube.com/watch?v=Mm1QAowgq_A.

17. The NGOs were Acre Arab Women's Association in Acre; Al-Fanar in Haifa; Al-Tufula Center in Nazareth; Al-Zahraa—The Organization for the Advancement of Women in Sakhnin; Arab Human Rights Association in Nazareth; Assiwar—Arab Feminist Movement in Support of Victims of Sexual Abuse in Haifa; Aswat Group—Palestinian Lesbian Women in Haifa; Isha L'Isha–Haifa Women's Centre in Haifa; Kayan—Feminist Organization in Haifa; Laqiya/Sidreh Weaving Project in Laqiya; Ma'an—The Forum for Arab Bedouin Women's Organizations in the Negev in Beer-Sheva; Mada Al-Carmel—Arab Center for Applied Social Research in Haifa; Mossawa Centre— The Advocacy Center for Arab Citizens in Israel in Haifa; Nissa Wa Afaq in Kfar Qari; Sanad (support) in Umm El-Fahm (a women's association focusing on motherhood and childhood established by the Islamic Movement in 1999); the Association of Women against Violence in Nazareth; the Coalition of Women for Peace in Tel Aviv–Jaffa; the Movement of Democratic Women in Nazareth; the Women's Association of Ara and Arara in Arara; and the Working Group for Equality in Personal Status Issues in Nazareth.

ONE

—𝔪—

EMBODIED CITIZEN STRANGERS

INTRODUCTION

The body serves as a deeply insightful entry point to the study of the struggle and the relationship between settler and colonized. Striving to restore an analysis of Israel's settler colonialist structure, rather than settler colonialist "tactics" or "outcomes," this chapter aims to demonstrate that Israel's encroachment of Palestinian women's bodies is not a concomitant phenomenon but the very heart of Zionist settler colonialism.[1] The research presented here enters rather uncharted academic territory and, overall, involves two challenges: First, it seeks to combine the theoretical framework of settler colonialism and the analytical lens of gender in its analysis of citizenship among Palestinian women in Israel.[2] Second, it aspires to establish a new angle of critique of citizenship in Israel and, by heavily drawing on ethnographic data, is primarily based on Palestinian women's own experiences and narratives.

The key research question of this chapter is twofold: What role does the body play in Palestinian women's experiences of citizenship in Israel? And, in turn, what do these experiences tell us about citizenship in Israel? In order to answer these questions, the chapter considers the multiple ways in which Palestinian women's bodies have been targeted by Zionist strategies since the *nakba*. Citizenship in Israel, as it is experienced and narrated by Palestinian women, is structured—in classic settler colonial fashion—along Zionist ideological categories. As a result, there are sliding scales of citizenship, which are gendered, racialized, and classed and, as a result, are all linked to the body. These scales allow the state to pursue new strategies to eliminate the native (Wolfe 1994, 96), for instance, through land dispossession and appropriation.

33

In particular, Israeli citizenship's persistent cultural assimilationist drive and political exclusionary inclusion (Molavi 2014; Robinson 2013) function to assert indigenous loss while preserving Jewish citizenship privileges.

On the basis of the ongoing metonymic link between the indigenous body and land in both Zionist discourses and Zionist practices, Palestinian women's bodies continue to constitute a pivotal site for the power struggle between settler and colonized today. The experiences and narratives of citizenship among Palestinian women in Israel are complex and contradictory. Most important, they are atypical and inherently political, unsettling many of the deep-seated discourses of power that entrench the vested interests of the settler colonial state and society. A reading of their experiences through the body reveals that the main function of citizenship is not to protect Palestinian women's bodies but to sustain their marginalization within and exclusion from the Israeli body politic. Their stories reveal that not only is settler colonialism indwelling in Israel's citizenship regime but that citizenship itself constitutes a central component of the Zionist settler colonial project.

TARGETED SINCE THE *NAKBA*

Structures of settler colonialism, sexist oppression, and violence are closely intertwined in Israel, where Palestinian women's bodies were turned into the primary targets of Zionist violence at least since the *nakba*, which constitutes a vital analytical point of departure of any feminist analysis of Palestinian women's bodies in Israel (Shalhoub-Kevorkian, Ihmoud, and Dahir-Nashif 2014). Even though the full extent of the use of violence by Zionist military forces in 1948 has yet to be revealed, it is common knowledge that the sexual violence against and the killing of Palestinian women during the destruction of Palestinian villages was used as a deliberate instrument to systematically massacre, terrorize, and evict the Palestinian people (Morris 2004; Sa'di and Abu-Lughod 2007; Masalha 2012; Sayigh 1979, 2007; Kanaaneh and Nusair 2010). Women's personal experiences of rape and other forms of sexual violence remained largely silenced by both the victims and perpetrators. All the more, fast-traveling news, threat, and fear of rape at the time played a crucial role in precipitating the flight of a great many Palestinians from their homes (Morris 2004; Hasso 2000; Sayigh 1979). This was particularly the case after the Deir Yassin massacre, after which a handful of women survivors gave harrowing descriptions of the atrocities they experienced to investigating Red Cross and British Mandate officials.[3] Colonial police officer Richard Catling, for instance, reported that

I interviewed many of the womenfolk in order to glean some information . . .
but the majority of those women are very shy and reluctant to relate their
experiences especially in matters concerning sexual assault and they
need great coaxing before they will divulge any information. . . . There
is, however, no doubt that many sexual atrocities were committed by the
attacking Jews. Many young schoolgirls were raped and later slaughtered.
Old women were also molested. One story is current concerning a case
in which a young girl was literally torn in two. Many infants were also
butchered and killed (quoted in Sayigh 1979, 77).

The fact that Palestinian women who had experienced or witnessed sexual
violence shared their stories despite their traumatization and reluctance toward
(male) British observers indicates the extent of their fright and despair. Moreover, Catling's quote suggests that Zionist violence against Palestinian women
did not occur simply as a corollary of Zionist military takeover but it deliberately targeted women across the board, including young girls, infants, and older
women. Today, plenty of evidence also suggests that there were no differences
between the regions in which the Zionist military forces operated.[4] Also, the
physical and psychological brutality, provocation, and demonstrativeness that
accompanied the Zionist attacks on Palestinian women's bodies—such as the
girl torn in two—points to a calculated use of rape as a tactic that targets not
only one woman's body, but one woman's body as a representation of the Palestinian people as a whole, as anthropologist Susan Slyomovics reminds us,
"Rape as a military tactic succeeds in so many societies because it targets more
than the woman; it threatens her male kin—father, brother, husband—who
cannot protect her, their *sharaf* and *'ird* (honor)" (Slyomovics 2007, 35). How
integral Zionist violence against Palestinian women was to the settler colonial
logic of total elimination of indigenous people was clearly demonstrated at Deir
Yassin when Zionist forces shot a woman who was nine months pregnant and
cut her open to extract her unborn baby. As in other colonial contexts, indigenous women were clearly perceived by the Zionist military as "threatening
because of their ability to reproduce the next generation of peoples who can
resist colonization" (Smith 2003, 78).

As mentioned, one reason Zionist forces specifically aimed at Palestinian
women's bodies was to offend traditional Arab notions of *'ird* in order to com-
pel Palestinian families to leave their homes to protect their families (Peteet
1991, 59). Particularly during the 1940s, men's honor in Palestine was closely,
though not exclusively, linked to land ownership and the maintenance of female relatives' virginity (when unmarried) or exclusive sexual availability
(when married) (Swedenburg 1995, 78–79). Indeed, contemporary research

in the Occupied Territories and Palestinian refugee camps in Lebanon and Jordan have carved out the protection of family honor embodied by Palestinian women as one of the key motives—if not the primary motive—of flight of a large number of Palestinians (Peteet 1991, 59; Warnock 1990, 23; Sayigh 1979, 90; Morris 2004, 592; Kassem 2011, 162). Incidents of sexual violence remained almost exclusively silenced, however, by notions of honor and shame among the Palestinians as well as notions of moral superiority among the Zionists: "They [the Palestinians] are, according to their perception, preserving their dignity in the face of defeat. This suited the attitude of the Zionist Jewish authorities, who silenced the cases of rape in order to demonstrate moral superiority" (Kassem 2011, 158).

Zionist strategic assaults on Palestinian women's bodies affected more than enormous physical and psychological damages on the women. Women's bodies also became more strictly controlled by patriarchal structures via both male and female family members, who sought to protect their daughters from sexual abuse by confining them to their homes (which in many cases turned out to be not safe places at all). For some women, homes became places of physical imprisonment (Kassem 2011, 159) as well as political imprisonment as their participation in the national struggle after 1948 became more strictly controlled by male family members—a military strategy that was used by other European colonial forces such as the French in Algiers (Daoud 2009, 51). Palestinian feminist scholar Nadera Shalhoub-Kevorkian stresses that this strategy of attacking Palestinian women's bodies in order to control their political activities continues to be used today as the Zionist state not only tolerates militarized sexual abuse of Palestinians (especially in the Occupied Territories) but also actively mobilizes violence against Palestinian women (and the threat thereof) in an effort to coerce Palestinians into collaborating with the Zionist state. The strategy continued to be employed, for instance, during the First Intifada in 1987, when the sexual abuse of Palestinians for political reasons became known in Palestinian discourse as *isqat siyassy* (downfall) (Shalhoub-Kevorkian, Ihmoud, and Dahir-Nashif 2014).

Another important aspect of Zionist attacks on Palestinian women's bodies is that of practiced symbolism and metaphoric representation erected by both Palestinian and Zionist men but maintained by many Palestinian women. In ethno-political and religious conflicts, control of territory and control of the female body and sexuality are commonly conflated: intrusion into national territory is perceived as an intrusion into women's bodies and as pollution of the nation and its territory (Spivak 1992; Peterson 1994). As a result, Palestinian nationalists came to regard violence that targeted Palestinian women's bodies, and thereby men's "honor," as a symbolic performance of Israeli superiority and domination over the Palestinian nation (Massad 1995, 471; Peteet 1991; Warnock 1990, 23). At the same time, in the aftermath of 1948, Israelis denied outright the rape of Palestinian women in order to maintain their claim of superior moral values and the myth of *tohar ha-neshek* (the purity of arms), which posits that weapons remain pure provided they are employed only in self-defense (Shlaim 1999, 173). "The familiar image of the nation as a female body" (Slyomovics 1998, 200–201) is extremely common among nationalist discourses. Particularly in settler colonial and colonial contexts, the invasion and conquest of native land is often perceived by nationalists as rape perpetrated on that female body (Enloe 2000). *Ightisab* (rape) and its derivations were often used and continue to be used to refer to the expropriation of national territory during the *nakba* by both Palestinian men and women (Humphries and Khalili 2007, 213), many of whom continue to link the rape of a woman's body and the invasion of Palestinian land by referring to them with the same phrase "when the Jews entered" (Kassem 2011, 161).

For many Palestinian men, the rapes of Palestinian women were not only a wholesale negation of their manhood, they also interpreted them as assaults on their political identities. Having constituted a central motive in the flight of the Palestinian people, the fear of rape came to be construed as detrimental to nationalist mobilization in nationalist discourses after 1948 (Hasso 2000; Warnock 1990). Before the advent of nationalism, many men prioritized the defense of women against rape over the defense of their homes (Warnock 1990), but the nationalist movement chose the slogan *al'ard qabl al'ird* (land before honor) to indicate the importance of preserving national territory at any cost. Because of this prioritization in nationalist discourses, narratives of sexual violence became increasingly associated with the guilt of losing the land, once again silencing women's memories of the atrocities acted against them (Humphries and Khalili 2007, 213, 223). In the process, Palestinian women's bodily experiences and memories of the *nakba* were nationalized (that is, absorbed into the mainstream national discourse) as their narratives were perceived as complicating and destabilizing nationalist narratives (Hasso 2000; Humphries and Khalili 2007).

Such were especially the perceptions of women's narratives, and many Palestinian women who witnessed the events of 1948 openly recognized sexual violence and the threat thereof (particularly after the Deir Yassin massacre) as a major incentive for male family members in their decision to leave their homes. Narratives collected in Fatma Kassem's *Palestinian Women* (2011) attest to this. Her research on gendered memory of the *nakba* of women from Lyd and

Ramleh illuminates and underscores the central role that these women attach to the often politicized and collectivized female body in their stories of the *nakba* as a site of experience, resistance, and memory. By rejecting the notion that it is the exclusive responsibility of men to protect the honor, the land, and the lives of Palestinians, her interviewees contest the gendered meanings of honor (Kassem 2011, 165) but also implicitly question Palestinian men's decision that families must leave their homes. Kassem interprets the women's silence on their personal experiences of rape and honor as "cooperation with Palestinian patriarchy" and the "reproduction of the presentation of men as sole protectors of the nation, women and territory" (Kassem 2011, 166). I believe Kassem's is a rather hasty conclusion. In fact, as Kassem points out herself, women would commonly describe their role as active agents in rebuilding, taking care of, and protecting themselves and the family at the peak of crisis and war (Kassem 2011).

WHY THE BODY?

The initial goal of my research was to investigate how Palestinian women in Israel experience and practice citizenship. Truth be told, I did not expect the body to emerge as an important topic when I started my fieldwork. From early on, however, I was struck by the surprisingly large number of women who shared intimate stories about their bodies. I was caught off guard by how many of the stories revolved around sexual violence: Almost two out of three of the women had experienced some form of sexual violence, either personally or as witnesses, within their families, communities, or circle of acquaintances. Their narratives included stories of rape by family members or within dating or marriage relationships; sexual harassment by relatives, acquaintances, colleagues, and strangers; sexual slavery; obligatory inspections for virginity; femicide; and forced marriages.[5]

Rather than casting themselves solely as submissive victims, however, my interlocutors' stories frequently cast their bodies as active and strategizing agents. Our conversations included stories about sexual activities and preferences, resisting oppressive and patriarchal sexual norms, sexual experimentation, and menstrual products. Naturally, I began to wonder how and why our conversations, which commonly started with questions such as "What is your citizenship?" could and regularly did end up involving very intimate topics. Only after several lengthy and thorough rereadings of my interviews and field notes over several months did it strike me that even when we did not discuss issues of the body directly, the vast majority of my research participants had cast their bodies, sometimes metaphorically, as a central site of their daily struggles with both the colonial state and various patriarchal powers. I decided to interrogate why women chose to tell their stories in such bodily and intimate terms and realized that, to a large extent, women's experiences of citizenship took place at the level of the intimate, which is predominantly experienced through the body.

For most of its history, the body has been understood as a biological object producing physical difference, particularly gender, race, and class. This conception was put forward primarily by those defending existing social orders, including that of gender (Connell 2009, 53). As a result, the body has enjoyed special attention within feminist activist camps and theory. Feminist theorists—such as Juliet Mitchel, Julia Kristeva, Michèle Barrett, Nancy Chodorow—and Marxist and psychoanalytic feminists committed to the idea of subjectivity as a social construct were particularly concerned about women's marginalization from public philosophical and political discourses on the basis of widely accepted notions that masculinity is associated with the mind and reason and femininity is associated with nature and the body. Notably, such a linkage in corporeality was also attributed to other bodies, such as colonized bodies and lower-class bodies (McClintock 1995; Alcoff 2006, 103).

Feminist revaluation of the body, which particularly undermined mind-body dualism, has led to an acknowledgment that bodies are not simply given by nature but are socially differentiated, while subjectivity and identity cannot be separated from specific forms of embodiment (Ahmed 2000). In *Volatile Bodies*, Australian feminist scholar Elizabeth Grosz (1994) famously argued that the body is always clothed as it is always inscribed within particular cultural formations. In other words, there is no "natural," "pure," or "real" body. Although the body can act as a canvas reflecting social images and imaginings of womanhood and manhood, its construction is also strongly affected by social processes, as pointed out by sociologist Raewyn Connell, who writes, "The way our bodies grow and function is influenced by food distribution, sexual customs, warfare, work, sport, urbanization, education and medicine, to name only the most obvious influences. And all these influences are structured by gender" (2009, 54).

Feminist explorations of the ways in which women's bodies have been disciplined to correspond to social ideals and the power relations working through such disciplinary social processes have made extensive use of the work of Michel Foucault, who analyzed the body as an object. Most thoroughly in *Discipline and Punish* (1995), he showed how disciplinary power and practices produce and police "docile bodies." Building on this idea, Judith Butler's (2004) performative approach to gendered subjectivity claims that the subjection of our bodies to such practices becomes not only a way in which already male and female bodies seek to approximate an ideal, but also the very process whereby sexed and gendered subjects come into existence in the first place.

The theorization of the body employed here mainly draws mainly on Connell's concept of the body as both agent and object. As outlined in her book *Gender* (2009), Connell does not conceptualize the body merely as an object of social process, whether symbolic or disciplinary. Instead, she claims, bodies are active participants in social processes: "They participate through their capacities, development and needs, through the friction and their recalcitrance and through the reactions set by their pleasures and skills" (2009, 57). Therefore, bodies are involved in a historical process through ongoing circuits of practices—which Connell refers to as "social embodiment." These circuits create and re-create social structures and personal trajectories that, in turn, provide the conditions of new practices in which the bodies of both individuals and groups are addressed and involved (2009, 67).

Palestinian women's bodies in Israel all have their trajectories through time and place: they are born into and raised by different families from various socioeconomic and cultural backgrounds based in different localities. They are nurtured, educated, and equipped with all kinds of skills for life by a plethora of individuals, groups, and institutions. They experience, resist, enjoy, suffer, or give in to accidents, displacement, loss, pleasure, violence, childbirth, disability, poverty, illness, surgery, and death. They are both objects and agents in daily social practices that bring them into contact with other bodies. Others regularly try to "read" Palestinian women's bodies, as they function as important markers of identity boundaries. Even before a Palestinian child is born in Israel, her body is marked by difference. In that sense, the relation between its body and that of others is not ahistorical. Conceived and grown in a Palestinian woman's womb, the baby inherits marks of difference including those imposed on him or her by hegemonic Zionist discourses. Sara Ahmed argues in her book *Strange Encounters* (2000) that difference, in this context, is not simply found *on* the body, but is established as the relation between bodies and the history of those relations. The history of the relations between Palestinian women's bodies and Zionist settler colonialism will be explored in the following section.

INTERLOCKING FORMS OF VIOLENCE

> I still feel that the state inscribes its power over my body and that is not easy.—Safah, university lecturer, 45

Recognizing the Zionist settler colonialist invasion as a structure, not an event (Wolfe 1994, 96) involves addressing the *nakba* not as an historical incident, but as the continuous Israeli invasion of Palestinian land and the destruction of Palestinian people in order to replace them with Jewish settlers, or what Patrick Wolfe refers to as the settler colonialist "logic of elimination" (2006). Accordingly, Zionist violence against Palestinian women's bodies continues today not as a by-product of settler colonialism but as an integral part of its very structure and as a logic that conflates Zionist invasion of indigenous women's bodies with Zionist invasion of indigenous land. Ongoing processes of Israeli occupation are thus maintained today by persisting threats on and control over the colonized body, including control over indigenous women's bodies and—because of their ability to reproduce—sexuality.

Violence that targets Palestinian women's bodies in Israel does not constitute an isolated exception to normal life but often is integral to the daily lives and social relations of colonized indigenous women, especially those living under severe deprivation and dispossession. The working of violence against Palestinian women in Israel is complicated by structures of settler colonial power, which based on its racialized machinery of domination and logic of elimination, explicitly targets native women (Shalhoub-Kevorkian et al. 2014), on the one hand, and internal patriarchal oppression that seeks to actively control women's bodies under the stresses of Israeli occupation, on the other. As a consequence, Palestinian women experience several forms of violence, including femicides, which have become increasingly prevalent since 1948.

No other issue calls the meaning behind Israeli citizenship among Palestinians in Israel into question as much as the violence perpetrated directly on Palestinian citizens by the state forces. The murder of numerous civilians and the excessive amount of violence against Palestinians by police and military officers, as well as decisions at the levels of the law enforcement systems, consistently indicate disproportionately harsh treatment of Palestinians (Ratner 1996). They further demonstrate how Israeli authorities perceive and treat Palestinians not as citizens to be protected but as internal enemies to be kept under strict control and surveillance. Between 2000 and 2015 alone, fifty Palestinians were killed by racist or state violence, more than the number killed by government forces.[6] During that period, the "October 2000 events," the murder of thirteen Palestinians, twelve of whom were citizens of Israel, by state forces marked a key turning point as the deadliest incident of state-sanctioned violence against the indigenous minority since the Kafr Qasim massacre in 1956.[7] Palestinian women are not spared from state violence, as can be seen in the recent case of the mentally ill Asra'a Zidan Abed, who was shot and injured by four police officers at a bus station in Afula.[8] The differential treatment of Jewish citizens is further emphasized by the fact that attacks by Israeli civilians or police officers on Palestinians never result in the indictment of the perpetrators of these crimes.[9]

Palestinian citizens do not have to break the law in order for their bodies to be treated as outlaws. This is particularly the case whenever Palestinians express their historical and political connection to pre-1948 Palestine publicly. Palestinian women's bodies are especially vulnerable to police attacks during public demonstrations. One of my interviewees, a young woman called Soheir, for instance, was shot in the head with a steel-coated rubber bullet while taking part in the July 2014 demonstrations against Israeli attacks on Gaza. The responsible police officer was not charged for Soheir's injuries. As commonly happens, violent Israeli right-wing mobs assaulted Palestinians and Israeli left-wing activists during antiwar demonstrations, causing the police to "intervene." Such interventions usually lead to many Palestinians, including an increasing number of women, being arrested and injured. Through the use of legal mechanisms, all types of Palestinian political protest are deprived of their political content by being collectively criminalized as a unified nationalist threat to the state (Rosenberg 2002).

It is important to note that Palestinian bodies come under attack not only through direct force but also through a lack of police protection.[10] The lack of protection of Palestinian citizens is firmly established and has a particularly severe impact on Palestinian women's bodies. One of the most insightful examples that I came across is the issue of femicide and sexual abuse, which continue to be prevalent in Palestinian society in Israel. Women who had been affected by sexual violence told me that they refrained from contacting the police because they did not trust Israeli police officers. They feared being ostracized and banned from their society, because "things might get even worse" or because they considered it politically problematic.

The number of academic explorations of the Israeli police's lack of protection of Palestinian women remain scarce. Among the few existing ones, sociologist Manar Hassan's exploration has revealed the ways in which femicide and state interests are often bound up with each other. Her research points to an accumulating number of cases of girls and women who have fled their homes out of fear that they might be murdered, only to be returned to their potential murderers by the police (Hassan 2002, 19). Hassan believes that the fundamental reason behind the cooperation between the Israeli government and patriarchal Palestinians leaders is the state's interest in stabilizing *hama'il* (plural of *hamula*[11]) in order to reduce the costs of their surveillance (Hassan 2002, 22).

In her very detailed investigation of Israeli police reactions to violence against Palestinian women, Nadera Shalhoub-Kevorkian supports Hassan's findings by revealing a large number of cases where police officers drew on what she refers to as the "cultural sensitivity approach" as a means of neutralizing their responsibility and justifying a noninterventionist approach (Shalhoub-Kevorkian 2004, 186). She emphasizes that police officers frequently refer the victims to "culturally acceptable" authorities (such as tribal heads or *mukhtars*, religious or village leaders) or return them to their abusive families under the pretext of cultural sensitivity. Shalhoub-Kevorkian considers such situations in the militarist and racist context in which they take place: The representatives of official or state agencies rely on military-based knowledge or authority in their reactions to violence against Palestinian women. As a result, she argues, they not only deny abused women their right to assistance and protection as citizens but actually harm them (187).

Particularly within the Israeli public domain, violent attacks on Palestinian women's bodies continue to be advocated as a potent weapon with which to advance Zionist constructions of the "Arab enemy" in order to complete the settler colonialist project of evicting the indigenous population. Sexual violence pervades the settler state and society and is frequently tolerated in an environment in which rape culture and male chauvinism are considered acceptable because of the power that resides within hegemonic, militant, and hypermasculinist Zionist discourses. Such discourses frame Palestinian women as threatening racialized enemies whose bodies must be destroyed in order to prevent enemy reproduction. Recent examples of this phenomenon include Israeli scholar Mordechai Kedar's statement in an interview with the Israeli broadcasting authority after the bodies of three kidnapped settler teens were found in July 2014: "The only thing that can deter terrorists, like those who kidnapped the children, and killed them, is the knowledge that their sister or their mother will be raped."[12]

Times of intensified conflict, such as the war on Gaza in the summer of 2014, especially incite public advocacy of sexual violence against Palestinian women in Israel. *"nesayen otam!"* (Screw them! / Finish them!) is a commonly used Hebrew expression to see off soldiers of the Israeli Defense Forces (IDF) on their way to battle. The city council and citizens of the Israeli coastal town Or Yehuda, for instance, prepared a banner of support during the war reading "Israeli soldiers, the residents of Or Yehuda are with you! Pound 'their mother' and come back home safely to your mother."[13] Shortly after the public hanging of the banner, a composite image of a woman labelled "Gaza" wearing a black Muslim dress that reveals her naked legs and red high heels was widely shared among Jewish Israelis via WhatsApp. Above and below it were the words "Bibi, finish inside this time! Signed, citizens in favor of a ground assault." By using the phrase "to finish" meaning "to ejaculate" in colloquial Hebrew, sexual violence against Palestinian women was openly espoused.[14]

Like many other colonized women, Palestinian women in Israel experience violence—whoever the culprits—as violence that cannot be disconnected from structures of patriarchal control, aggravated by both Zionist forceful eviction and Zionist occupation of the Palestinian people and land. This explains a statement of one of my interviewees, a young Palestinian woman who grew up in Canada and Jordan, where she experienced sexual slavery as a child perpetrated by her father over years, as well as repeated sexual assault by her ex-husband: "I wish I was never Palestinian. . . . It has brought me so much pain. . . . I wish I was never Palestinian." This sentiment is echoed in Andrea Smith's findings during her work as rape crisis counselor for native women: "When a native woman suffers abuse, this abuse is not just an attack on her identity as a woman, but on her identity as a Native. The issues of colonial, race, and gender oppression cannot be separated. . . . Their experience is qualitatively different from that of white women" (Smith 2003, 71).

Although sexual violence perpetrated by colonial forces and perpetrated by Palestinians against Palestinian women cannot be separated from one another, they can be experienced in contradictory manners and apparent safe spaces can emerge in the openings or frictions between the two oppressive layers. For example, state violence against Palestinian women but also the state's failure to implement social reforms to provide a decent level of health, welfare services, and the protection of women from violence allow social institutions such as the family, community, or tribe to take on more powerful roles in women's lives. These social units may provide protection and apparent safe spaces from state violence and control, but they can also use their increased power over women to produce violence and reinforce patriarchal gender relations within Palestinian society.

The contradictory and complex nature of the synergy between apparent safe spaces occasionally offered to women by both patriarchal Palestinian society and Zionist oppressors was best illustrated to me through the story of Amal, a young businesswoman in Haifa, who told me about her trip to Ramallah. Amal dismounted a public bus on the Jerusalem side, crossed the Qalandia checkpoint into Ramallah, and waited on a corner to be picked up by her friend who lives in the West Bank. Wearing a long hippie dress revealing parts of her shoulder, Amal was approached by several strangers:

> There were men, young men, and they started street-harassing me. It was really bad. Those beasts said to me, "Hey love, you're so beautiful. You're so tall." Then a soldier in an IDF jeep comes by and stops and pulls down the

window and says to me in Hebrew, "Are you okay? Is everything okay? Do you need help?" Imagine: an Israeli jeep in front of Palestinians! And that moment, Kim, was by far one of the worst moments of my life. How do I dare to feel a bit safe for the fact that this soldier who works at a bloody checkpoint to come by and protect me from "my people"?! That answers your question of how the women's and Palestinian struggle interplay for me. Somehow—and I can never forgive myself for this—I felt safe.

Amal did not feel comfortable about telling me this story and the significance of it did not lie in the question of whether one form of oppression was worse than the other or that it came as surprise to her that she found herself in a situation in which an IDF soldier showed some concern for a Palestinian woman. Amal's discomfort about being in a place in which she felt she was physically threatened and in which, simultaneously, she found herself at an Israeli soldier's mercy, and worse, in which she admitted to herself that she felt safe because of the presence of somebody she did not want to feel safe with, somebody whose main task was the eradication of her people, demonstrates the interwoven and complex ways in which violence, and also threats of violence and safety, can be experienced by Palestinian women.

Amal clearly felt she had to share the story with me in a context in which we were discussing violence against Palestinian women. Even though she could have just told me about the Palestinian men harassing her, the soldier's role was central to her story. A man's power over a woman is built on his access to her sexuality and body; this access includes the "protection" of her sexuality and body or, in the context of the soldier, his power to protect her, which, in a way, further consolidates masculine and colonial power and control over her. As a Palestinian woman, Amal's ownership over her body was violated by an assault on it made at the intersections of colonial and patriarchal powers, where gender and racialized orders enforced each other in what looked from the outside like a reenactment of "white men are saving brown women from brown men" (Spivak 1988).

OTHERED AND "MARKED" BODIES

Palestinian women's bodies in Israel are also targeted in much subtler ways by the Zionist state and society. Subtlety does not necessarily imply that its actions should be interpreted as somehow less violent. As indigenous bodies that managed to remain on their homeland, Zionist efforts to uproot Palestinians from their homes, their land, and nation in Israel differ from strategies employed outside the 1948 territories. The logic of Zionism dictates that occupied territory, settler colonialism's "irreducible element" (Wolfe 2006, 388), is strictly reserved for the Jewish people and, according to this logic, it is the Jewish body in Israel that constitutes what Moira Gatens refers to as the "unmarked body" (1991, 82). She considers such an unmarked body as a body that is "at home" or "in place," and it is metonymic with and defines the body politic. Bodies that are marked as different, bodies that are marked "out of place," are excluded from the body politic: "Slaves, foreigners, women, the conquered, children, and the working class, have all been excluded from political participation, at one time or another, by their bodily specificity" (Gatens 1996, 23). The notion of political exclusion being based on corporeality was very much reflected in statements made during my fieldwork, statements such as "It is physically impossible for us to be citizens here." In *Strange Encounters: Embodied Others in Post-coloniality* Sara Ahmed builds upon Gatens's notion of "unmarked bodies" by suggesting that the process of forming the boundaries of "unmarked bodies" has an intimate connection to the forming of social space—territory marked as "homeland" (2000, 46). Thus, the containment of certain bodies in their skin (bodily space) is a mechanism for the containment of their social space.

The othering of Palestinian bodies plays a central role in Israelis' own national identity formation. Sara Ahmed (2000) argues that, although identity operates through the designation of others as "strangers," it is through daily encounters with others that this identity formation takes place. Indeed, Palestinian bodies are turned into targets of discrimination via daily encounters with Israelis who not only seek to identify them as strangers by reading signs on their body, or by reading their body as a sign, but also perpetually reconstitute themselves as subjects during these encounters. As Ahmed points out, the encounter through which the subject assumed a body image and comes to be distinguishable from the Other is a racial encounter (Ahmed 2000, 43). Difference as a marker of power on the body is not simply found on the body, which often makes attempts to "read the body" such a challenge, but is established as a relation between bodies, the history of this relation, and ongoing encounters (44).

In Israel, these relations between bodies produce important corporeal hierarchies according to which citizenship rights are accorded to specific bodies along the lines of race and gender, thereby also playing a central role in the production of class in Israel. As Israel's founding group and their descendants, the Ashkenazim, occupy the most powerful positions within Israeli state and society while enjoying the maximum of citizens' rights, frequently dominating Sephardim and Mizrahim, who were not part of the original Zionist plan but were mobilized by the Zionist project mainly to support Israel's labor force and boost the Jewish demographics since the 1950s and 1960s. Ethiopian Jews, brought to Israel in several mass transfer operations in the late 1980s and early 1990s, experience overt racism and discrimination, as has been demonstrated again most recently by the Israeli police brutality exercised against them.[15] The state separates non-Jewish groups such as Palestinians again into religious and ethnic groups such as Muslim, Christians, Druze, and Bedouin. Last in the hierarchy are those with no citizenship: foreign workers (mostly Asian) and refugees (mostly African). Overall, one can observe a doubly racialized system of power and privilege: Although Zionist constructions of race based on religious membership produce the underpinnings of Jewish racial privilege that translates into political hegemony, within both Jewish and non-Jewish citizen groups, another Zionist classification of race regulates the distribution of power according to the idea that of people of color are biologically inferior.

In an environment in which Palestinians are under pressure to make their bodies "disappear" while they yet remain "marked," failures to read their bodies are frequent, as Anan, a student from Kafr Bir'im, brought home to me: "For some stupid reason they do not think that there are any blonde or blue-eyed Arabs and I also don't speak Hebrew with an Arabic accent. . . . So they always look at me surprised: 'Oh, you're an Arab?' It's like I should carry a sign around me saying 'I'm an Arab' because they cannot recognize and tag me easily enough."

One of the most common examples of when Israelis' failure to "read the body" of Palestinians that was shared with me was during apartment rentals. Jewish landlords would invite Palestinian potential tenants to look at apartments, show them around apartments, agree on a price for an apartment, and cancel on them (or end the contact) as soon as they looked at the Palestinian IDs during the signing of the rental agreement. Zuhur, a Palestinian female artist in her early twenties, for instance, had already been looking for a room to rent in Tel Aviv at the time of our interview in early 2013. She had visited many available rooms that she had found online and even received some confirmations. The landlords, however, changed their minds whenever they learned her national identity. Usually, they would either disappear or argue that they couldn't accept Zuhur as a tenant because of her dog—an odd argument considering that, unlike other metropolises, it is very common in Tel Aviv to rent an apartment with a dog—and considering that Zuhur would always bring her dog with her during the apartment viewings. A year after our interview, she posted this on Facebook:

> I find a good apartment on the internet. I call the owner on the phone (and) I say, "Hey, this is Zuhur." Of course, their minds automatically translate my name into "Tamar" or "Smadar" or any other name that is not Arabic! Then I go see the flat. Sometimes I like it and give the owner the best offer he could

get for the apartment and of course he agrees! But . . . when things become
more serious and he asks me to send him details about myself (ID and stuff)
he simply disappears! I tried to get my Jewish friends to call from their own
numbers and ask about the apartment and as expected: they were invited
to come and visit. . . . I've been looking for an apartment for over year now
(meanwhile I've been living in different sublets) and I'm starting to lose the
last few drops of hope I had on this sick place!

In contrast, "passing as the Other" through their fluency in Hebrew, imitations
of Israeli clothing style, imitations body language and gestures, has emerged as
a valuable counterstrategy by women who were born and raised as citizens in
Israel. Many women told me proudly about their ability to "pass as the Other,"
which was especially common among women who grew up around Jewish Israelis such as a Druze woman who went to a religious Jewish kindergarten and
Ghayda, a law student whose parents decided that, because of her blindness,
she was better cared for and supported in a Jewish kindergarten and school.
Ghayda told me rather proudly:

> Israelis usually don't believe me when I say that I'm Arab. I speak Hebrew
> almost since birth . . . but also their body language, their attitude. . . . I can
> do that without looking like an Arab. I always went to a Jewish kindergarten
> and school and I'm glad about it. People sometimes ask, "What are you?
> Moroccan or what?" At university, I took part in political conversations but I
> never had a problem with anybody, no matter whom . . . because I know how
> to talk to them.

Strategies of "passing as the Other" are frequently used by Palestinian women
to access resources and benefits (education, job opportunities, accommodation, etc.) that are reserved for Jewish Israelis, but also to avoid trouble or protect themselves from potential threats (e.g., body searches and physical and
verbal attacks). By transgressing racial boundaries constituted by Zionist discourses, "passing" can be regarded as a "sign of racial duplicity which threatens
to undermine the stability of racial categorization" (Young 1996, 85).

INNER ENEMIES

At the heart of Israeli Othering of Palestinians lies an inner contradiction:
On the one hand, Palestinians are coerced to assimilate, "de-Palestinize,"
and lose their connections to pre-1948 Palestine, including language, dress,
and culture. On the other hand, however, as potential threats, their bodies
are expected to remain identifiable in the eyes of the colonizer. In daily life,

Palestinian bodies are marked as strangers not only in order to be kept out of Israeli social space but also in order to be identified as threats to the Jewish body in Israel. Sara Ahmed refers to this dynamic as "stranger danger," a discourse that produces the stranger as someone who must be expelled from "the purified space of the community, the purified life of the good citizen" (Ahmed 2000, 22). Janan, a feminist researcher in Haifa shared with me several stories of how she experienced the stranger danger phenomenon through an everyday encounter in Haifa's Wadi Nisnas, where, because of her light skin and fluent Hebrew, she was often mistaken for a Jewish woman: "I got off a bus and a woman came closer to me and asked me, 'May I go with you a little bit?' I thought in my mind—woman to woman—'of course!' Maybe she felt more comfortable this way for some reason. And I said 'of course, do you need any help?' It sounded like she wasn't born in Israel. . . . Maybe she was a Russian immigrant. And she said, 'Yeah, I've heard that there are a lot of Arabs here.'"

As Frantz Fanon famously argued in his book *Black Skin, White Masks*, colonialism leaves its imprint on the body of the colonized by inscribing oppression on it, thereby objectifying blackness (Fanon 1967). One of the most salient settler colonial inscriptions on Palestinians in Israel is their construction as internal enemies. Since the establishment of the state in 1948, perceptions of the Palestinian national minority as a (demographic) threat and danger have been expressed in manifold ways (Pappé 2011, 3). More than a third of Jewish Israelis openly declare that they regard their fellow Palestinian citizens as "inner enemies."[16] Public discourses of the sort entail serious consequences for the daily lives of Palestinian women and men in Israel. The severity of this representation is expressed, for instance, in the fact that almost half of Jewish Israelis are in favor of removing Palestinian citizens from the country.[17]

The construction of Palestinian citizens as enemies of Israel is not limited to passive perceptions or individual incidents. It permeates Israeli state and society and is actively and frequently propagated in public. In July 2014, Knesset member Ayelet Shaked, for instance, publicly declared that the "entire Palestinian people" were the enemy and called for their genocide on Facebook. Her post received thousands of "likes" and did not prevent her from becoming the current Israeli Minister of Justice. One excerpt from her post read "Now this also included the mothers of the martyrs, who send them to hell with flowers and kisses. They should follow their sons, nothing would be more just. They should go, as should the physical homes in which they raised the snakes. Otherwise, more little snakes will be raised there."[18] This depiction resoundingly echoes classic settler colonial imaginings and constructions of indigenous women as threatening, which are primarily based on women's ability to give birth to future generations of indigenous inhabitants. Thus, Palestinian children, too, are dehumanized and demonized as "snakes," biblically symbolizing evil and viciousness. This racialization and criminalization of Palestinian children and women comes into being through the settler colonial "organizing grammar of race" (Wolfe 2006, 388), according to which the continuation of indigenous presence, manifested through indigenous homes and children, is the prime motive for the elimination of the Palestinian population. Notions of danger-ousness, civilization, religion, and ethnicity play a major supporting role but do not constitute the cardinal inducement for elimination.

This passage also demonstrates that Zionist constructions of the inner enemy are not only racialized but also gendered. Shaked's portrayal of the Palestinian woman as the mother and reproducers of the indigenous (usually male) terror-ists is a classic and common representation of Palestinian women as threats to the State of Israel. Israeli imaginings of Palestinian women as inner enemies are not limited to the terrorist's mother as I ascertained through my conversations with women such as Soheir, a young professional who lives and works in Haifa. Like many other women her age, she was born and raised in a Palestinian village in the Galilee and moved to Haifa to study at Haifa University. Her appearance quickly caught my attention, as her long, black curls, flamboyant style of dress, big, shiny jewelry, and heavy smoky-eye makeup made her stand out in the crowd of people who were packed into the tiny café in which we agreed to meet for our interview. Soheir proudly identified as a feminist but also made sure to emphasize to me the distinctiveness of Palestinian women's struggles in Israel. One of her stories was about her experience at the university:

> One of my English classes was taught by this American Jewish professor, who made Aliyah[19] and openly identified as a Zionist. . . . I think he enjoyed getting into discussions with me even though he clearly didn't like me. I was called to a disciplinary panel because I took part in a demonstration against the killing of Palestinians in Gaza. . . . I had exceeded the maximum of possible disciplinary warnings, and they told me that if I didn't start playing by the rules, I would never get a degree from an Israeli university. Luckily, there were a few professors who defended me. After the session, this professor stopped me in the hallway and said, "Come to my office!" In his office he said, "Listen, do you want to be kicked out of the university?" I said, "No, why?" He said, "Listen to me carefully. It's not that I agree with everything you say, or that I support your ideas, but you need to understand that you are a threat to this country and you are a threat to the existence of this country. You are a threat to Zionists and you and the people like you are the people that Israel is scared of. The hijab-wearing terrorist woman who is stuck in her home won't

be listened to but you, you are educated, feminist, proud to be Palestinian
and fighting—you will be listened to."

Soheir's account illustrates how the "Palestinian woman enemy" is currently
constructed, feared, and attacked in Israel, even within academic environments: Her professor confirmed the binary "good" (i.e., nonreligious, educated, modern) versus "bad" (religious, uneducated, "terrorist") constructions
of Arab-Israeli women, emphasizing the potential danger that she posed with
her education, outspokenness, self-confidence, and potential to mobilize more
women. This fear is particularly relevant in educational environments, where
Palestinian connections to their pre-1948 history or Palestinians outside Israel
are frequently criminalized. Again, the body played an important role in this
context: As conceived by her professor, Soheir's physical appearance poses a
threat, and he interprets it as evidence for her rebellion against her patriarchal
society. For that reason, her feminism destabilizes stereotypes of Palestinian women as oppressed subjects within their "backward" traditional society.
Moreover, her appearance does not fit the stereotypical frame and makes her
body less recognizable as the inner enemy, thereby frustrating the colonizer's
desire to "read her body" and to identify her as a potential threat.

Palestinian women's bodies such as Soheir's become increasingly collectivized, politicized, and criminalized within the Zionist state. Nevertheless, they
are not simply passive objects to colonizer's practices and readings but subjects
that produce and perform social meaning (Butler 1990). It is often through means
of the body that they carefully navigate their lives through the tensions between
modernization and tradition in Israel. Soheir's choice of clothing, for instance,
the dropping of the traditional long and full covering common in her village for
tight dresses, still takes place within the framework of what is considered appropriate within Palestinian urban society. Though her clothing style appropriates
some Western fashion styles, her Palestinian identity is divulged by wearing
traditional jewelry, eye-makeup, and occasionally a *kaffiye*[20] (particularly during
demonstrations and at university). As will be further explored in the following
chapters, the ways the body is dressed can also pose a political statement, as Soheir claims her right to be in the very place that seeks to delegitimize and erase
Palestinian existence. In that regard, clothes are important in understanding the
performance of the female body as an agent of both resistance and compliance.

THE MAKING OF THE ARAB-ISRAELI WOMAN

Racialized and biologized as internal enemies and, hence, obstacles to the Zionist project, Palestinian women in Israel are excluded from Israel's body politic.

Zionist strategies to mark them as bodies out of place are practiced by both the
Israeli state and society. Most overtly, these strategies include stripping Palestinians of their national identity, their history, and their feelings of belonging to
the Palestinian nation. Examples include the imposed designation of Palestinians in Israel as Israeli Arabs or Arab Israelis, a historical distortion that aims
to interrupt the continuity of their national existence by separating Palestinians in Israel from Palestinians in the Occupied Territories and those in exile.
Other strategies, however, take on more corporeal forms, such as segregation
on Israeli buses and in schools, differential treatment by the Israeli police both
in protecting (Shalhoub-Kevorkian 2004) and, as shown earlier, in attacking
Palestinian bodies of men, women, and children alike, as well as the charges
filed after police misconduct.[21]

A thorough understanding of the estrangement experienced by Palestinian women in Israel needs to consider the Arab-Israeli woman—which is how
Palestinian women in Israel are referred to and constructed by the Israeli state
and society. The naming politics of the term itself carries some important
expectations about Palestinian citizens, including the de-Palestinization of
their identity and the interruption of their relations with Palestinians outside
Israel. Most important, the State of Israel has historically avoided the term
Palestinian in its vocabulary to avoid the implied historical claim of Palestinians to their homeland within the 1948 territories. The tools employed to de-
Palestinize the indigenous population are no less eliminatory than violence
itself. They include diverse and far-reaching methods of what Ilan Pappé has
coined "cultural memoricide" (Pappé 2006), which include not only systematic scholarly, political, and military methods of written hegemonic history
but also materialized history (destruction of material evidence of Palestinian
history), toponymicide (the erasure of ancient Palestinian place names and
their Hebraization—replacement with newly coined Hebrew toponymy). The
quotidian construct of the Arab-Israeli also carries some important messages
about how Palestinians in Israel should appear and carry themselves within
Israeli society and in respect to the outside world.

The "Arab-Israeli," "Israeli Arab," or "good Arab" has come to signify the
Palestinian in Israel who is thankful for her or his citizenship, loyal to the
State of Israel, politically apathetic, and quiet. She or he is often depicted as
progressive, which, in this context, means abandoning historical and cultural
ties to Palestinian land and people and, it is important to note, being willing to
cooperate with state officials, for instance, by betraying information about fellow Palestinians to the national secret service (Cohen 2010). The incentive for
becoming docile "Arab-Israelis" is receiving a share of Israel's modernization

project, which entails generous health, education, and housing benefits for its Arab citizens. As pointed out by Shira Robinson, it is the coexistence of the good and bad (i.e., hostile, menacing, intransigent) that came to embody the construct of the Israeli Arab: "One part of him was tied to the state and its future, the other was a reminder of his potential to slip back into his true essence—a rationale why they would always keep him at arm's length" (Robinson 2013, 151).

In this context, the good Arab is often pitted against the bad Arab in public discourse, when, in fact, the Palestinian people as a whole remain an oppressed minority, regardless of their behavior. The selective drawing on both good and bad Arabs serves to communicate an essentially empty promise of democratic inclusion. Rhoda Kanaaneh's research on Palestinian soldiers in the Israeli military, for instance, reveals that even Palestinians who go as far as to serve in the Israeli Defense Force do not receive the same citizenship rights as their Jewish Israeli counterparts: "Even when people are willing to go to great lengths to accommodate the state, becoming Zionists, soldiers, Likudniks, or whatever else, the power and privileges they acquire does not change the Jewish nature of the state or their non-Jewish positioning within it (2003: 15)." Despite of these soldiers' willingness to essentially fight their own people, they are nevertheless subject to strategies of elimination such as systematic house demolition (Kanaaneh 2003).

The Zionist construct of the assimilated good Arab in Israel is not only racialized but also gendered. Accordingly, there are established notions of the good Arab woman who, oppressed by the traditions and customs of her "narrow-minded" and "backward" community, should consider herself lucky and thankful for the social and political opportunities offered to Arab women by the State of Israel. Contemporary constructs of the Arab woman are produced by various Zionist discourses, including those that refer to themselves as liberal and left-wing. Their discourses frequently include celebratory and exploratory narratives about Palestinian women, such as the "Arab female spring" of Palestinian women entering Israeli political institutions like the Knesset or local councils, "revolutionary events" within Bedouin women's education, or reports of sexual violence against Palestinian women as violence that takes place exclusively within the boundaries of the Arab communities and is isolated from the state.[22]

In many ways, the strategy of modernizing Palestinian women has functioned as a measure of the legitimacy of power in Palestine for Zionist, Arab, and British leaders (Katz 1996, 39; Katz 2003; Fleischmann 2003; Chatterjee 1993). Israeli normalization of the racialization of Palestinian women's bodies frequently deploys a modernization rhetoric toward the Palestinian society, which is condescendingly referred to as *migzar ha-aravi* (the Arab sector). The status of Palestinian women constitutes a key role in racializing Palestinians as backward, sexist, and traditional Others, regularly in an attempt to legitimize Israel's differential treatment and discriminatory policies toward them. Such modernizing discourses date back to an early Zionist ideology that, in European colonial and Orientalist fashion, framed the Jewish people as the bearers of European civilization in the face of what they perceived as a culturally backward region and people living on an uncultivated land. Even today these perceptions contribute to the foundations of Israeli modernization discourses and are part and parcel of Israel's struggle to secure its own modernity (Kanaaneh 2002, 252). They are endured by and experienced by Palestinian women as consistent patterns of selective negligence. A Bedouin interviewee, for instance, explained thus: "On the one hand, the state sees us as out-of-control breeders. On the other hand, they don't give us education. I say, 'Give us educational opportunities!' and you will see, we will have fewer children . . . if that is what the state is worried about." The settler colonial state casts itself as the "savior of the Arab-Israeli woman" on three levels: Politically, it stages itself as a democratic and modern system that not only invites and welcomes Palestinian women to participate in the local and national political frameworks provided (and controlled) but also insists on their doing so. Particularly in the face of patriarchal *hamula* and tribal politics that continue to dominate Palestinian local politics, the state seeks the opportunity to enter the stage as an actor who, in contrast to Palestinian society, celebrates the increasing number of Palestinian women who decide to run as candidates for local elections, most recently in the local elections in 2013.[23]

On the socioeconomic level, the state has cast itself since its very establishment as the savior of its Arab-Israeli women by providing them with significant education and career opportunities. Public portrayals of the State of Israel in the media and political representation make great efforts to draw attention to the government's efforts to improve the living standards in Palestinian localities. Women are frequently displayed as the key beneficiaries of the "social revolution" made possible by its new government. Of course, the state's efforts stand in sharp contrast to the numerous reports of the poverty experienced by Palestinian women, particularly those living in the countryside, the continuing difficulties Palestinian women face when trying to enter the Israeli labor market or academic field, and the gendered ways in which particularly Palestinian women suffer from the inequality between Jewish and Palestinian localities in terms of electricity, running water, public transportation, functioning sewage systems, and so on.[24]

Finally, on the state level, Israel represents itself as a savior of Palestinian women's physical health and safety by providing them with public health-care services, and "protecting" them from violence, particularly domestic violence perpetrated by Palestinian men. Again, this image stands in sharp contrast to the reports on the inequalities between the health-care services provided to Jewish and Palestinian women and research revealing the neglect of Palestinian women's safety by Israeli authorities (Shalhoub-Kevorkian 2004).[25] Nevertheless, by reinforcing Israel's image as the white knight of Palestinian women, hegemonic portrayals of the indigenous population as sexist, barbaric, and backward are solidified by drawing on and stressing classic settler colonial imaginings and narratives of the "dirty native mind" that not only tolerates but upholds savage traditional practices such as polygamy, forced marriage, and domestic violence.

CONCLUSION

This chapter argues that the body plays a central role in Palestinian women's experience of citizenship in Israel. Their experiences are significantly marked by violence, including sexual violence and harassment, police violence, and the enhancement of violence against women that take place in patriarchal Palestinian communities. It is through their bodies that these women experience differential treatment in everyday life by Israeli state officials and society, especially at national borders, when applying for housing or jobs, when taking political action in public, and in daily racist encounters. In particular, examples of the last have demonstrated that Palestinian women's bodies are marked by difference in Israel. Even though the difference was imposed on women's bodies by the colonizer, the colonizer has also failed significantly in its attempts to read this difference from Palestinian women's bodies. Having arisen from the history of the relationship between settler and colonized, this difference is in constant flux as it is destabilized and renegotiated by both colonizer and colonized in the present.

In contrast, and as a result thereof, the narratives of my research participants have revealed that their bodies constitute a central site in their experiences of citizenship in Israel, which continue to be dominated by the struggle between colonizer and colonized. Their experiences demonstrate that it is, in fact, through citizenship that the state seeks to control their bodies as colonial subjects. The state's use of violence (and threats thereof) and constructions of Palestinian women as inner enemies constitute central tools in the production, maintenance, and legitimization of domination and subdomination. It is

important to note that this targeting of indigenous women's bodies by Zionist strategies is not a side effect but is central to the structural logic of settler
colonialism, which conflates indigenous women's bodies and indigenous land.

The recipe for citizenship for Palestinian women in Israel is, thus, ready-
made, insofar as the ingredients and their portions are predefined and fixed: the
making of the "Jewish state" is an exclusionary idea—both prior to and since
the establishment of the settler colonial state—whose realization, by nature,
relies on a logic of elimination. Settler colonialism destroys the indigenous
society in order to replace it with a settler-colonial society. Because invasion in
a settler colonial context constitutes a structure rather than an event (Wolfe
1994, 96), strategies of elimination are continuous and take on various forms
of dispossession and land appropriation, as well as assimilation, which, it is
important to iterate, is not less eliminatory.

Assimilation is particularly relevant to 1948 Palestinian women, whose collective memory and identity is targeted through the body by various Israeli
policies that aim to transform Palestinian women into "Arab-Israeli woman"
and recruit them into the state's culture in order to keep them under firm control. Assimilation through citizenship in this context is an effective strategy
of elimination, primarily because it "does not involve disruptive affront to
the rule of law that is ideologically central to the cohesion of settler society"
(Wolfe 2006, 402). At the same time, it serves the state's aims to uphold its
democratic facade and self-identification as modern. Lorenzo Veracini, who
has led recent efforts to theorize settler colonialism as an important global
phenomenon, posits that settler colonialism is "characterized by a persistent
drive to supersede the conditions of its operation" (2011: 3)—that is, to make
itself seem "natural without origin" (and without end) and, thus, inevitable.
Palestinian women's bodies resist this drive by providing valuable alternative
knowledge that dismantles deep-seated Zionist myths of "equal citizenship"
and settler colonialism as a "thing of the past." By doing so, these bodies are
transformed into potentially powerful sources of defiance, which are capable of
subverting dominant historical narratives but also of continuously unsettling
and complicating the boundaries between colonizer and colonized.

NOTES

1. The need to restore settler colonial structure to an analysis of the
continuing subjection of Palestinians by Israelis has been emphasized, for
instance, by the authors Omar Jabary Salamanca, Mezna Qato, Kareem Rabie,
and Sobhi Samour in "Past Is Present: Settler Colonialism in Palestine" (2002) a
special issue (issue 1) of *Settler Colonial Studies volume 2.*

2. Some of the notable exceptions include Nahla Abdo (2011) and the research by Nadera Shalhoub-Kevorkian, for instance Shalhoub-Kevorkian (2012).

3. On April 9, 1948, more than one hundred inhabitants of Deir Yassin were murdered by the Zionist paramilitary group Palmach and the Zionist terrorist organizations Irgun and Lehi. The massacre became widely known for the atrocious ways in which the villagers—more than half of whom were women, children, and the elderly—were killed. Cases of mutilation, decapitation, disembowelment, and rape were widely publicized in Zionist radio broadcasts in order to terrify the Palestinian population and incite their flight.

4. C. McGreal, "Israel Learns of a Hidden Shame in Its Early Years," *Guardian*, November 4, 2003, http://www.theguardian.com/world/2003/nov/04/israel1.

5. Since the late 1990s, Palestinian feminists, led by Nadera Shalhoub-Kevorkian, have insisted on using the term *femicide*, or *qatl al-nisa*, instead of "honor crimes" so as to refuse any legitimization and justifications that bestow "honor" on the killers and abusers of women.

6. See Mossawa Center, "Arab Civilians That Have Been Killed 2000–2015," January 20, 2015, http://www.mossawa.org/en/article/view/402.

7. During the massacre, forty-nine Palestinian citizens were shot dead by the *Magav* (the Israeli Border Police) while returning to their village during a military curfew.

8. Ma'an News Agency, "Video: Palestinian Woman Shot after Alleged Stab Attack in Afula," October 9, 2015, https://www.maannews.com/Content.aspx?id=768112.

9. Adalah, "The October 2000 Killings," November 8, 2020, https://www.adalah.org/en/content/view/8639.

10. B. McKernan, "Amnesty: 'catalogue of violations' by Israeli police against Palestinians," *The Guardian*, June 24, 2021, https://www.theguardian.com/world/2021/jun/24/amnesty-catalogue-of-violations-by-israeli-police-against-palestinians.

11. *Hamula* is traditional, patriarchal kinship social (and political) structure, sometimes simply referred to as "clans" among Palestinians who are part of the same extended family and who tend to live in the same village or town.

12. O. Kashti, "The Only Thing That Will Deter Terrorists: The Knowledge That Their Sister or Their Mother Was Raped," *Haaretz*, July 21, 2014, http://www.haaretz.co.il/news/politics/1.2383281 (Hebrew).

13. T. Saar, "What Does Sex Have to Do with War at All?" *Haaretz*, July 29, 2014, http://www.haaretz.co.il/gallery/mejunderet/.premium-1.2389676 (Hebrew).

14. A. Shams, "Israeli Discourse of Sexualized Violence Rises amid Gaza Assault," *Ma'an News Agency*, August 6, 2014, http://www.maannews.net/eng/ViewDetails.aspx?ID=717908.

15. A. Smith, "Israel: Promised Land for Jews . . . as Long as They're Not Black?," *Middle East Monitor*, May 4, 2014, https://www.middleeastmonitor.com/20140504-israel-promised-land-for-jews-as-long-as-they-re-not-black/.

16. D. Harmann, "Poll: More Than a Third of Jewish Israelis see Arab Citizens as 'Enemies,'" *Haaretz*, January 20, 2016, http://www.haaretz.com/israel-news/.premium-1.698370.

17. M. Newman, "Nearly Half of Jewish Israelis Want to Expel Arabs, Survey Shows," *Times of Israel*, March 8, 2016, http://www.timesofisrael.com/plurality-of-jewish-israelis-want-to-expel-arabs-study-shows/.

18. B. Norton, "Netanyahu Appoints Ayelet Shaked—Who Called for Genocide of Palestinians—as Justice Minister in New Government," Mondoweiss, May 6, 2015, http://mondoweiss.net/2015/05/netanyahu-palestinians-government/.

19. "Making Aliyah"—literally meaning the "act of going up"—refers to Jewish immigration to Israel.

20. A *kaffiye* refers to a traditional Palestinian checkered black and white or red and white scarf, usually made of cotton, that is worn around the head or neck.

21. J. Khoury, "When It Comes to Arab Citizens, the Police Are Quick on the Trigger," November 10, 2014, Haaretz, http://www.haaretz.com/news/israel/.premium-1.625476; H. Matar, "Jerusalem Police Shoot 10-Year-Old Palestinian Boy in the Eye," +972 Magazine, May 21, 2015, http://972mag.com/border-police-shoot-10-year-old-palestinian-boy-in-the-eye/106956/; M. Zonszein, "Jewish Women Can't Volunteer at Night—to Avoid 'Contact with Arabs,'" +972 Magazine, October 17, 2013, http://972mag.com/jewish-women-cant-volunteer-at-night-to-avoid-contact-with-arabs/80527/; J. Khoury and Y. Kubovich, "Police Officers Won't Be Charged in November Death of Israeli Arab," Haaretz, May 5, 2015, http://www.haaretz.com/news/israel/.premium-1.655084.

22. J. Khoury, "The Female Spring: How Arab Women Change the Face of Israel's Local Elections," *Haaretz*, November 2, 2013, http://www.haaretz.com/news/israel/.premium-1.550148; M. Shmulovich, "Israeli-Arab, female and headed for the Knesset," *The Times of Israel*, January 22, 2013, http://www.timesofisrael.com/israeli-arab-female-and-headed-for-the-knesset/; L. Gradstein, "Revolution in Beduin Women's Education," *Jerusalem Post*, November 21, 2013, http://www.jpost.com/Features/Magazine-Features/Revolution-in-Beduin-womens-education-329283; J. Khoury, "Israeli-Arab Women's Reports of Physical and Sexual Violence Increase by 20%," *Haaretz*, February 13, 2012, http://www.haaretz.com/print-edition/news/israeli-arab-women-s-reports-of-physical-and-sexual-violence-increase-by-20-1.412535.

23. J. Khoury, "The Female Spring: How Arab Women Change the Face of Israel's Local Elections," *Haaretz*, November 2, 2013, http://www.haaretz.com/news/israel/.premium-1.550148.

24. Working Group on the Status of Palestinian Women Citizens of Israel, *The Status of Palestinian Women Citizens of Israel*, December 2010, http://www 2.ohchr.org/english/bodies/cedaw/docs/ngos/WomenCitizens_of_Israel_for _the_session_Israel_CEDAW48.pdf.

25. See also, for example, Mohammad Khatib, *Health of Arab Women in Israel*, Policy Paper (Shefa-Amr, Isr.: Galilee Society, 2012), https://www.gal-soc.org /wp-content/uploads/2019/11/health-of-women_en.pdf.

TWO

—ɯɯ—

BORN WITH A PLAN

DECONSTRUCTING PALESTINIAN PATRIARCHY

Most of the women who participated in this research are members of the third generation of Palestinians after the *nakba*. They are highly educated and working women and, as such, their experiences cannot be read as representing the lived realities of every Palestinian woman in Israel. Born into an indigenous national minority who, at the time of their birth, had lived under a settler colonial state for decades, these women's daily lives take place within multiple interwoven and deep-seated expectations about them. On one side are Zionist expectations for them to disappear or assimilate (i.e., transform into "Arab-Israeli women"), as discussed in chapter 1. On the other side, they are expected to fulfill the gender roles assigned to them by a highly diverse but fundamentally patriarchal Palestinian society. As a result, a persistent tenet that permeates both official Palestinian feminist discourse and existing scholarship about Palestinian women in Israel is the assertion that they live under "compound discrimination" or "two layers of oppression" because they are both members of an indigenous national minority in a settler colonial state and women in an inherently patriarchal society (Working Group on the Status of Palestinian Women Citizens of Israel 2016).[1] But how pertinent is the term "Palestinian patriarchal society"? This chapter concentrates on a deconstruction of the phrase and sheds some critical light on the commonly accepted notion that the patriarchal oppression experienced by Palestinian women within their communities is somehow on a par with Zionist settler colonial oppression.

Although patriarchy is one of the most overused analytical concepts within feminist theory, it also remains, by and large, one of the most undertheorized

(Kandiyoti 1988, 274) and highly contested terms. The lack of theorization also applies to existing research about Palestinian women in Israel. For instance, one of the common lines of argument of this scholarship is that the State of Israel works to reinforce Palestinian patriarchal oppression over Palestinian women in order to present it as backward and inferior because of its misogynist customs (Sa'ar 2007; Shalabi 2010). But, in the distribution of power and material resources, the oppression of women is endemic and integral to most social systems, particularly nationalist, religious, and settler colonial states such as Israel. Therefore, without considering the state as a patriarchal system itself, this argument fails in its mission by essentially implying that the State of Israel is somehow "less patriarchal" (i.e., "less backward") than Palestinian society. Put differently, is there a social system that does not qualify as patriarchal in Israel? And if not, why do we continuously refer to Palestinian society as patriarchal but not, for example, the Zionist state, neoliberal capitalism, or religious institutions, *all* of which affect Palestinian women's lives?

It is not my intention to review feminist theories of patriarchy here, but I believe that the imprecise usage of the term patriarchy necessitates a clarification of what I mean when I refer to patriarchal society. The concept of patriarchal, as it is used throughout this book, draws on Floya Anthias and Nira Yuval-Davis's approach in *Racial Boundaries* (1993), in which they write, "We would like to retain the use of the term patriarchal as a descriptive term which denotes relations between men and women that subordinate women. But we do not believe such patriarchal relations are explicable by deploying the term patriarchy as a distinct social system" (109). Notably, the authors emphasize that patriarchy is not independent of other types of social systems such as capitalism and racism (1993, 106–9). The idea of linking systems of oppression has already been introduced by Hisham Sharabi (1988), who proposed the concept of "neopatriarchy" as the outcome of modern Europe's colonization of the patriarchal Arab world or, in other words, the marriage of imperialism and patriarchy.

The notion of patriarchy employed here takes into account the ways in which women can be active agents both in their subordination and in the struggle against it (Kandiyoti 1988). The former role is particularly relevant, as patriarchy implies the rights of not only males but also elders, including elderly women, which are usually justified by kinship values that are frequently supported by religion. Patriarchy neither emerges nor exists isolated from other forms of oppression. It is not a distinct or universal social order. Therefore, the concept of patriarchy considers the various collective social structures in which the daily lives of Palestinian women are embedded. Such structures include a settler colonial and religious state, the labor market, higher education, and various ethnic communities, among others, which all function as patriarchal orders. Moreover, they all construct the nature and quality of their patriarchal social orders in juxtaposition with, and in relation to, each other. For instance, religious institutions in Israel, such as religious courts, construct their patriarchal social order in relation to the patriarchal order constructed by the Zionist settler colonialist (and religious) state and the other way around.

Likewise, the continuation of women's marginalization and oppression within Jewish religious institutions and spaces is also constructed in relation to the Zionist state, which relies heavily on paternal Jewish social orders in order to complete its settler colonialist project. The interplay of these various patriarchies forms the context of both Palestinian women's oppression and their struggle and bargaining strategies with patriarchal orders or, as Deniz Kandiyoti has claimed, "Different forms of patriarchy present women with distinct 'rules of the game' and call for different strategies to maximize security and optimize life options with varying potential for active and passive resistance in the face of oppression" (Kandiyoti 1988, 274).

In addition, we need to avoid the pitfalls of interpreting all actions as ultimately linked to patriarchy alone, thereby misrecognizing and misinterpreting what are, in effect, reactive behaviors to other issues such as insecurity, poverty, or personal choices. For example, the decision of some of my interviewees to wear a hijab is frequently interpreted as an extension of traditional Arab customs and a violation of women's rights. This interpretation ignores the fact that some women choose to wear a hijab for a plethora of reasons, including to protect themselves from public sexual harassment (by Jewish Israeli as well as Palestinian men), to rebel against their family (sometimes their family members do not support it), or simply to express their religious identity.

Even though limiting patriarchy to specific social institutions (Walby 1990), historical periods (Pateman 1988), or geographical regions (Moghadam 1994; Kandiyoti 1988) constitutes a step toward differentiating patriarchies, patriarchy is not independent of other social relations of power, such as subordination along the lines of race, religion, physical ability, or class—or, as Yuval-Davis writes, "Gender, ethnicity and class, although with different ontological bases and separate discourses, are intermeshed with each other and articulated by each other in concrete social relations. They cannot be seen as additive and no one of them can be prioritized abstractly" (1997, 8–9). In other words, different women experience patriarchy in different ways that depend on their membership in such categories, and, ultimately, there is no one-size-fits-all definition of patriarchal society for Palestinian women. Some feminist theorists have convincingly argued that sexism is the form of oppression that is experienced

by *most* people and is socially acceptable to most (both as oppressor and oppressed), but acceptance does not render the intimate links between all forms
of oppression in any way less crucial. The "overly monolithic" (Kandiyoti 1988,
274) use of the term *patriarchy* as the common enemy, that is, the universal
existence of male domination over women based on biologists' assumptions
about the inevitable conflict of interests between men and women as practiced
by radical feminists (Firestone 1970), has led to a hegemonizing of the interests
of white, Western, middle-class women. At times, I have observed a similar
hegemonizing of interests among middle-class Palestinian feminist activists
who have marginalized or dominated the voices of religious and black Palestinian women. One of the directors of a feminist organization, for instance, in
her effort to stress her argument that women's oppression, including that of
Palestinian women, is the oldest and most severe form of oppression, said, "I
believe that woman is the nigger of the world," which exemplified her oblivion
for the struggle of black Palestinian women.

The present research strives to counter the persistent assertion that ap-
prehends Palestinian women as being confined to "Palestinian women" as an
essentialist category and, thereby, prevents a truly holistic analysis. While Palestinian society can be described as patriarchal, it is not a homogeneous, closed,
or absolute social order, as Deniz Kandiyoti puts forward in the notion of the
"patriarchal bargain" (188) according to which women strategize within the
negotiable boundaries of patriarchal gender orders to gain more security and
autonomy. Systems of class, religion, sexuality, and race, too, create a rich diversity in Palestinian women's experiences in Israel and are also, in turn, shaped
by women themselves. It is important to remember that these categories play a
crucial, mutually constructing role in determining the extent to which oppressive patriarchal and colonial strategies affect the lives of individual Palestinian
women. Moreover, constantly changing social norms and traditions need to be
considered, as well as the overarching influences of global capitalism, liberalism, and the attached notions of modernity.

The assumption of a unitary category of Palestinian women allows the experiences of black and LGBTQI women, for example, to remain largely unrecognized,
resulting in a failure to incorporate the effect of racialized and gendered social
relations into the account of Palestinian women's lives in Israel. This chapter outlines some of the ways in which individual women experience plans made for their
lives in the form of gendered expectations for them on the basis of their marital
status, class, or ethnic or racial background. In an effort not to compartmentalize
oppression, I will describe how these individual experiences take place within
collective structures, which are often neglected by mainstream scholarship.

Seeking to move beyond the double discrimination model, I take a more nuanced look at Palestinian women's situatedness by proposing the alternative notion of Palestinian women being—as one of my interviewees phrased it—"born with a plan." While I take seriously the common use of the double discrimination model among Palestinian feminists in Israel, I observed that this portrayal is problematic when used to represent all Palestinian women. For instance, I found that Bedouin women, while discussing their struggles as women, seldom, if ever, used the phrase "patriarchal society" to describe their community. In general, it can be said that the deeper and more informal our conversations, the more all my interviewees described their individual stories in terms of a plan that they were born with. The double discrimination model, which is expounded by a rather privileged group of scholars and activists, in many ways marginalizes the voices and input of some women in Israel, in terms of both its representation and its construction. For that reason, and because of the intersectional nature of women's daily lives, I found the concept of Palestinian women being "born with a plan" in Israel—a plan that by nature is marked by their backgrounds—more inclusive of all my research participants.

WORKING WOMAN, WIFE, AND MOTHER

The plan that Palestinian women's society, communities, and families designed for them was explained to me by almost all the women I interviewed as revolving particularly around one central patriarchal institution and ultimate purpose and goal in life: marriage. At best, as Areej, a young professional in Nazareth asserts, "once we are married and once we are mothers, we can do anything we want. It's a rite of passage. For the feminists, too. So often we have children, not because we want them, but as a status." As a terminological note, I will refer to "arranged marriages" and "love marriages," the latter indicating those arranged by couples themselves. However, this binary is obsolete as the matter of marriage is frequently a combination of love and arrangement and rarely either-or. Even love marriages bring in the larger extended family at some point. A plethora of behaviors are often expected of Palestinian women from an early age in order for them to increase their marriage prospects and prepare for their lives as wives and mothers. Some Palestinian families expect a code of behavior to be followed that includes women's sexual abstinence, not providing any cause for scandal, and what can be described as "general obedience" to male and elder family members, which all contribute to the honor of the family. The family's duties lie in the guardianship and "preservation" of their daughters.

In her essay "Growing Up Female and Palestinian in Israel," Palestinian feminist scholar Manar Hassan (2005) describes the purpose of Palestinian women's lives: "From the moment of her birth, the patriarchal society, through the agent of the nuclear and extended family, operates a system of conditioning designed to transform the child into the epitome for male lust and desire, and a mother. The success of a Palestinian girl is determined by her ability to measure up to the social expectations transmitted to her through the family.... The Arabic term which best defines the status of the Palestinian woman is *qasar*, meaning 'handicapped,' or 'minor,' that is irresponsible, undeveloped, immature, irrespective of her age, education, or social status" (181–82).

The shattering experiences of the *nakba*, situated within wider regional developments such as increasing industrialization and urbanization and the universalization of education sweeping though Palestine and resulting in social and cultural rifts within Palestinian society, ultimately translated into significant changes to the traditional plan. As a result of the mass killings, expulsion, and displacement of the indigenous Palestinian people and the destruction of their agricultural base, an impoverished, largely male, workforce emerged, who increasingly depended on the goodwill of their colonizers. Palestinian women's everyday lives also changed radically as they started to pursue higher levels of education in increasing numbers, but also—though primarily out of necessity—as they entered the workforce. Faced with these profound transformations of their social organization and under the growing stress of a settler colonial state, Palestinian society sought to preserve itself by turning increasingly inward and holding onto traditional values. Despite their new opportunities and challenging responsibilities, women's obedience was expected all the more strongly as their education and work experiences came to be regarded more as an additional asset to their marriage value rather than as an opportunity for women's self-realization.

Notwithstanding the financial and social benefit that families and husbands receive when women work, many men wish to control all decisions about women's education and work and continue to do so, and they frequently prefer women to stay at home. Naturally, this plays into the hands of the state's representation of a "backward and misogynist Arab minority" and its liberal self-projection as the "savior" of Palestinian women. Examples include publicly declared targets for the inclusion of Palestinian women in the Israeli labor market by the Equal Employment Opportunity Commission (Chief Economist Department 2015). Statistics published by the Israeli Ministry of Labor in mid-2019 state that the number of Palestinian women who were registered as being in the workforce remains at a very low 38.2 percent, in comparison with, for example, an employment rate of approximately 76 percent among Haredi (Jewish Orthodox) women.[2] Notably, many Bedouin women whom I spoke with linked their lack of options for self-realization as both working women and mothers to the limited education and job opportunities provided to them by the settler colonialist state: "They say 'Bedouin women are busy with making children'—that's not true. My mother gave birth to nine daughters and two boys, and I only have two boys because I have to work and study. If you give education and work to the women in the Negev, they will naturally have less children. I think with Israel's policies they encourage women to have more children. These women have more time. So all I'm saying is the state is not very clever" (Areen).

Women in urban areas, especially older women who lack education, stressed that they find it difficult to find local employment that will allow them to continue to take care of their household. And work outside the local market is difficult to reach because of the state's neglect of infrastructure throughout Arab-Palestinian localities, resulting in women's increasing social disparity with and dependence on men. Palestinian feminist researchers in Israel, such as Himmat Zoabi, have argued that "structural, political factors (more than social factors) are impeding the employment of Palestinian women" (2009, 5). Nevertheless, I found that among my research participants, including the younger, educated, and urban ones, the difficulty of juggling work and family life was often a major concern. In fact, these women were predominantly concerned with their impression that the majority of men preferred to marry educated and successful working women such as themselves for their future expected income, not for their knowledge or minds.

In an environment with limited opportunities for indigenous people in general, society often reserves education and work opportunities for indigenous men. While Palestinian boys who wish to pursue paths of self-fulfillment are commonly met with sympathy, admiration, and support by their families, girls who express a desire for higher education, careers, or travel are sometimes regarded by their family members as shirking responsibility (Hassan 2005). Amal, a twenty-six-year-old businesswoman in Haifa, explained the situation of Palestinian women as follows:

> The Palestinian woman in Israel was born with a plan, even if you don't want this plan. The society already has this plan for you. You are born a woman—perfect. So you go to school, you go to university, if you are born into a liberal family, but then you get married, have kids, and live in a house with your family. To be a rebel is quite a challenge and the exception. Not once or twice have I heard from my parents and other family members that

"It's time now! Yallah (come on), put some effort into it!" Of course you need to marry someone from the same "level" as you in terms of social, economic, [and] cultural status. I had a very hard time going against my parents telling them I want a successful career, travel, live abroad. It was very hard for them to accept that. They said, "No, problem, but with a man!" Of course my career makes them proud, but still there is this thing missing.

Amal's description of the situation of young women in Palestinian society was very common among my interviewees who were about her age. All the women had, at some point in their lives, struggled with the plan that was imposed on them by their families or their society. Usually, the first barrier they had to confront was situated within their own family. The most common points of conflict into which the plan had materialized were around issues of relationship, marriage and divorce, career, and sexuality. As can be read from Amal's statement, some young women perceive marriage as the bedrock of Palestinian society, which considers it the natural and desirable state. Although the amount of decision-making agency they had in regard to the choice of husband varied among my research participants, family pressure to marry was high among the majority of young women.

Across all the groups of women interviewed for this study, and as expressed in Amal's statement earlier, being married—as a social status—can provide some Palestinian women with significantly more leverage and freedom to work, travel, and express themselves in public than they would have as single women. Throughout the years of being in contact with Palestinian women in Israel, I have observed some of the most outspoken feminist critics of marriage getting married, not seldom in a quite lavish or even conservative fashion. While I assume that not all these women experienced a sudden conversion experience, based on my observations and conversations, many appeared to enjoy the freedoms, and sometimes the status, that comes with being a married woman.

In some families, I have encountered a continuous pursuit of scaling of women to their marriage candidates. Only a minority of the unmarried Palestinian women in Israel who I spoke with said that their family members did not mind whom they marry in the future. The majority of women explained that there was a plan, without always referring to it as such, as well as traditions and important preferences society and their families held. While family members' preferences for their daughters and sisters to marry a man (rather than a woman) of certain socioeconomic standing, often from a specific community or family, one should keep in mind that holding such preferences are common in families more generally and regardless of geographic context. Nevertheless, intermarriage between members of the different Arabic-speaking communities—Druze, Christian, and Muslims—is rare in Israel.

A number of women drew on commonly used paradigms that allocate specific ideas of modernity and tradition to men based, for example, on their hometowns. The identities of Palestinian villages, in particular, are frequently associated not only with notions such as wealth and modernity but also with the qualities of potential husbands. For example, there were villages described as offering "more opportunities for women" and villages characterized by more open-mindedness than others. Hence, men from some villages were narrated as more modern and, accordingly, more receptive to women's wishes for self-realization than others. Notably, these villages were usually Christian and Muslim villages and, even more so, Druze villages were depicted as rather traditional (by women of all religious affiliations). Many of my interviewees, particularly in those same villages, enthusiastically adopted the binary reference frames of tradition and modernity.

Love marriages that were not approved by family members, particularly among interreligious partners, were often regarded by women as a challenge to families, potentially causing the breakdown of a family or women's relationship with her family. While only a small number of women had witnessed an unapproved love marriage in their family, the majority of my interviewees said that they did not think that their families would support them marrying a husband who did not share their religion. Israeli settler colonialism, particularly its divide-and-conquer policies, has significantly affected marriage within Palestinian society. As a result, sustaining Palestinian family structures, including the hamula, and their values and politics, has become a crucial defense mechanism against settler colonial oppression (Hassan 2005, 185). Historically, land has played a central role in Palestinian marriage making, which aimed to create alliances in order to safeguard livelihood through land ownership. Research on the matter conducted by Majid Al-Haj (1987) and Henry Rosenfeld (1968) has revealed a strong correlation between the number of children and the size of family land holdings among Palestinian villages. The research explains why certain forms of traditional marriage such as polygamy and *badal* (exchange marriage) have become more frequent (Abu-Rabia 2011) as land has become more contested under the colonizing state.[3]

Another major concern expressed by the women pertained to the expectation about them juggling family and work life. Therefore, married working mothers often emphasized the challenge of combining their family and their work, particularly in a society that accepted, if not actively endorsed, their desire to enter higher education and find demanding jobs and also expected them to primarily not only manage but master their families' domestic tasks and take care of their children. Some women pointed out that such expectations for them are further aggravated by their perception that they also have to prove within Israeli society that Palestinian women can be just as smart, successful, and emancipated as Jewish Israeli women. Indeed, the Israeli government plays an active part in contributing to the difficulty of Palestinian women juggling work and family life, as out of 1,600 government-funded day-care centers for children under the age of three, only 25 operate in Palestinian communities (Zoabi 2009).

As in many other societies, the bigger part of Palestinian society perceives new education and career opportunities for women more as augmenting the normative consensus on domesticity than as contravening it. In addition to the gendered division of labor, women frequently deal with greater social changes after their wedding, as they are often expected to move to their husband's place of residence and need to adjust to a new social life. In her study on Palestinian careers and working women, Khawla Abu Baker points out the important contrast between women's often *changing* and men's rather *static* roles: "Palestinian women have found, as elsewhere, that adding work outside of the house to their lives does not necessarily entail a systemic change in the operation of the household. While Palestinian women share family income responsibilities with men, men refuse to change their traditional social roles and their cultural allowances, and in this they are strongly supported by social, political, historical, cultural, and religious norms" (2002, 86).

In some communities, I have noted that jobs were also frequently classified as appropriate or inappropriate for women. For instance, appropriate ones include becoming a teacher or a social worker and not—as particularly Bedouin women pointed out to me time and again—a nurse, because nurses work night shifts, something that cannot be reconciled with looking after children. Nuzha, however, a Bedouin nurse herself, was a mother of four who drove forty minutes to work a few days and nights a week. She lodged me for many weeks and explained her "problem with feminism" to me as follows: "Look, I don't care if a woman wants to work. So she works! But then why does she have children also? A mother that always works and is never at home is not good for a child." If discourse is any indication, whenever I had the chance to discuss feminism with "nonfeminists," one of their biggest concerns with what they dubbed "feminist talk" was their concern about who would take care of the children once all women realized their "self-fulfillment." Even though these women not seldom constructed feminists as callous mothers on the basis of stereotypes, they appeared to have no problem with working women in general but, often from their own experiences, knew how hard it was to combine work with childcare.

Marriage within Palestinian society in Israel is marked by not only continuities, often amplified under the stresses of Zionist settler colonialism, but also significant changes caused by both external influences and radical internal changes. The laws of engagement that apply to the third *nakba* generation have in some areas relaxed significantly. For example, intermarriage (such as Muslim-Druze, Christian-Muslim, and Bedouin-Muslim Jerusalemite) remains exceptional but, according to my research participants, had increased over the years. Many of the women who intermarried married for the second time. This relaxation also includes groups considered among the most traditional and patriarchal, such as the Bedouin tribes in al-Naqab. Throughout the last decade, Bedouin families have increasingly agreed to their children's marriages outside the extended family (though not outside the tribe), which means that love marriages have very likely become more frequent. Many women have placed themselves in direct confrontation with traditional norms of marriage by adhering to liberal notions of partnerships and lifestyles. Subsequent conflicts or clashes between women and their families, husbands, or society as a whole often result in rapid burnout either of women's careers or their marriages (Abu-Baker 2002, 86).

UNMARRIED AND DIVORCED WOMEN

There is a psychosocial element in large parts of the wider Arab society according to which marriage constitutes the crucial stage in the lives of both women and men, at which they attain the maturity required for true womanhood and manhood. In spoken Arabic, a woman is frequently called *bint*, which literally means "girl," until she has sexual intercourse for the first time during her wedding night. Women who remain single continue to be referred to in spoken Arabic as "girls," not as "women." Hence, regardless of their age, married women are expected to be psychologically and socially more mature than unmarried women. Older, single women, on the other hand, often suffer from negative social judgments. Young unmarried women are called ʿazbaa (not yet married), but the term is used in most Arabic countries to refer to women under the age of thirty. For unmarried women over thirty years old the derogatory term used is ʿaanis (spinster), which implies that they no longer have any chance of marrying. The fact that there is only one word to describe the unmarried status of men of all ages, 'azab (bachelor), indicates that the determined, socially acceptable window of opportunity for marriage is gendered.

Being divorced is not considered "part of the plan" for Palestinian women. In fact, in many regards, it constitutes the lowest status of women in the family hierarchy, as society usually blames women for their divorce and interprets it as her failure to understand her husband's needs and psychology. A woman who is divorced is not seldom treated as a woman who has failed in her most important mission, and the term *muṭalaqa* (divorcée) sometimes connotes disgrace and condemnation. Primarily because of their treatment by society, and the difficulty of a religious state that leaves all family law issues in the hands of a sectarian religious and religious court system, the number of Palestinian women filing for divorce in Israel remains small.

According to social customs and the stories that I was told, a divorced woman has no chance of marrying a man who has never been married before. At most, a divorced, older, or widowed man may consider her as a potential marriage partner. Because of the fact that they have sexual experience, divorcées are often perceived and represented as sexual predators or as "on the prowl for men" (i.e., other women's husbands). 'Aanis, widows or divorced women, all of whom lack a relationship with an official, male spouse, are required to abstain from sexual relationships and avoid all social scandals. These three types of single women are differentiated by the social support they receive and the deference granted to their situations. Widows are given the most social sympathy, but divorced women and 'aanis are treated as though they are to blame for their marital status. All three groups of women usually experience great difficulty in finding a spouse of their own age and social status. The fact that the stereotypes attached to unmarried women and divorcées continue to affect such women's lives severely and negatively is reflected in a Jordanian cartoon that was widely shared within a Facebook group of Palestinian feminist activists. It reads, "She wasn't in love with him but afraid of the word 'spinster.' That's why she married him [top]. She wasn't happy with him but afraid of the word 'divorcée.' That's why she never left him [bottom]." (See fig. 2.1.)

Many divorced women that I spoke with felt that they were expected to move back in with their parents and had few alternatives. In cases where the woman had custody of her children, she had to accustom herself and them to the new conditions. There are also important material issues, such as the wealth of the woman and her family of origin, that play a role in determining whether she may continue living as an adult or whether she must return to go back and live as a dependent child in her family's home. This possibility is

Figure 2.1. The Spinster/Divorcée. © 2013, Hajjajcartoons
.com. From Facebook page "Emad Hajjaj."

one of the reasons that—despite the relaxation of the role of family approval—
many women are reluctant to marry without their parents' approval; they want
to maintain the family safety net. All the women who had gone through a
divorce described this period of their lives as the most difficult. Such was especially the case for those women who had to convince their parents that they
wanted to rent a flat and live by themselves in a city. It was described as even
more difficult for those who had children.

LGBTQI WOMEN

The hegemonic discourses and customs that make up the plan for Palestinian
women's lives usually presuppose cisgender heterosexuality. Although I did not
actively look for women belonging to the LGBTQI community, my research
participants included lesbian, bisexual, queer or questioning, and intersex
women. Evidently, issues of homosexuality, transgender, and intersexuality
are scarcely talked about in public or at home among Palestinians in Israel.

As with sexuality and sexual health more generally, these topics are also not part of the formal school curriculum. As a result, I found that there was a lot of confusion, especially among Palestinian teenagers, about the meanings and differences between homo-, trans-, and intersexual, except for when their parents worked in the field of sexual education themselves. At the same time, reactions toward homo-, trans-, and intersexual people were blatantly bold and usually expressed through sexist attitudes and masculinist bullying of noncisgender and homosexual persons.

Palestinian LGBTQI activists have started to gather and organize themselves since the early 2000s, which has resulted in the establishment of two organizations: Aswat—Palestinian Gay Women in Haifa and Al-Qaws for Sexual and Gender Diversity in Palestinian Society, based in Jerusalem. The former was founded in 2003 as an offspring organization of Kayan-Feminist Organization, which includes women living in present-day Israel. The latter, established in 2007, includes Palestinian queers in Israel and the West Bank. Both organizations have made it their mission to promote education about sexual and gender diversity, combat ingrained stereotypes, and create a safe space for LGBTQI individuals and activists.

Only a minority of Palestinian lesbian women come out of the closet to both their family members and society. This minority often had the advantage of being born into families who support and respect their sexual orientation. Unfortunately, most parents' reactions are negative, and daughters are often ostracized by their families. Some go as far as to react with violence or death threats. Some women told me about their experiences of being beaten and some even feared that they might be murdered by relatives. A number of women felt that they had no choice but to flee to women's shelters in Israel or move abroad. As a result of the continuing power of stereotypes and social stigmas, coming out is not an option for most women. Instead, they live what many have described as double lives: one life is as Palestinian single women in front of their families and communities and in the second they live out their sexuality and what they referred to as true identities in spaces that they consider safe, usually spaces far away from family and community circles. For instance, many of the lesbian women whom I spoke to moved to Tel Aviv after school or university graduation to experience living in an anonymous space in which they felt they could be openly gay. It is here that many of them had their first chance to actually explore their sexuality and start relationships with other women. It was not uncommon for these women to describe this phase in their life as liberating. Upon reflection, however, many of them told me that, at a later stage in life, the Tel Aviv lifestyle was no longer an option for them, as they became increasingly aware of how the gay scene in Tel Aviv contributes to the Zionist project of *pinkwashing* the occupation of Palestine.[4]

Palestinian women go about their homosexuality in various ways while navigating some of the heteronormative and homophobic social environments into which they were born. Some women had sought arranged marriages outside Israel (usually to gay men), in order to please their families by marrying, but, really, in order to enjoy the freedom abroad, away from their society. Others had consciously decided "against their sexual orientation" and married men, thus, continuing a double life in Israel. For a lot of these women, such marriages failed to work out, and they eventually separated. The new double life as separated women poses serious challenges for women from their status as "divorcée":

> At this stage, I was more at ease with my sexuality. I knew that I want to date women, but never really thought about coming out. Now that my father is no longer with us, it seemed too overwhelming and far-fetched even [to] consider coming out to my mom. She too endured the pain of losing my dad, suffered the "shame" of my divorce, and constantly worries about her single-mom daughter, so it felt too much to burden her with one more truth—the truth about her lesbian daughter (quoted in Abboud 2010, 54–55).

As in most other countries, Palestinian transgender and transsexual women live under extreme pressure in Israel, as sex change is still widely considered an abnormal or unnatural phenomenon. Often bullied in school, work, and family environments for their feminine gestures, body language, and appearance, transgender women rarely find people whom they can trust and share their stories with. Parents often feel overwhelmed and confused about the transsexuality of their children and, as a result, usually send their children to therapy, hoping that what they consider a psychological problem will be fixed there. According to the personal experiences of one transgender woman cared for by an organization which I interned with, the experience only prolonged her pain.

Having to deal with a constant lack of understanding, medical needs, ostracism, psychological stress, loss of jobs, and family hostility (as well as major difficulties in sexual relations) are commonplace experiences among Palestinian transsexual women in Israel. Although I did not have the chance to speak to any transgender women directly, through my continuous contact with the Haifa Women's Coalition, I witnessed many cases of transgender women who, after coming out to their families, had to flee their homes in order to find shelter at the homes of activists.

Everyday images constructed by society of transgender women scorn acknowledging the fact that they were born in the wrong body. Perhaps paradoxically, spaces in which women's transsexuality is normalized include both sexist, patriarchal, and Zionist colonialist spaces. For instance, I was surprised about the apparent normalcy of the presence of transsexual women and transvestites and the openness of Palestinian men and women around them at a New Year's Eve party in a club in Bethlehem, which I attended with a group of friends. Even though I doubt that this particular group of transsexual women were sex workers (although I cannot say for sure), many transsexual women do work as sex workers in order to pay for their expensive sex-change operations. Thus, as a result of their impossible embodiment, transsexual women often have no choice but to break several social and gendered taboos at once. This is a real problem, as the gender regime, once it tolerates the sex change, expects them to adhere to its rules and power hierarchies *a fortiori*. In other words, even if there is a certain clientele of straight men who are excited by and mingle with transsexual women, this does not mean that they respect them (Connell 2009, 113).

The fact that this interaction often strengthens the gender regime is reflected in a statement by a transsexual member of Aswat, the Palestinian Feminist Center for Gender and Sexual Freedoms, who wrote in its collection of stories, *Waqfet Banat* (colloquial Arabic for "Women take a stand"), about her mother's reaction toward her being born a woman stuck in a man's body: "There was one sentence that she said that I will never forget: 'Be a girl, but don't be a whore'" (Abboud 2010, 71–72). Transgender women frequently come under extreme psychological pressure, and, at worst, they become suicidal, as they feel increasingly displaced by other people and often excluded from both genders: "I wasn't allowed to walk with girls because people might still think that I'm a girl, and I wasn't allowed to talk to boys because people might think that there was something sexual going on between us. I became so depressed" (Abboud 2010, 73).

The intense intersectional quality of their oppression exposes transsexual women all the more to targeting by Zionist Orientalist discourse. While they might experience temporal normalcy within some Israeli spaces, these experiences do not automatically imply that they are respected as women or indigenous women within these spaces. One of the most public examples are the 2016 Miss Trans Israel elections, which were won by Talleen Abu Hanna, a transsexual woman from northern Israel (previously crowned "Miss Israel" in 2004). Talleen was repeatedly quoted within Israeli media for her statement "I wouldn't be alive if I had grown up in Palestine."[5] This statement was taken out of context, as by "Palestine" Talleen was referring to the Occupied Palestinian Territories, but she was portrayed as essentially ascribing some kind of gratitude for the occupation of her homeland within the borders of 1948. Moreover,

Talleen's story was constantly told in contrast to that of another participant, Caroline Khouri, who was forced to flee her home after a male relative threatened to kill her and was, eventually, "rescued by the Israeli police" (Abboud 2010, 73).

This is not to say that there is nothing empowering or liberating for Talleen in the public celebration of her body and beauty, but events such as Miss Trans Israel also produce a space in which indigenous women become more vulnerable to and targeted by a settler colonial desire to strengthen Israel's Orientalist presentation of Palestinian society as uncivilized and backward while bolstering its self-representation as the liberator of indigenous women, including transsexual women. As pointed out by Jasbir Puar's article on Israel's gay propaganda war, this kind of pinkwashing is a "potent method through which the terms of Israeli occupation of Palestine are reiterated—Israel is civilized, Palestinians are barbaric, homophobic, uncivilized, suicide-bombing fanatics."[6] Moreover, by focusing on Palestinian transsexual women, Zionist pinkwashing is a distraction from the homophobic and sexist oppression of Israel's own many LGBTQI people.

BEDOUIN WOMEN

Ashirat Al-Sana

Because of the extreme transformation of their special relationship with their ancestral land, the central role of genealogical knowledge, and the maintenance of the 'asl (Arabic for "nobility," "origin," or "ancestry") of their families, the plan for Bedouin women and their experiences are rather distinct from those of other Palestinian women. Even though it might appear that this section takes us too far afield, I believe that, because of their long and particular history in the region, a thorough acknowledgment of the specificities of the Bedouin context is fundamental to grasping Bedouin women's experiences in Israel. The importance of tribal affiliations and heritage among al-Naqab Bedouins, though addressed by some, is often understated in contemporary studies about Bedouin women. I understand that, at times, the omission is due to the effort made to emphasize their shared experiences as a Palestinian minority. I believe, however, that these aspects are central to Bedouin life and must be considered in order to gain a coherent understanding of the multifaceted experiences of the indigenous Palestinian minority in Israel, of which the Bedouins constitute a crucial part.

The Bedouins are made up of three groups with different socioeconomic origins, some of which date back to the 1300s (Biasio 1998, 24): the *a'rāb* (Bedouins who consider themselves "original Bedouins" based on their Saudi Arabian roots, also known as *sumran*, "the landowning"), the *fellaheen* (landless "peasants," also known as *humran*), and the black Bedouins, former slaves who are referred to by others only as *'abeed*, a derogatory term that they themselves perceive as essentially racist. Despite the fact that the term *'abeed* is still widely used within both academia and among both *fellaheen* and *a'rāb*, I will refer to "black Bedouins" in this book because of the ongoing racism they experience. The name *badawiyyun* (desert dwellers) includes all three groups and was originally given to them by settled Arabs. The *fellaheen* were predominantly landless after their move from Egypt to al-Naqab in the period 1830–1948. As a result, they lived as clients, basically in dependence on *a'rāb*, until 1948. Almost all black Bedouins were forcibly moved from Sudan to Saudi Arabia, where they were bought by wealthy Bedouins from Palestine during their pilgrimages to Mecca (Biasio 1998, 24). When the Ottomans abandoned slavery in the early twentieth century, they started to align themselves with *a'rāb*, with whom, like the *fellaheen*, they eventually assimilated in their dialect, living accommodations, clothing, and stock rearing. Up until today, written scholarship about the history and experiences of black Bedouins remains scarce (especially so in the English language).

Throughout my fieldwork, I almost exclusively engaged with Bedouin women in al-Naqab, specifically members of the al-Sana tribe, as one of my friends is a member of this tribe and was willing to take me in almost weekly in the recognized Bedouin township Laqiya (northeast of Bi'r as-Sab'). The al-Sana tribe belongs to Al-Tiyaha, the second-largest *gaba'il* (confederation) out of the seven to which belong the twenty-eight Bedouin tribes north, east, and southeast of Bi'r as-Sab' to the edge of the Dead Sea and south of Hebron. The tribe, or *'ashirah* in Arabic, is part of a *saf*, a group of tribes with territorial and political affiliations, called *'kdeirat*. (See fig. 2.2.) Although important for Palestinians in general, land and family roots are the linchpin of Bedouin life. In order to gain a thorough understanding of Bedouin daily life in Israel, I decided to concentrate my fieldwork on one *'ruba* (subtribe). It is important to note that only *a'rāb* are organized within an *'ashirah*, a territorially and precisely defined unit called a *dirah*, where they enjoy the right to water and livestock farming. Tribal membership runs along patrilineal lines. In other words, women belong to their father's kin throughout their lives, whereas their children belong to their husband's family.

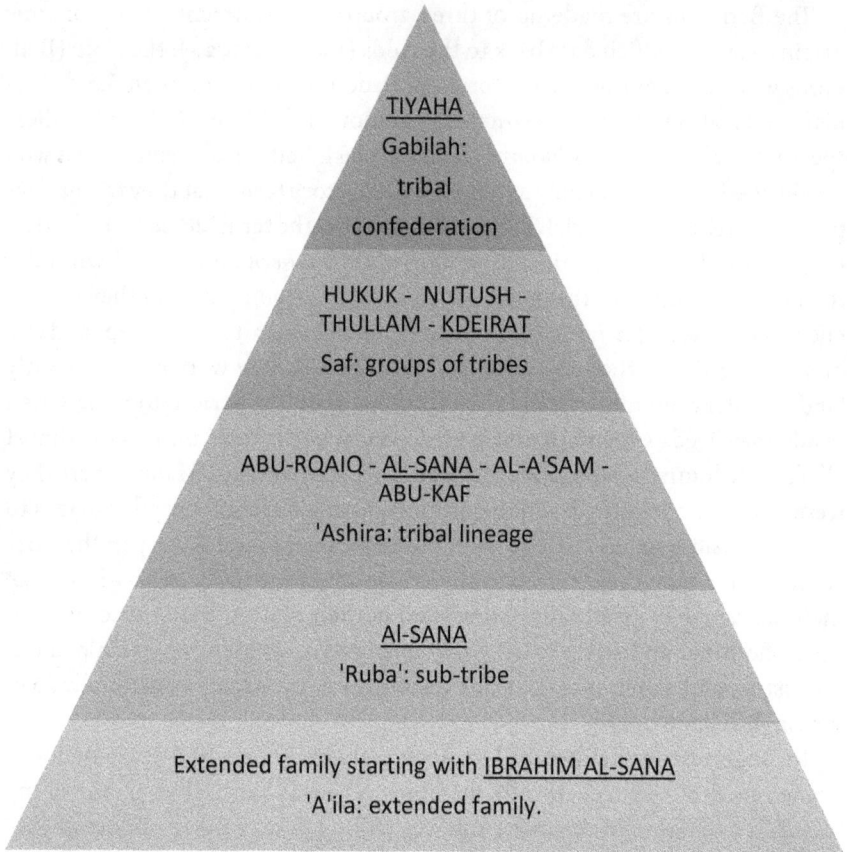

Figure 2.2. Bedouin tribal and family structure of the Al-Sana family. © 2014, Kim Jezabel Zinngrebe.

While much of the existing literature on al-Naqab Bedouins claims that changes in the Bedouin way of life preceded the *nakba* (Dahan-Kalev and Le Febvre 2012, 35), the narratives that I collected throughout my fieldwork strongly indicate that the *nakba* was experienced not only as a pivotal turning point in history but also an ongoing struggle of Bedouin life. When I asked my friend's mother, Sana, about her memories of the *nakba*, for instance, she replied, "What '*nakba*' do you mean? This is still the *nakba*!" The forced resettlement and abrupt transition to an urban way of life turned Bedouin women's lives fundamentally upside down. Before 1948, Bedouin women fulfilled central roles as shepherdesses, producers of agricultural goods, and managers of home economies. The loss of land that arose in the elimination of the Bedouins' agricultural basis of life entailed serious consequences for women, as they lost their central function and were left with no economic alternative. As a result, women's dependence on men, both economically and socially, increased significantly, solidifying their inferior status. The urbanization of their daily lives, imposed on Bedouin women by the state, was not followed up by any measures to support the transition. Today, Bedouin women's access to education, public transport, and work remains vastly limited, particularly in villages that are unrecognized by the state.

The loss of land and women's traditional roles is felt not only by the women who experienced the 1948 war. Bedouin women pass on their stories and experiences orally from generation to generation. This way, many young Bedouin women of the third *nakba* generation, despite not experiencing traditional Bedouin life on their ancestors' land, continue to have strong connections to their ancestral land and way of life. Many times, young Bedouin women expressed a longing for the days of the past. Despite the fact that many of these women have experienced city life through work or attending university, most emphasized that they cannot imagine living anywhere else but on their homeland. In a collection of poems, recipes, and stories of Bedouin women written by young Bedouin women, I came across a poem entitled "They asked me to live in the city," which captures this sentiment very nicely:

> They asked me to live in the city:
> And I know that the sky is the roof of my house
> and the ground is my place of sleep
> and the moon is my light
> and the rooster calls me to my prayers
> and the herd is my fortune
> and nature is an exit for my narrow breaths
> and the fire is my mate at night
> When I think of my life, my destiny.
>
> They asked me to live in the city:
> I feel the walls as mountains on my chest.
> No animals, no nature, no fireplace.
> This is death for me.
> I chose to die rather than city life.
>
> Say I am a Bedouin:
> Courage, horse riding, and unity are my place within myself,
> Through them I fight every friend and enemy.

Desert and mountains are my home,
Sheep and camels
Constitute my pride and livelihood.
I cannot live without them:
I am a Bedouin.

(As with most folktales, the poem has no known author.)

Bedouin Women and ʿAsl

Notions of ʿasl continue to be of central importance among al-Naqab Bedouins. Literally translated as "ancestry," "origin," or "nobility," notions and
meanings attached to ʿasl refer to a range of qualities and genealogical characteristics that essentially serve to differentiate Bedouins from non-Bedouins
(Abu-Lughod 2016). In other words, ʿasl decides whether one qualifies for
tribal membership. Specific qualities that were associated with ʿasl include
generosity, honesty, loyalty, keeping one's word, assertiveness, pride, and
self-control. As will be discussed at a later stage, even though these notions
are gendered, the attainment of ʿasl qualities and the construction of meanings of ʿasl is by no means reserved for Bedouin men. Indeed, women play a
central role in various aspects of ʿasl, including adhering to ʿasl ideas of moral
character and narrating ʿasl, particularly through passing on genealogical
knowledge, child-rearing, arranging marriages, keeping up networks, and
passing on advice to their children.

At the time of my fieldwork, I was under the impression that knowledge about
internal workings, tribal affiliations, and family networks that constitute al-
Naqab Bedouin society is mostly reserved for Bedouins themselves, and information about them is, even today, routinely either omitted by many tribal members or presented rather intricately to outsiders. For that reason, I felt privileged,
not only by being "allowed in" as an external person, but also by being able to
inquire again and again about complicated details that I was confused about.
Moreover, observing Jalilah, an indispensable supporter of my research, persis-
tently finding the answers to my questions or, alternatively, arranging for me to
meet the people who could help, essentially meant that I watched her actively
practicing ʿasl in some form or another. I observed significant generational differences, mostly those between Jalilah and her mother, who, unlike Jalilah, never
relied on anybody else's knowledge to tell a story or answer a question, and still
less on social media to introduce me to somebody she thought I should meet.

It quickly became clear during my stays that Bedouin women fulfill a central
role in maintaining the ʿasl of their tribe, as their ways of storytelling differ from

the storytelling of Bedouin men and, characteristically, their narratives constitute a vital contribution to the complementation and completion of 'asl. Throughout my collection of oral histories among the al-Sana tribe, one of the names that
was frequently mentioned was Sheikh Hajj Ibrahim al-Sana, or simply "Ibrahim,"
Jalilah's grandfather. Bedouin family histories often focus on a common, single
ancestor in order to emphasize and strengthen a shared descent, and differences
between women's and men's storytelling were clearly noticeable when I spoke to
both Sana and her brother Muhammad about their father Ibrahim. While both
half-siblings told me Ibrahim's story in a neat, chronological order, Muhammad's
narrative was much more structured, while Sana would stop and focus on specific
episodes in detail. Her genealogical and geographical knowledge was just as ac-
curate as that of Muhammad, but she described the characteristics of both places
and people with much more descriptive detail. Whereas Muhammad backed up
his facts (as many other men I spoke to did) by showing me materials such as
photographs, books, and photocopies of important documents, Sana recounted
the past solely from her personal memories. Muhammad praised his father's
leadership qualities and his protection of the tribe and contribution to Arab
nationalism. From his perspective, Ibrahim was very solution-oriented, always
finding a way out for his tribe at critical moments in time: during the waves of
Jewish immigration and land sales, the forced displacement in 1948 and in 1952
when the tribe was let down by the Jordanian king. Sana's portrayal, on the other
hand, focused on Ibrahim's personal traits, particularly his "big heart" and generosity toward both his family and the tribe more generally. Her story included a
thick description of everyday life rather than a focus on specific historical events.

Marriage and Motherhood

While marriage and motherhood continue to play central roles for women's
status in not only their nuclear but also their extended families and tribes,
some major changes in Bedouin women's lives also occurred that I identified
throughout my fieldwork. Many Bedouins perceive the primary function of
marriage to be the strengthening and stabilizing of the tribe as a social and
territorial unit. As a social institution, marriage assists in the definition of
group relations and the maintenance of true Bedouin origin. Marriages are
usually arranged by parents, without whose blessing a marriage seldom takes
place. Marriage arrangements are a lengthy and complex process that has
to follow strict rules and respect careful leveling between the two families
in question. Most commonly, marriages take place within the same tribal
confederation or tribal lineage according to the practice of unidirectional

endogamy. Preferred marriages are paternal cousin marriages between persons who are first-generation cousins to fifth-generation cousins (Dahan-Kalev and Le Febvre 2012, 34). This practice continues to be considered the ideal form of descent in which members may claim undisrupted genealogical descent with past *badu* people, allowing them to not only justify their true origins but also differentiate themselves from the *fellaheen*. Marriage rarely takes place across *safs*. Intermarriage between black, *fellaheen*, and *a'rāb* Bedouins is extremely rare. In exceptional cases, *a'rāb* men may marry a *fallaheen* woman, but no *a'rāb* father would give his daughter to a *fellaheen*. Despite these gendered practices, women play a central and powerful part in the marriage arrangements of their children, for instance, via the creation and upholding of formal and informal networks of information about marriage candidates.

Bedouin marriage customs have maintained their importance and centrality, but I noticed various ways in which the rules of marriage among *a'rāb* families have been bent. As an example, some families have come to accept their daughter's decision to marry a Bedouin man from a different *saf*, or even a non-Bedouin. The families in question were all families of high standing with close connections among the family members. While they all struggled with these developments, it should be emphasized that the struggles, which were followed by the eventual acceptance of the families, took years to resolve. Even though, in these cases, nuclear family ties trumped traditional marriage rules, Bedouin marriages never take place within the confines of the nuclear family, and therefore complex bargaining with numerous (and often less understanding) relatives was part of the eventual acceptance of a woman's love marriage.

The loosening of the marriage regulations of the *a'rāb* has also been affected by the *nakba*, as Bedouins historically aimed to extend their territory and access to water and pasture areas. One of the post-*nakba* factors is the forced restructuring of the Bedouin tribes after 1948: in 1953, the Israeli military administration conducted a census. In order to obtain an Israeli identification card, and thus citizenship, every individual had to align with one of the nineteen tribes whose sheikhs were recognized by the State of Israel. Because the leaders and many members of smaller Bedouin groups had fled, the remaining people were absorbed into other tribes, including the *fellaheen* and black Bedouins, with the *fellaheen* eventually establishing their own tribe.

Engagements among Bedouins are a very lengthy and structured affair. Preconditions for a man to get engaged to a woman are preferably membership in a family and tribe deemed appropriate, an ability to provide a house (or, in some cases, a modern flat), and a specific amount of money in his account in order to prove his ability to provide for his wife and future children. In some of my friends' cases, months, if not years, of bargaining between the families (and partners) were involved in arranging an engagement.

Married Bedouin women, especially married women with many children, and particularly sons, enjoy a higher status than single women, while women with daughters only, or no children at all, have a significantly lower status than married women with sons. Frequently, husbands of the latter continue to take second or third wives in order to increase their chances of having sons. On these grounds, polygamy is frequently tolerated or even encouraged. The majority of Bedouin families whom I met, however, consider polygamy old-fashioned. Most Bedouin women, backed up by their families, would not tolerate having to share their husband with another wife. Nevertheless, women took seriously the expectation for them to bear male offspring. A mother's higher status is also always vulnerable to the will of her husband and is constantly at risk from the uncontrolled right of men to get another wife (which is not very common in the more prestigious families). Under these circumstances, the role of mother-in-law is the highest status a woman can achieve in the patriarchal structure, even though the role remains contingent on the support and tolerance of men.

Throughout the past few decades, polygamous marriages among the Bedouins have consistently increased, regardless of age, level of education, or socioeconomic standing (Abu-Rabia 2011, 467). This development has not taken place in isolation, essentially operating at the intersection of settler colonial and patriarchal power. In her in-depth research on polygamy in the Bedouin society of al-Naqab, Rawia Abu-Rabia (2011) argues that, as a result of a colonial power that supports the traditional tribal system and condones polygamy, Bedouin society is internally segregated. At the same time, Bedouin women remain invisible before the law, as their issues continue to be exoticized or ignored, justified by Israeli civil services under the pretext of a supposedly culturally sensitive approach.

Unmarried women have little or no status within Bedouin society, which usually recognizes women as individuals only once they have married. When a Bedouin woman bears children, particularly sons, her status is greatly elevated. This increase in status is also accompanied by the task (and often burden) of the fact that she alone will be in charge of caring for all the household chores and, often in addition, supporting outer family members with their households and children or elderly parents. Time for voluntary work and activism is minimal, and the chances of keeping a job are tiny for most women.

Divorces remain an absolute exception; but, during times of marital conflict, many married Bedouin women stay with or move in with their parents.

As husbands usually rely on their wives to cook for them, the commonness of such occurrences helps demonstrate their reliance on, and hence the power of, their wives. Not uncommonly, wives who leave their husbands in order to stay with their parents also leave the children with their husbands. I usually witnessed this method when women of the family experienced domestic violence or when they were verbally insulted by their husbands.

In contrast to notions of virginity in other parts of Palestinian society, within Bedouin society, virginity still has to be demonstrated during the wedding night referred to as *leylat al-dokhola* ("the night of the entrance"). In the past, as I was told through several stories, a blood-stained sheet had to be displayed publicly to a large group of family members waiting outside the house in order to demonstrate that the family had kept its good name and duly delivered a virgin bride to the groom. Even though, today, these old customs are considered old-fashioned by most Bedouins and preparing the bedroom for the married couple—in which I once participated—is a rather sober and stressful affair, virgin brides are still expected to bleed during their wedding night in front of her husbands, or as a friend told me, "If I don't bleed during my wedding night, I'm in trouble."

BLACK WOMEN

While the existing scholarship has acknowledged the way in which gender, religion, and geographical backgrounds converge to shape the features of Palestinian women's experiences in Israel, to my knowledge, little attention has been paid to issues of race. I found this striking in light of the fact that, from very early on during my fieldwork in various Palestinian communities, the marginalization of black women from Palestinian feminist and women's rights discourses emerged rather quickly. Black women were rarely included in my snowball sampling, which began with middle-class, urban-based, largely secular women. It turned out to be rather difficult to get in touch with black Palestinian women, except within the Bedouin community. Nevertheless, it is argued here that only by including the experiences and narratives of black Palestinian women can a thorough understanding of the plan for Palestinian women in Israel be possible.

Black Palestinian women in Israel largely belong to communities that Israeli policies of spatial and economic suffocation target, policies that are regularly justified as security measures. As a result, such communities commonly struggle with problems such as high unemployment rates, poverty, poor infrastructure, crime, and lack of education. Specific localities that I encountered include the village of Jisr az-Zarqa (Arabic for "Bridge over the Blue"), the only Arab town on the Mediterranean coast; Bab al-Majles, an African-Palestinian neighborhood in Jerusalem; and various Bedouin villages in al-Naqab. I also met Palestinian women of color and mixed-race women throughout the Galilee and Triangle[7] region, many of whom identified as "black."

The workings of racial formation are different in every place and are the product of a particular history and politics. This fact reinforced the need to draw on intersectional theory and, more specifically, an intracategorical-complexity approach that interrogates boundary-making and boundary-defining processes and acknowledges the stable and durable relationships that social categories represent at any given time (McCall 2005). Black Palestinian women cannot be regarded as one cohesive group; they are women with various and individual historical and geographic backgrounds. Some of their ancestors include fifteenth-century African Muslim pilgrims from Chad, Senegal, Sudan, and Nigeria. Predominantly they were Sudanese people who were largely kidnapped and enslaved by various Bedouin tribes throughout the centuries. African women were specifically targeted by the Arab slave trade as wet nurses and domestic helpers but mostly as sex slaves. This slave trade, also known as the "Islamic Empire slave trade" or "Eastern slave trade," took place throughout the last fourteen centuries and was not prohibited until the Ottoman authorities did so at the beginning of the twentieth century.

Language, Power, and Identity

Class structure in Palestinian society, as in Arab society more generally, has always been shaped by a racial politics of color. The lasting effects of the power relationship that emerged with the Arab slave trade between white and black Arabs, it will be argued here, are kept very much alive through language and spatial segregation. The narratives that I encountered among black women were marked by many contradictions, some of which, I believe, were a result of the presence of white listeners such as myself and, at times, a mutual a'rāb friend. For instance, while black Bedouin women condemned the racist nature of the state policies toward the Bedouins, they also emphasized—in front of the a'rāb friend—that there was no racism among the Bedouins themselves. Yet it could easily be noticed that socioeconomic relations are very much linked to racialized power relations, as wealth among the Bedouins is distributed according to a power hierarchy based on color. For instance, all the Bedouins whom I met in Laqiya and who served in the army were black. Black Bedouins' lack of professional prospects was generally greater than that of other Bedouins. They also shared many more stories about loved ones being murdered, indicating that the crime rate experienced within the black Bedouin community is higher. Also, lengthy participant observation showed me that black Bedouin women rely much more heavily on social benefits from the state.

The most interaction that I witnessed between black and white women was within the Bedouin community in which I stayed. As I started to explore the complex family structures within the al-Sana tribe, I quickly noticed the many times when black Bedouins were referred to as 'abeed (slaves) by a'rāb women. While, historically, 'abeed also included a minority of white slaves, today the term is an expression of anti-Black racism. Some a'rāb even went as far as to continue to add to their names the names of the tribes that they used to serve, for instance 'Abd Al-'Atawnih, enforcing their perception of the black Bedouins as being of mean birth. Black Bedouins themselves, on the other hand, preferred to call themselves after an ancestor of the solidarity group that they had decided to follow after the abolition of their slavery. I was particularly disturbed by the fact that contemporary scholars, too, employ the term whenever writing on the subject of ethnic groups within the Bedouin community: "Finally, there are the 'abd (pl. 'abeed) people of African descent who migrated or were enslaved by various tribes throughout the centuries" (Dahan-Kalev and Le Febvre 2012, 32). Older research draws on even more racist language: "The term 'abd is still applied today, even by the negroes to themselves" (Marx 1967, 67). The lack of exploration of, or reflection on, this kind of terminology among anthropologists is particularly problematic since they themselves note that black Bedouins do not, in fact, identify or refer to themselves as 'abeed but, in fact, as "sumor" (the blacks) (Kressel 1992, 85).

Black Bedouin women were very clear to me about the derogatory meanings and racist implications in the use of the term 'abd. In fact, the first woman I asked about the meaning of 'abd, while we were chatting in a group of women in her living room, felt offended just by my question and responded, "If you ever use that word again, we will have to slap you! I slap everybody who uses that word. It is a bad word, a painful word. Don't use it!" Another woman, Manar, a young teacher from Rahat, told me that, while she loathed the word 'abd, she was proud of being black and hence preferred to be referred to as samra (black). We were casually socializing in a group of common (a'rāb) Bedouin friends when I realized that, even among younger women, internal racism was hardly discussed and, if so, mostly in a joking manner (perhaps especially so in front of me). An important point here is that Manar's experience confirms that within the Bedouin community racism is an integral part of black women's daily lives. The seriousness and painfulness of this experience is, again, underlined by Manar's description of her defensive reaction to people whenever they use the word ʿabd.

> Manar: I'm a teacher in a school where everyone is mostly white and in the class that I taught, they kept calling me "Ya ʿabda." It drove me crazy!
>
> Kim: How did you react?
>
> Manar: I didn't say anything to them because I didn't want to speak to them.
>
> (She gets very quiet and wrapped in thought.)
>
> Manar: Now the students have stopped using the word because they have observed that I get angry whenever they use it. I grabbed one of the students who used it and said, "Why do you say this?!" and I slapped them. I slapped one of them in front of the whole class and now they stopped using the word because they know how I react to it.
>
> (She turns to one of her friends.)
>
> Manar: These are my friends. Look, all of them are white. Ask her what she said to me!
>
> (She points at her friend Amnaa.)
>
> Amnaa: The first time I called her ʿabd and then I said samra. Now I always say samra. She is a beautiful black [woman].
>
> (Amnaa grabs Manar's face and kisses her forehead. They joke around.)
>
> Manar: I have more white than black friends, you know.
>
> Amnaa: Yes, because the blacks don't like you.
>
> Another friend jumps into the conversation: Whites also don't like her!
>
> (All of them laugh out loud.)

While black Bedouin women were very much aware of and offended by the derogatory implications of the word ʿabd, most of my aʿrāb acquaintances were unaware of the implications. In fact, the use of the term ʿabd was normalized and common among aʿrāb Bedouins. I thought this was striking, considering they were all close friends, lived near each other, and essentially had grown up together. Once, for instance, Jalilah told her father that we would head out to visit her (black) friend, shouting, "Bye, dad. We will be at Hussein's house," as we were standing in the doorway about to leave. Her father did not understand who she meant by "Hussein" and asked again and again until she said, "Hussein al-ʿabd." He then immediately understood who she meant and nodded. According to black Bedouin women, the term is much more commonly used within small villages than within Bedouin urban centers such as Rahat, which are deemed more open-minded and less racist. In general, there is no doubt that it is used widely. Black Bedouin women themselves said to me that they use it only jokingly among themselves and, as one woman emphasized, "never when there is a white person in the room!" According to black Bedouin women in Laqiya, only one Bedouin family is officially allowed to be referred to as Al-ʿAbd, a black Bedouin family whose actual surname is ʿAl-ʿAbd and who live in a small forest outside Laqiya that they refer to as "the jungle." Aurora Ellis, a researcher on African diaspora studies, has pointed out that throughout Arabic-speaking Africa, ʿabeed is a term primarily used in a derogatory manner about blacks, black citizens, and black foreigners alike, but I encountered the term only among the Bedouins.[8]

Outside the Bedouin community, black women predominantly used the words ʿaswad and ʿasmar. While ʿaswad can be read as the Arabic equivalent of "black" as a political identity, used within very similar contexts, most women preferred to use the word ʿasmar, which refers to light black skin color. One black woman described to me that it meant "something like 'less than black.' It's a sort of polite way of referring to very dark persons who might otherwise be called 'black.'" I observed a vivid discussion about which terminology the women thought was right in discussions on women's Facebook statuses. At times, black women or women of color would even pick on or correct each other about which term to use. A black woman named Violet, for instance, who proudly identified as black also as a political identity, for instance, commented on a fellow women's rights activist who used ʿasmar to refer to herself in her status, saying that she should write ʿaswad instead and "use it proudly!"

Marriage Discrimination and Hypersexualization

Black Palestinian women—regardless of their community—are discriminated against, in particular, in the context of marriage. Anthropological studies of the Bedouins in al-Naqab pointed out the extremely high rate of group endogamy as early as the 1960s. In his study on social hierarchy, kinship, and marriage among former Bedouins in the Ramla-Lod area, Gideon M. Kressel, for instance, found a 100 percent rate of endogamy among the black Bedouins for both brides and grooms in the early 1970s (1992, 68). Kressel explains the lack of interracial marriage as being based on the treatment of the black Bedouin community as a lower caste by a'rāb and fellaheen (69). While a'rāb clearly do not encourage their children to marry black Bedouins, I found that explaining the discouragement of intermarriage solely by a'rāb racial supremacy is rather incomplete and lacks the other side of the coin. Manar, for instance, explained to me that she was against the marriage of her sister to a white man for the following reason: "If they were married and they had kids, the family of the man would call the children ʿabeed. I don't want my sister's children to feel hurt like that." Later on, she pulled about thirty passport-sized photographs out of her wallet, including one photograph of her niece, and said, "Look, they call her *samra* because she is of color. If you're half black, you're black, you're *samra*."

While Manar explained to me that the situation of black women in the north is better, that they experience less racism there and that, as a result, interracial marriage is more common, I failed to find a single mixed-race married couple in the country. Instead, I encountered only many rumors about distant acquaintances, which were told over and over again, including a story about a white woman and a black man from Rahat who had to flee to the United Kingdom in order to protect the woman from relatives who wanted to kill her for marrying a black man. In fact, I found that the racial discrimination against black women in marriage could be seen among black Palestinian women all over the country. Several of these women shared their personal experiences with me about how they were tolerated as girlfriends of *a'rāb* or white Palestinian men only as long as the men's mothers thought the relationship was not serious. Afra, a very successful businesswoman from the Galilee, broke down in tears toward the end of our interview:

> To be a black girl in the Arab society is the worst thing. . . . I really don't want to go into this but really for me this was one of the main obstacles that I faced as a woman . . . and not from my family but from the society. This is one of the obstacles I face as a Palestinian feminist: an empowered Palestinian woman also wants to get married and have her own family. If nobody wants to get married to her this is a huge obstacle! If you're older than thirty and you're not married, you'll get depressed very easily. You're not having sex, you don't have a partner by your side, you don't have children. . . . In my village they called me *samra*—this connotation felt awful. Our society expects us to be white. . . . I really don't know why by the way . . . because most Arab people are not white . . . but at some point, society decided that the woman you're going to marry should be white. I'm still very sensitive about this issue. . . . Most Arab men look for blonde women and I don't want a man to whom this is important.

Afra's statement caught me off guard on several levels: first, most of the rest of our conversation had revolved around a totally different subject: Palestinian women in the Israel labor market. Second, perhaps because of Afra's outstanding professional success and stunning good looks, I have to admit I was prejudiced and never would have expected her to feel insecure about her appearance. The internalization of hegemonic white beauty standards described by Afra was a recurrent theme in my other conversations with black women, as was the frustration in trying to find a husband who did not adhere to racist standards. In an article confronting antiblack racism in the Arab world, Palestinian novelist Susan Abulhawa explains the roots of these standards as follows:

> An extension to Arab anti-black racism is an aspiration to all that our former—and current—colonizers possess. Individuals aspire to what is powerful and rich, and the images of that power and wealth have light skin, straight hair, small noses, ruddy cheeks and tall, skinny bodies. That image rejects melanin-rich skin, coiled hair, broad or pointy noses, short stature, broad hips and big legs. So we, too, reject these features, despising them in others and in ourselves as symbols of inferiority, laziness, and poverty that's why the anglicizing industries of skin bleaching and hair straightening are so profitable (Abulhawa 2013).

But black women's bodies are not targeted only by Arab beauty standards representing notions of power and privilege. The elevation of whiteness over blackness by Palestinian society is strengthened by the fact that it takes place within a settler colonial state that also adheres to a system of white supremacy: Ethiopian Jewish women rank below Mizrahi, and Mizrahi rank below Ashkenazi women. Controlling images of white beauty standards are virtually impossible to escape throughout the country. As a result, Patricia Hill Collins writes in *Black Feminist Thought* that black women frequently experience "the pain of never being able to live up to prevailing standards of beauty—standards used by white men, white women, black men and most painfully one another" (2000, 98). Thus, the experiences of black indigenous women in Israel take place at the intersection of a settler colonial state and an indigenous society, both of which produce and mutually reinforce gendered and racialized hierarchies in which black indigenous women are placed at the bottom. As a result, indigenous black women's bodies, as the most deprived and vulnerable, are the discursive and physical terrain where settler colonialism and social patriarchy, both structured by sexist and racist logics, converge.

A demonstration of the settler colonial interlocking systems of racism and sexism took place right on the spot of my interview with Afra, when she was catcalled by two Orthodox Jewish men who walked by, on separate occasions, with the macho pickup lines *"Chag sameach"* (happy holiday) and *"Ma ha-matzav?"* (what's up?), winking at her. The hypersexualization and exoticization of black women's bodies is part of the social imagining of both Arab and Israeli society. Rooted in the history of black women's violent enslavement as sex slaves, black and dark-skinned women continue to be seen by both Palestinian and Israeli men as sexually promiscuous and available. This experience is very similar to that of African American women, whose allegedly deviant sexuality becomes constructed around controlling images such as "jezebel," which again originated during the slave and imperialist eras and provide a crucial rationale for widespread assaults by white men (Collins 2000, 89). Like the Afro-American "jezebel" or "hoochie," black Arab women's hypersexualization manifests itself in Arab-speaking popular culture, most notably in the fetishization of the *"samar"* (black woman) and her lascivious sexuality, which pervades daily life and culture.

The association of blackness with sexual appetite goes back to the Middle Ages, when sexuality itself was referred to as "the African sin" (McClintock 1995, 113). During the long periods of Western and Eastern slavery and imperialism, black women became even more closely associated with a "primitive sexual appetite." "Scientific" medical examinations and the public exhibition of black women's supposedly excessive genitalia, such as the famous exhibition of the Khoisan woman Saartjie Baartman as "The Hottentot Venus," aimed to demonstrate external signs of this temperament in the name of "race science." As has been pointed out by feminist scholar Anne McClintock in *Imperial Leather*, "Victorian men of science found a fetish for embodying, measuring, and embalming the idea of the female body as an anachronistic space (1995, 41)." Important among their claims are alleged proofs that female genitalia are more primitive than those of men, which essentially also has served the purpose of the subordination of Victorian white women.

NOTES

1. The working group's members are the following NGOs: Adalah, Al-Tufula, Assiwar, Arab Women in the Center, Arab Association of Human Rights, Kayan Feminist Organization, Ma'an, Mada Al-Carmel Arab Center for Applied Social Research, Mossawa Center for the Rights of the Arab Citizens of Israel, Muntada, Sidreh, Yasmin Al-Nagab for the Health of Women and Family, Women against Violence.

2. "Coronavirus Unemployment Crisis Deepening for Arab Israelis," *Jerusalem Post*, May 24, 2020, https://www.jpost.com/israel-news/coronavirus-unemployment-crisis-deepening-for-arab-israelis-629133.

3. *Badal* marriage is when a sister and her brother are married to a brother and his sister from another family.

4. *Pinkwashing* refers to Israel's public promotion of gay rights in order to present itself internationally as a liberal democracy while trying to cover its violations of Palestinian human rights.

5. Y. Schwartz, "Meet the Arab Woman Who Has Just Become the First Miss Trans Israel," *Time*, May 31, 2016, http://time.com/4352201 /talleen-abu-hanna-first-miss-trans-israel/.

6. J. Puar, "Israel's Gay Propaganda War," *Guardian*, July 1, 2010, https://www.theguardian.com/commentisfree/2010/jul/01/israels -gay-propaganda-war.

7. The "Triangle" is a group of Palestinian towns and villages adjacent to the Green Line.

8. See M. Williams, "Black Women's Resistance to the Legacy of the Arab Slave Trade," *teleSUR*, April 10, 2015, https://www.telesurenglish.net/analysis /Black-Womens-Resistance-to-the-Legacy-of-the-Arab-Slave-Trade-20150410 -0016.html.

THREE

—~∿~—

DEFYING BODIES

INTRODUCTION

When it comes to the intimate politics of the body, there is enormous pressure for Palestinian women in Israel to stick with the plan. In all parts of the world, bodies and the people who inhabit them are subject to social norms of looking and behaving in specific ways (Bobel and Kwan 2011, 1). Norms are diverse and yet particular, as they are the product of the history and politics of a specific time and place. For this reason, the ways in which Palestinian women's bodies in Israel act can be analyzed only in terms of the norms and expectations in which they are embedded. Such expectations include practices particular to age, class, gender, sexuality, and race as they apply to both settler colonial imaginings of "Arab-Israeli" and patriarchal imaginings of Palestinian women's bodies. Notably, informed by both sets of norms, these expectations work in unison with each other more than they impede each other in their parallel striving over the control of Palestinian women's bodies. Body norms are powerful means through which to invade and infringe on women's intimate body politics and thereby exert this control or, as Chris Bobel and Samantha Kwan write in *Embodied Resistance*, "to state the obvious, norms *normalize*, they exert a near-magnetic effect on people, compelling them, often unwittingly, to fit in or risk censure, condemnation, and in some instances, danger" (2011, 1). Body norms' function to normalize control takes on a specific meaning in settler colonial contexts, wherein the creation of specific kinds of subjects and bodies is fundamental to the making of a body politic that sustains settler supremacy. In Israel, the occupation and colonization of indigenous bodies and minds is a sustained and incomplete part of the Zionist project. Settler colonial body norms imposed on Palestinian women seek a normalization of the occupation and entail the paradox of assimilating Palestinian women's bodies while, concurrently, keeping them recognizable.

What happens when Palestinian women's bodies act in ways that are considered inappropriate, encompassing actions that are deemed unfeminine, disgusting, indecent, or immoral? What can we learn from the quotidian intimate politics of Palestinian women's defiant bodies in Israel pertaining to how they reveal, fortify, or challenge wider structural and political forces? Defiant bodies, sometimes called undisciplined bodies or body outlaws (Edut 2004), are understood here as bodies that not only resist hegemonic body norms but also venture a step further: they cross and redraw the contours of Palestinian womanhood according to women's own desires and imaginings, thereby destabilizing both the settler colonial and patriarchal social orders.

This chapter scrutinizes and is structured by the following three areas of Palestinian women's intimate body politics: (1) the politics of menstruation, (2) tattooing, and (3) dress. I investigate areas that revolve around social taboos in these areas. Women's strategies to defy the plans for their bodies are as multifaceted as the plans themselves. The personal stories that will be analyzed in the following sections should not be mistaken as voices that represent a given group of resisters (i.e., there is no group of Palestinian women who come together as "menstrual activists" or an organized subculture of self-identified Palestinian "tattooed women"), which, in a way, makes them all the more exceptional and intriguing. Instead, attention will be paid to women's individual stories and experiences that take place in the lived, complex, and messy daily realities of Palestinian women in Israel. Even though the women included here are from diverse social and ethnic backgrounds and political and religious orientations, they by no means capture all forms and accounts of Palestinian women's intimate politics.

Rather than looking at embodied resistance, my interest lies in resisting bodies or what I call "defying bodies." To that end, this chapter aims to contribute to the growing number of empirical works that examine the body "reacting back and affecting discourse" (Shilling 1993, 81). Several studies not only scrutinize how women's bodies are not merely embodying or acted on by social and political relations of power, which transform them into disciplined or resistant bodies (Foucault 1995), they also draw attention to the resisting doings and "not doings," as Mullaney's (2006) title frames it, of bodies. (See also Davis 1988; Pitts 2003; Weitz 2001; Gimlin 2002.) They further draw attention to the fact that we cannot depict their stories as "one of two," as every action potentially contains both elements of resistance and compliance. Defying bodies' refusal to negotiate between resistance and compliance has usually been preceded or continues to be accompanied by personal journeys of women's self-discovery: What makes them feel comfortable and beautiful in their own bodies? It is important to note that all the women whom I have written about in this section have struggled or continue to struggle throughout their daily lives on their journey to corporeal self-determination as they imagine and desire it.

"LEAVING MARKS": THE POLITICS OF MENSTRUATION

Having spent months living in other women's places, I noticed the common practice of putting out toiletries in the bathroom, which usually included wet wipes, menstrual pads, panty liners, and, at times, tampons. Whenever I asked women, usually women around my own age, for a tampon I realized that the use of tampons was not very common. I did not really think about it that much until I had a few chats with women who said that their parents disliked them using tampons, as there was still a preconception that they might injure the hymen and thereby put their virginity at risk. Upon researching around the issue, I found that the use of tampons is unpopular among some Arabs because of traditional notions of menstrual blood being impure and unhealthy if it "lingers in the body" (El Feki 2013, 61). Haneen, a twenty-four-year-old student and a virgin, for example, told me, "I bought tampons in order to go swimming during our family trip in Germany. So, I put the box in front of my parents ... and I'm totally confident with that. But still, it's awkward. Even though they let me do it, ... it's still seen as a 'strange thing' or an 'unusual thing' to do."

Haneen's experience is representative of many young women's when they choose to use tampons. Often these women, all from very educated backgrounds, described the contradiction between their parents' lack of real concern about their virginity and their outdated concern about the tampons injuring the hymen. As my curiosity about the contradictions between social perceptions and practices around the issue of female menstrual hygiene grew, I also observed how, even within the homes of feminists, tampons would be removed from the bathroom whenever a mother or an aunt came to visit so as to not offend them or make them feel uncomfortable. To my mind, the contrast between the open display of women's menstrual hygiene products in bathrooms to most guests (including to visiting men) but the removal of tampons from the sight of older family members (usually women) was striking. When I addressed the practice of removing tampons to a friend, I could not help but be irritated by the fact that she did not want her own mother, a very open-minded and progressive woman with whom I once had an extensive discussion about condoms, to know about her using tampons. I was also struck by the speed with which she started to point to the Haredim (Orthodox Jewish) community and describe all kinds of details about the *niddah* (menstruating woman) custom of separating a wife from her husband for seven days during her menstruation, and how any object, or even person, that she may come into contact with during this time would become "ritually impure."

At first thought, I interpreted her pointing out another community and its customs as a way of distracting me from my initial question, which, perhaps, put her on the spot about her feminist politics too much. On second thought, I reminded myself that her decision to hide her tampons from her mother so as not to offend her did not take place in a social vacuum, and so I began to question what practices around menstruation represent in a wider context of existing power relations, what meanings women's decisions about menstrual hygiene might carry and the possibility of them having not only social but also political implications. Because women's bodies, behaviors, desires, pleasures, and appearances are a product of wider power relations (Grosz 1994, 32), in most societies, women's handling of their menstruation is, to a large extent, policed by hegemonic cultural norms. It will be argued here that reading women's practices and decisions about menstruation can give us valuable insights into women's experiences of and their resistance to such norms and politically oppressive systems.

The policing and fetishization of women's menstruation take place in numerous cultures and are often expressed through the obsessive regulation and ritualization of women's bodies, even in the most intimate settings such as the family (Laws 1990, 32). Building on Haneen's example of the Haredim community, there is a whole register of terminology about menstruation in Judaism, describing the time, material, and practices and, even the people involved in women's periods, such as the days during which the woman is likely to see her menstrual flow, the people who come into contact with menstruating women, the children who are conceived when their mother is in *"niddah"* (menstruating), and the cloth with which to check whether menstrual blood has finished, among others. The close involvement and central role of rabbis in identifying which blood qualifies a woman as *niddah* or not demonstrates the extent of the masculinist invasion of women's bodies in order to keep track of their cycles and time of ovulation for their main purpose: reproduction. Hegemonic masculinity significantly relies on women's ability to menstruate as a justification for the creation and continuation of the public-private divide (De Troyer et al. 2003). It is used, above all, to relegate women's place in the nation to that of mothers.

Even though there are extensive anthropological investigations of various cultural practices around menstruation, including both severe social restrictions and privileged treatment of menstruating women (Mead 1949; Shuttle and Redgrove 2005; Knight 1991), feminist explorations have only sporadically really built on these existing works. Feminist scholarship extensively discusses the politics of the body in terms of sex and sexuality, but the politicization of menstruation has remained comparatively neglected. The perceived conflict between women's roles as mothers and as political beings has led many Western feminists to regard the female body and its cycles of menstruation, pregnancy, maternity, and lactation as a hindrance to women's struggle for the rights and privileges that patriarchal society accords to men. Even though some feminists have come to perceive the female body as a means of accessing valuable knowledge, within Western feminist camps menstruation continues to be perceived as a physical and emotional impairment, a limitation for women more than a means of power.

A significant amount of literature investigates the central role of Palestinian women's bodies in particular—their targeting by settler colonial and patriarchal violence, and their giving birth to the nation. None of it, however, addresses menstruation as a site of women's struggle against patriarchal and settler colonial oppression. In other words, not much has been written either about how Palestinian women's menstruation is used as a site by Zionist forces to control and discipline them as indigenous women or about the potential significance of menstruation as a defying tool against violent domination.

Manar Hassan's essay, "Growing Up Female and Palestinian in Israel" (2005) is a rare kind of publication that illustrates the feminist sociologist's perception of how menstruation is experienced among Palestinian girls in Israel:

> The menarche appears as a bolt from the sky or as a mysterious illness. When the women of her family discover her state, the feeling of illness is exacerbated by a sense of guilt and sin. The subject is discussed in whispers, far from the ears of men. The teenager is given no scientific explanation of the physiological phenomenon; yet the menses themselves become a monthly proof of her sinful state.... These instructions carry additional concealed messages. The menstrual flow is to be absorbed with cotton wool, which, of course, must be hidden before use and burnt clandestinely afterwards. Even the toilet paper, which may be thrown into the bathroom wastebasket, as is the practice in many Palestinian households, has a lower negative impact. Thus a completely normal physical process becomes a focus of guilt and conveys a feeling of perpetual pollution.... The mother as a trained agent of the patriarchal system, must report to the father that his daughter has

> become a walking time bomb, liable to sully the so-called family honor. . . .
> Supervision is increased. . . . The feeling of guilt becomes a permanent element
> in the life of the adolescent female (2005, 183–84).

The policing of women's menstruation is enabled through its social tabooing. In this context, the primary tool is the link of women's menstrual blood to various forms of uncleanliness. Menstruating Palestinian women are often perceived and represented as dirty, polluted, vile, and impure (Douglas 1966; O'Brien 1981; Laws 1990, 32). Similarly Orthodox Jewish religious protocol requires women to immerse themselves in the *mikvah*, a ritual purification bath, immediately after they stop menstruating. Such menstrual etiquette (Laws 1990, 42) ensures a sense of fear, embarrassment, and shame for women about their menstruation. The association of menstruation, menstrual blood, and therefore women, with dirt is not unlike the attitudes that dominant groups hold toward oppressed groups. As Sophie Laws suggests in *Issues of Blood* (1990), power relations have frequently been solidified by dehumanizing both the lower classes and various ethnic minorities as dirty:

> Pollution beliefs can be read as statements about power relations in society.
> They define, according to the dominant ideology, what is "matter out of place"
> and this in turn makes it clear who has control of such social definitions. Thus
> the idea that people with certain characteristics are dirty is very often found
> as part of the attitudes of a dominant group towards a less powerful one. It
> is a persistent feature of racism and anti-Semitism as well as of misogyny. In
> relation to class, too, the upper classes have habitually made a distinction
> between the "respectable" poor and "the great unwashed." Dirt represents
> lack of self-control, and those whom the powerful wish to control are
> expected to be eager to demonstrate their compliance (Laws 1990, 36).

Although in-depth explorations remain scarce, menstruation also takes on a special role within settler colonial contexts, where indigenous women's menstrual bleeding, because of its sexualization, its tabooing, especially among patriarchal indigenous societies, and most of all its symbolization of ongoing indigenous existence and potential reproduction, has been used as a means of oppressing indigenous women. In a context in which indigenous peoples are already constructed as dirty and wild, settler colonial discourses and attacks on indigenous women's menstrual bleeding serve to reinforce such notions. In her comprehensive book on the removal and assimilation of indigenous children in Australia and the United States in the early twentieth century, *White Mother to a Dark Race*, historian Margaret D. Jacobs (2009) pays special attention to the central role of white women in the project of assimilation. In exploring the aim of white female educators to control indigenous girl's bodies and sexuality, Jacobs outlines how menstruation was a particularly crucial site for the settler colonial assimilationist attack. Whereas, in their indigenous communities, many girls would have received a special puberty celebration, the settler institutions treated their menses strictly as a "source of shame and mystery" (311). While one can assume that the settlers did not treat menstruation as a subject of discussion among their own daughters, the supply of only the bare necessities to indigenous girls by white women and chiding them as dirty for asking for information about what they were experiencing reflects a political strategy that is best expressed in their ongoing close monitoring of indigenous girls' bodies (e.g., diaries were kept about girls' menstrual bleeding) (Jacobs 2009).

The taboo nature of menstruation has been used in various interrogation practices against both men and women. For example, Laleh Khalili writes about a female American interrogator at the Guantanamo Bay prisons who slapped—what the prisoner believed to be—menstrual blood on a prisoner's face in order to make him talk (2010, 1482). It is not surprising that menstruation was also a special means to target Jewish women in Nazi concentration camps, where women were killed for showing any "unaesthetic" bloodstains despite not being provided with anything to conceal their menstruation (Sereny 1977). Menstruation has also frequently been used by the Israeli military to pressure and attack Palestinian women prisoners, though—because of the taboo of menstruation—it has scarcely been reported. In her book about Palestinian women's anticolonial struggle within the Israeli prison system, Nahla Abdo writes about how menstruation is used as a tool to enervate women prisoners and detainees as part of Israeli psychological and sexual torture: "Women complained about the refusal of the interrogator or the prison guard to provide them with sanitary pads during menstruation. Detainees who were sentenced and placed in prison rooms would rip some of the rags used as bed sheets or covers and use these; others in solitary confinement, in isolation cells or during interrogation would be left bleeding all over their only pants" (2014, 165).

Supporting this claim, the Public Committee against Torture in Israel (PCATI) submitted two group complaints two years before the publication of Abdo's book, in which nine Palestinian women detainees and former prisoners testified that there was an intentional absence of hygienic conditions and a denial of sanitary pads to women who were menstruating during interrogation.[1] Overall, Palestinian women's ability to menstruate and the taboo associated with it increases the value of Zionist threats and punishments on their bodies.

Theresa O'Keefe writes about a comparable situation, the use of menstrual blood as a tool for the oppression of republican women prisoners in Northern

Ireland. Like Palestinian women prisoners of Israel, these women were severely intimidated and humiliated by frequently being denied menstrual products and the use of sanitation facilities. During the so-called Dirty Protest, initiated by their male counterparts, the women in Armagh prison started to refuse to use the bathrooms and instead smeared their own excrement on the walls of their cells as a means of protest. Compared to the excrement of their fellow male prisoners, however, the women's menstrual blood was perceived as particularly deterring (O'Keefe 2006).

During my talks with many women who were about my own age, I came across the exceptional story of Maryam, a young feminist activist who also decided to use her menstruation as a site of resistance in her workspace, a law office in central Tel Aviv:

> I moved to work in a private law firm ... very rich with white men leading it, a very patriarchal place. I had my period and there was one man who was leading the firm and the staff were women, the lower ranks were packed with female secretaries. . . . It was quite hierarchal. It was my second working day there and I used a towel (pad) and put it into the bin and then another woman, a colleague, came into my office and asked me to make sure that I had put it into the bin "properly," meaning in a way in which nobody would see it. Wrap it in toilet paper so we don't see the red color. And I said "Why?" Why would I hide the fact that I have my period? I was shocked. We had a unisex toilet and she just wanted to make sure that the men didn't feel "uncomfortable" looking at the red color in the bin. I mean it was in the bin ... who looks into the bin? I intentionally leave marks when I'm on my period so people understand that a period is not something blue and shiny like in the tampon adverts. I intended to put it into the bin like that. I felt that my colleagues were completely overwhelmed by my decision and that the atmosphere was getting tenser. So we met again to talk about it. And I declared that I was very proud of my period, the red color is beautiful, and they thought that I was completely crazy. I said to them, you are marginalizing me from the unisex toilet. Every man can leave his marks ... and they do! But as a woman I cannot leave marks.

As mentioned earlier, the power of menstruation, for both the oppressor and those resisting oppression, lies in the fact that it is widely constructed and considered a taboo matter (O'Keefe 2006, 536). Challenging the constructed taboo around menstruation can be a powerful way for women to seek to disrupt the hegemonic societal order. Maryam's explicit refusal to cover up bloodstained menstrual pads in the wastebasket of her office's unisex bathroom was directly linked to her rejection of the social norms and expectations that were upheld and imposed on her by her colleagues. Maryam's action expressed defiance against and destabilization of the plan in several ways.

First, in a male-dominated work environment where women's bodies are tolerated as a minority but their reproductive functions are subject to strict codes of secrecy, her action was shocking for both the men and the women who were actively complying in upholding the gendered social order. Among them was her female colleague who reminded her of her duty as a woman to make sure to cover up all traces of menstruation. This duty is anchored in a deep-seated historical association with women's "duty of cleanliness," that is, their assigned responsibility to take care of the household and keep their children clean (Leddy 1995, 261). In contrast, men, such as Maryam's male coworkers, who also leave marks, albeit of a different nature, are "naturally" associated with a certain extent of dirt based on their historically often dirty jobs. As a result of the history of male jobs and status, men continue to be provided with the freedom to indulge in soiling their body, clothes, and environment more than women, for whom such behavior would entail "failing to be feminine." Moreover, dealing with one's menstruation in the way Maryam did is perceived by both men and women as disgusting. Julia Kristeva's theory of objectification helps to understand this "naturally felt" disgust as a reaction to the ambiguity of menstrual blood. Menstrual blood is neither part of, nor separate from, the body and, as a result, cannot be conceived as either subject or object, inside or outside; rather, it is abject. Ambiguity defines the abject as "what disturbs identity, system, order. What does not respect borders, positions, rules. The in-between, the ambiguous, the composite" (Kristeva 1982, 4). Because of its disturbance of the existing order, menstrual blood is othered as an object of disgust.

In her chapter "Menstrual Meditations," Iris Marion Young explores cultural attitudes to menstruation and illuminates the importance that women attach to concealing their menstruation by following a myriad of practical rules (1997, 106). All these rules spring from the assumption that menstruation is dirty and must be kept secret, an assumption that is fed to women by patriarchal medicalized discourses in particular, as well as by the capitalist industry of menstrual products. Advertisements for menstrual products and drugs to deal with menstrual discomfort frequently present menstruation as a restriction on physical and social activity: the menstrual cycle is a "hygienic crisis" (Brumberg 1997), a medical malady or a problem that requires treatment (Tavris 1992; Angier 1999; Ussher 2006; Vostral 2008). Simultaneously, menstruation is considered an indiscreet matter and so, the logic goes, menstrual blood must be kept hidden and is represented by blue liquid in advertisements. Within Israel, a country in which sexualized self-representation is fed, in particular, to young girls, female soldiers, and other women, being "clean" and hiding any traces of menstruation is particularly desired. The message is enforced not only by the so-called femcare industry, but also within schools, the army, and workspaces. In fact, even mainstream advertisements for menstrual products (see fig. 3.1), which, as Maryam stated, camouflage menstruation with shiny blue fluid and suchlike, still deeply disturb a large number of both religious and secular Jewish Israeli women (Barak-Brandes 2011).

Maryam's blatant refusal to adhere to this menstrual etiquette was based not only on her protest against being an object of patriarchal discipline and normalization but also on her desire to feel comfortable and proud of her own body with all its functionings. Her decision not to hide her menstrual traces and to openly discuss the issue destabilized the separation between the private and public spheres as they were constructed in the office. Moreover, Maryam directly challenged Palestinian patriarchal norms, which dictate when women must demonstrate that they bleed (during the time of the loss of their virginity) and when they must not show any signs of bleeding (during menstruation). Maryam's action was more, however, than a protest against patriarchal discipline because it took place in an overall hierarchical workspace dominated by Jewish Israeli male workers. Maryam was not only new and surrounded by many superiors she was also the only *indigenous* woman worker. Simone de Beauvoir's theorization of "Woman as Other" is fundamental to women's oppression through menstruation as menstrual activist and scholar Elizabeth Kissling writes in *Capitalizing the Curse*: "The social construction of menstruation as a woman's curse is explicitly implicated in the evolution of woman as Other: 'the blood, indeed, does not make woman impure; it is rather a sign of her impurity' (quoting Beauvoir). That is to say, menstruation does not make woman the Other; it is because she is Other that menstruation is a curse" (2006, 4).

It is important to observe that Maryam was not Othered simply as a woman but as an indigenous woman. Thus, the resistance against her menstruation as something dirty also implies a resistance against her whole body, that she was being subjugated and dehumanized as a dirty indigenous person. As a result, there is a hierarchy of propriety that not only encompasses men and women but also settler and colonized. As pointed out by Elizabeth Grosz, despite being ejected from the body, menstrual flow still has something bound up with bodily fluids—which is why they are objects of disgust, loathing, and repulsion as well as envy and desire (1994, 81). Menstrual blood takes on particularly noteworthy meanings, as blood is an indicator of both life and death. In a context of militarized conflict marked by a great amount of blood loss, indigenous menstrual blood constitutes a distinct and powerful oppositional force in the eyes of the

Figure 3.1. A Tampax commercial in Tel Aviv, 2013. The commercial reads "He enters the water now. What about you? Don't miss any opportunity just because of your period. Go for Pearl Tampax." ©Tampax.

settler colonizer, signifying, not only symbolically but also physically, the on-going indigenous existence as well as potential reproduction.

By claiming the freedom to leave marks, Maryam essentially turned around the patriarchal and colonialist construction of menstruation that was intended to discipline and to make her vulnerable, thereby resisting the policing and control over her body, taking over space, and, ultimately, transgressing the behavioral codes imposed on Palestinian women by the plan. By not respecting these borders, Maryam not only destabilized the disciplinary power that inscribed femininity in the female body (Bartky 1997) but also defied and disturbed the colonialist drive that inscribes assimilation in the indigenous female body. Maryam's act of defiance was radical not only because of the ongoing tabooing of menstruation among many Palestinian feminists themselves, but also because of the space in which it was enacted. While in O'Keefe's (2006) study of Irish women prisoners, menstrual blood resulted in unwanted trespassers being warded off as wardens entered the cell only when they absolutely had to, Maryam's office constituted a very different space: a space in which she was at the bottom of a racialized, gendered, and professional hierarchy on which she relied in order to make a living.

TATTOOS: BADGES OF SELF-DETERMINATION

Nahla and I had known each other since my first stay in Haifa in 2011. I stayed with her family in a small Palestinian village in the northern Galilee multiple times, including during the Christmas holidays. Even though by the time I conducted my fieldwork we had become close friends, I was amazed by the fact that it took us two years to reveal our tattoos to each other. To me, this was particularly puzzling in light of the fact that most tattooed people choose to "get inked," as the saying is, in order to decorate their bodies with symbols, messages, or stories with which they have an intimate relationship and that they proudly display, at least in front of friends. Despite the fact that I have never regretted any of my tattoos and share the sentiment of being proud of one's tattoos, I felt very uncomfortable about revealing some of my tattoos during my fieldwork. I frequently caught myself as I strategically displayed and hid certain tattoos in Israel, usually to obtain free passage, to show solidarity, or simply to provoke, the choice depending on where I was or the people I was with at the time.

I felt particularly uncomfortable about a Hebrew tattoo, which I made sure to cover throughout my fieldwork. With an excerpt from a religious song tattooed on the crook of my right arm, I would wear clothes that covered my elbows; this, combined with my preference for knee-length skirts, led many Jewish Israelis to believe that I was, in their words, "religious" (i.e., Orthodox Jewish). Showing my tattoo did not usually clarify their false belief, as they still believed I was religious, just in a more "Boho" or "hipster" way, and I did not mind that because it frequently made me appear less sexually available to Israeli men.

Revealing my Hebrew tattoo to Nahla, however, was a totally different thing. I was terrified that she might suspect that I wore it to express some kind of sympathy for the Zionist movement and that revealing the tattoo might have serious repercussions for our friendship, especially our mutual trust. But when she revealed her own tattoo (a phrase in Elfish) to me, we overcame our initial irritations within seconds and burst out laughing. Naturally, we shared and exchanged the stories behind our tattoos—when we received them, where, and what they symbolize for us—and I could tell that both of us felt significantly relieved afterward.

A nontattooed person might ask why we covered our tattoos in the first place. There is a common and persistent assumption that "people who have tattoos get them for the viewers or for the outside gaze, that tattoos are some sort of personal advertisement" (Bell 1999, 56). Women seldom acquire tattoos, however, in order for them to be read and thereby attract attention. In fact, as Beverly Yuen Thompson's research on heavily tattooed women in the United States points out, women "start their collection in spite of the attention they begin to receive, not in order to receive it" (2015, 161). Tattoos (that are received of one's own volition) as they are discussed here need to be conceptualized as an extension of the body and, as a result, any kind of display of tattoos can be equated to a display of the body itself, which is something the women discussed here struggle to reclaim ownership and control over. Women's desire to control the audience of their tattoos is also rooted in what Christine Braunberger refers to as their "anxieties of misrecognition" (2000, 1): the fear that tattoos might be misread or misinterpreted. Another reason for women to hide their tattoos from the public gaze is that some tattooed women simply feel that their body art, just like any other parts of their body (whether they perceive them as "beautiful" or not), are too intimate to be revealed to another person or in public.

Envisaging the female body as more than a mere canvas and tattoos as a chosen (decorative) extension of that body, I consider tattooed women's bodies as more than simply "inscribed bodies." It will be argued here that women's tattooed bodies not only passively embody messages through which power can be read, but that they are also bodies that speak and thereby actively contest and participate in power struggles. Thus, this chapter argues in line with scholars who have called for a greater focus on the body as subject rather than as a material object, or, as Thomas J. Csordas phrased it, the body as "being-in-the-world" (1994). Such scholars, including Terence Turner (1994, 1995), Pippa Brush (1998) Sara Ahmed and Jackie Stacy (2001), have critiqued theories of the disembodied poststructuralist body, or what Turner calls "antibodies" of postmodernism and poststructuralism (1994), which, to them, are too devoted to the idea of the metaphorically inscribed body, the body as a text on which social reality is inscribed (Foucault 1984, 83; Derrida 1976, 1978). As a modification of the skin, the largest organ and natural border of our bodies, tattooing entails a physical transformation that is layered with intimate meanings, especially for women (Mifflin 2001, 4). Whether or not tattoos are motivated by a feminist ideology, by becoming tattooed women redefine and blur the boundaries—they participate in what Fleming calls "border skirmishing" (quoted in Schildkrout 2004, 320)—they redefine the relationships between not only the self and the other, the self and society, the private and the public, but also the personal and the political through the skin.

Tattoos are all about intimacy: (1) the intimate meanings or stories that we attach to the drawings or symbols that we choose, whether they entail a religious text, the memory of a passed or living lover, friend, or family member, a political statement or a pop culture reference; (2) the intimacy that is involved in the act of getting a tattoo—its location under the skin, perhaps also in a place that is considered intimate by the tattooed woman, but also the intimate relationship created through the trust that we put in the tattooist; and (3) the intimate politics involved throughout the process of getting tattooed.

From choosing a design to getting inked, Palestinian women are seldom driven by the mere idea of enhancing their looks. This section interrogates the motivations behind Palestinian women's decision to get a tattoo: Are they revolting against prevailing hegemonic notions of beauty? Are they reclaiming ownership over their bodies? Who tattoos them? When do they prefer to cover their tattoos? What are the reactions they receive? Do the relationships between a tattooed woman and her spouse and family members change as a result of her tattoos?

When Palestinian women in Israel decide to transform their bodies through tattoos, they do so in a particular social, political, and historical setting in which they defy the plan of being good Arab-Israeli women on several levels. By not only claiming, but actively practicing, ownership over their bodies, they resist both the patriarchal control over their bodies but also patriarchal hegemonic notions of feminine beauty, which they reject and redefine for themselves. In addition, they demonstrate this ownership over their bodies to a settler colonial state that favors either their disappearance by acting as stereotypical oppressed Arab-Israeli women or their assimilation as liberated Arab-Israeli women. Ultimately, the women who participated in this research rejected both and, moreover, renegotiated their relationships with their families, society, and the state by demonstrating self-determination through their bodies, thereby repracticing Palestinian womanhood. Their tattooed bodies manifested the existence of both tattooed Palestinian women and Palestinian tattoo culture in Israel in general, and they refused to participate in Israeli tattoo subculture and its Zionist modernist discourses. Their bodies contest the emergence of new forms of Zionist settler colonialism (such as Hebrew hipsterism) by telling stories of heritage, personal relationships, and values about religion, family, identity, and history in the eyes of fellow students, colleagues, or passersby. Notably, they were never hidden from the eye of the settler (in contrast to some family members). Embedded in a wider movement of an increasing number of young Arabs who express their identity through tattoos, Palestinian women strengthen not only their national identity but also their cultural and emotional links to Arabs outside Israel.

As with Arab women in other parts of the world, tattooing has become increasingly popular among young Palestinian women in Israel, even if some of them, like my friend Nahla, choose not to display them publicly all the time. Most of the women who participated in my research stopped collecting tattoos after receiving between one and four and therefore are what tattoo sociologist Beverly Yuen Thompson calls "lightly tattooed" (2015, 4). Warda, a young professional in Haifa, for instance, has two tattoos: a delicate lily on her wrist with the inscription *libertas* (Latin: "freedom"), and a colorful iris on her ankle. Even though Warda and I had met during my fieldwork in Haifa, I asked her for a chat on Skype so that I could get another glance at her tattoos before writing about them. After allowing me to take a good look at her body art, Warda smiled at me through the camera and said, "it's addictive, isn't it?" and I knew that it was because we are both tattooed—even though she had emphasized how proud she was of her tattoos—that we could talk about them rather openly. Like myself, Warda had the motif for her first tattoo in mind and started to save money for it years before she actually received it. She also hid her tattoo for a while from her parents. In contrast, she received her second tattoo much more spontaneously during her honeymoon in Japan. Transitional life moments such as honeymoons are classic moments to get a tattoo. We spoke while she was still in her Israeli workspace, where, she told me, she did not have to cover her tattoo: "Freedom means a lot to me and that's why it says 'libertas.' I got flowers simply because I love flowers. My name is the name of a flower. In the future, I would love to get an elephant but with a flower on its head. (Laughs.) There's a theme on my body, you know? I definitely want to get my mother's name, which is also the name of a flower."

From the perspective of heavily tattooed women, Warda's tattoos may appear to be within the parameters of acceptable femininity for women in the West: they are delicate and small and feminine in design and are located on feminine parts of the body (Thompson 2015, 5), Warda herself said that she chose her wrist and ankle as locations because she simply found them sexy. She talked me through her tattoos with pride in both them and her body in general and I could tell that her tattoos combined with her curly red hair and her facial piercings were her way of not only defining her own beauty standards but also practicing them by displaying them openly.

The fact that tattoos have become more popular does not mean that women also display them more frequently in public. Indeed, I did not meet many women who would display their tattoos as openly throughout their daily lives as Warda did. Tattooed women are often expected to hide their tattoos at their wedding with special makeup or skin-colored cloth (Thompson 2015, 51), as weddings constitute the most prominent event of the enforced beauty culture. Warda, however, not only rejected such notions but regarded her wedding as an opportunity to show off the artwork on her body in front of all her guests and in her official wedding photographs and her wedding video.

As expressed in Warda's tattooed *libertas*, many Palestinian women experience tattooing and the rejection of the patriarchal beauty culture that it entails as liberating. All the tattooed women I spoke to expressed a sense of heightened self-confidence that they gained as a result of their tattoos and that becoming tattooed made them feel "more in line with their own self-image" (Sweetman 1999, 68). Regardless of their size and location, women's tattoos defy socially sanctioned standards of feminine beauty and force the recognition of new, largely self-certified ones. Particularly in patriarchal societies women feel that tattoos not only inscribe the body with alternative forms of power (DeMello 2000) but also contest existing power relationships by claiming power through their bodies. First and foremost, this power is linked to the control over their own bodies, as Janan, a young teacher from Nazareth, related: "I was really against tattoos when I went to high school. If you had told me back then that I was going to get a tattoo, I wouldn't have believed you. On a basic level, I think they're beautiful. I also like the way in which I can change my body and have control over it. If I dye my hair, put on makeup, these are things that I choose, that I control."

As in other cultures, beauty standards for Palestinian women largely continue to be dictated by patriarchal and male-dominated fantasies, imaginings, and definitions of women's beauty. Thus, Palestinian men strive to guard and supervise Palestinian women's bodies, including their skin. On this note, Janan told me, "It's a big deal that I'm tattooed because I'm a girl. If one of my brothers was tattooed it wouldn't be such a big deal. For men it's definitely easier to get tattoos. Some of my male students, they're fourteen or fifteen years old, got tattoos. . . . I cannot imagine what would happen if any of the girls that age was to get a tattoo. The reactions would be really bad." Janan's tattoos include detailed work that symbolizes the complicated relationship to her mother, who was not very enthusiastic about her body art. Among her five tattoos are also motifs that represent her relationship to Palestine as a national, historical, and emotional identity. One of them includes a pomegranate that she said she was very fond of because, according to her grandmother's stories, it functions as a national symbol of Palestinian culture on several levels.

There are not many things that are as much subject to the whim of historical epochs as the ways in which women's beauty is defined. While today Palestinian women's tattoos are often read, by both men and women, as indicators of their living wild lives or being sexually promiscuous, tattoos were socially acceptable enhancers of Arab women's beauty until the late 1920s. The Arabic saying that "tattoos enhance the allure (*lil-hila*) of a girl" (van Dinter 2005, 177) resonated in the women's common participation in tattoo culture within the wider Arab region. As expressions of women's secret desires (which were impossible to express throughout their daily lives), tattoos were formerly used as a means of enhancing women's attractiveness to men. This was, for instance, the case with the Arabic and Kurdish *deq* tradition of facial tattooing among Syrian women refugees in Turkey, especially in the province of Urfa, and the last generation of tattooed women in Algeria.[2] The women of both of these groups are now between sixty and seventy years old and their husbands continue to pay special tribute to the women's tattoos.[3] Similarly, until recently, among the Iraqi Marsh-Arab tribe 'Al bu Muhammad, men refused to marry a woman who was not tattooed (van Dinter 2005, 178). In Palestine, admirers of women with tattoos include its national poet, Mahmoud Darwish, whose most famous poem, "A Lover from Palestine," testifies to how tattoos were very much a part of the idea of Palestinian beauty:

Her eyes and the tattoo on her hands are Palestinian
Her name, Palestinian
Her dreams and sorrow, Palestinian
Her kerchief, her feet and body, Palestinian
Her birth and death, Palestinian.

(Darwish 1982)

Although tattoos are still worn by older members of Bedouin tribes, I did not manage to find many women who engaged in traditional Palestinian tattooing. I asked my friend's mother Sana about the small tattoo on her forehead, which reminded me a lot of the *deq*, particularly as she was a member of the same generation of women but also because the symbol of her tattoo resembled a moon and earth symbols that were commonly used for *deq*. Like the women with the *deq* tattoo, Sana's main motivation for receiving the facial tattoo had been to enhance her looks (rather than healing, fertility, or other motivations, which were also common). But unlike Kurdish or Algerian women with facial tattoos, Sana was not particularly proud of her tattoo. In fact, she was glad that at the time she received the tattoo her cousin interrupted the tattooist (a friend) and reminded her that it was *haram* (a sin according to Muslim religion). The *deq* tradition, too, stopped as a result of the mainstreaming of Islamic religious beliefs, according to which altering the body with tattoos is *haram*, so it may well be that these ideas arrived in Palestine before they did so among Kurdish women. Both groups of women also expressed the idea that tattoos were simply no longer modern but old-fashioned. When I first complimented Sana on her tattoo, she laughed at me and said, "Don't be silly. It's not modern!" Often, parents' reservations about or objections to their daughters' tattoos are also based on not only patriarchal notions of beauty but also a sincere concern about preventing their children from making "a mistake" if tattoos eventually become out of fashion.

Relatives' reactions are also revealing about the relationship between tattooed women and their families: Like many other tattooed women, including myself, Warda told her mother about her first tattoo before she told her father. Fathers were usually narrated as more adverse to their daughters' tattoos than mothers. Family reactions to tattoos reflect the established relations of trust and acceptance but also control and domination. Most women could anticipate their parents' responses because they already knew their parents' feelings about tattooing.

> Warda: My mum was cool with it because, you know, my mum is cool (*laughs*). My dad forced himself to be okay with it. I think he was relieved that it wasn't anything bigger. (Laughs).
> Janan: I didn't really think about what my parents would say. My brothers didn't care, my father doesn't know and my mother was shocked. She is a Muslim Palestinian mother and, in a way, I understand. . . . They have made us, our bodies. When I got my two larger tattoos, her reaction was like "but why? Why would you do this to yourself?" And somehow, I think it is beautiful and sad at the same time. I'm hiding my tattoos from my grandmother. That's the only

person really. She was furious about the tattoo on my back when she saw it by chance.

Janan's story reveals some important contradictory elements in relatives' reactions to women's tattoos. Even though she said that she did not take into consideration her parents' reaction when she chose to get a tattoo, implying that it did not matter to her, she hides her tattoo from her grandmother, who is strongly opposed to it. Notably, many of her tattoos tell a story about her relationship to both her grandmother and her mother. Janan respects her mother's and grandmother's opinions and opposition to her tattoos as she perceives her own body as her mother's artwork (and therefore her grandmother's). This perception is significantly gendered, as she reclaims ownership over her body not from her mother's, but from her father's side. Overall, Janan narrated her tattoos as empowering because of their reclaiming this ownership from her father and simultaneously intensifying the close relationships between her female relatives, despite the fact that all of them are opposed to her tattoos.

While tattoos do not of themselves make women feminists, the historical periods of greater interest and participation in tattooing among women have frequently been times of women's rights breakthroughs (Mifflin 2001, 8). "As an extrovert art form," Margot Mifflin writes, "tattooing appeals to the iconoclast in many women" (2001, 4). In contrast to tattooed men, tattoos often function as emblems of self-determination for tattooed women. This is particularly so when issues of sexual violence, abortion rights, and women's health reinvigorate the question of who controls their bodies. For these women, the significance of a tattoo can lie in the mere act of getting inked (as a form of rebellion or a way of reclaiming the body after rape or sexual abuse) or in the timing (to commemorate milestones such as marriage or divorce, or in remembrance of dead friends or relatives) (2001, 4).

As tattoos are intimately linked to ideas of control, the question about who tattoos their body is very important to some women. While, to me, the issue mattered a great deal, Warda, for example, did not really attach a lot of importance to who did the tattoo, as for her it was a simple exchange of money for body art. She received her first tattoo on Haifa's Masada Street in a small studio led by a male Israeli tattooist, which closed shortly afterward. Janan's experience was very different as she received her first two tattoos from a Palestinian male artist and then switched to a female Israeli artist. She made it very clear that she preferred her second tattooist for several reasons. Most important, Janan was much more satisfied with her work (one of her first tattoos made her so unhappy that she seriously considered a corrective tattoo). Moreover, she described how she "connected and identified" with her art, which was very simple and yet paid attention to fantastic details. Nevertheless, being tattooed by an Israeli was still an issue. "If there was a Palestinian artist whose work I was happy with, of course I would prefer the Palestinian tattooist, but there is nobody like this." Janan's boyfriend was particularly unhappy about her body being tattooed by an Israeli artist, again emphasizing the importance of women's bodies as a site of the struggle between settler and colonized.

Like many other tattooed women, Palestinian women are drawn to women artists for a variety of reasons. In Janan's case, her preference for a woman tattooist was primarily based on her art; other women preferred the comfort, safety, and openness of a female space. While not all women tattooists' work is alike, it is a common narrative that women tattooists are gentler because of their firsthand knowledge of the female body. Many women artists, so it is argued by some, have brought a new sensitivity to tattoo design and placement (Thompson 2015, 138). Notably, the Palestinian women's preference for a woman tattooist was never a matter of their boyfriends' or husbands' refusal to let "their women" be touched by another man.

Even though the women whom I spoke with did not become involved in the Israeli subculture of tattooing, I was stunned that most of them entrusted their body decorations with Israeli tattoo artists. An additional reason for getting inked by Israelis is of course the simple fact that the vast majority of tattoo studios in Israel are owned by Jewish Israelis. The Israeli tattoo scene is booming; it peaked with the launch of the first Israel Tattoo Convention in December 2014. This annual convention brings "all of the major tattoo artists of Israel under the same roof" and at it they display their work to an international crowd of tattoo lovers.[4] Hosting international tattoo artists, the tattoo convention is a major opportunity for Israeli propaganda, or *hasbara* (explanation): like other cultural events, such as the annual Tel Aviv gay pride parade, the Israeli Tattoo Convention promotes Israel's liberal culture or gay-friendliness, also known as whitewashing or pinkwashing, essentially "white-inking" the occupation. Despite the overall emphasis on the fun and art elements, the mainstream Israeli tattoo scene, like any other, is deeply embedded within a sociopolitical context and history.

As in the tattoo scenes in the United States and Western Europe, race, gender, and class play important roles in the Israeli tattoo subculture, in which most customers and tattoo artists remain by and large white, Ashkenazi, middle-class men. Even though tattooing has become more mainstream in general, associations of tattoos with criminality, darkness, and mystification linger. In certain locations, tattooed women can experience such associations, as one of my interviewees did during her trip to Japan: "I didn't know that the Japanese connect tattoos with the mafia. People would stare and move away from me, so I had to cover my tattoos whenever we traveled on public transportation. They have gorgeous public baths, but there is no way you can enter those as a tattooed person, so we went to a private one instead."

In Israeli society, the association of tattoos with criminality and imprisonment has its own loaded history, which includes the German Nazis' use of tattoos as a way to dehumanize Jewish prisoners in the extermination camps of Auschwitz-Birkenau. Despite the invention of the electric tattoo machine in 1891, the Nazis chose to use a tattoo technique that served to enforce the intended effect of degradation: after metal stamps were pushed into the prisoners' flesh, the wounds were covered with ink. Tattooed like cattle, Jewish prisoners, among them toddlers, were not only criminalized but also dehumanized. That the experiences of tattooed Shoah victims and survivors are still relevant to today's Israeli tattoo culture was demonstrated by the controversy and public discussion caused when grandchildren of tattooed Shoah survivors chose to be tattooed with the same number as their grandparents as a testimonial to their history.[5]

The idea that tattoos dishonor Shoah victims resonates with many Israelis, as tattoos are prohibited by *halaḥah* (Jewish religious law), which draws on Leviticus 19:28: "Ye shall not make any cuttings in your flesh for the dead, nor print any marks upon you" (quoted in van Dinter 2005, 38). Even though the beliefs that tattoos will hinder Jews' ascent into heaven or prevent them from being buried in a Jewish cemetery remain widespread, the number of ink-wearing Jews, particularly those with religious and Zionist symbols, is growing.[6] Taking into account the sensitive history and ongoing controversy about Germans tattooing Jews, I was struck by the large number of German tattooists attending the Israeli Tattoo Convention, an annual event that has taken place since 2016, especially so considering that there is only one single Palestinian tattoo artist.[7] Similarly, the existence of Palestinian tattoo artists—except for the renowned Razzouk family, who specialize in Christian tattoos in Jerusalem—has been disregarded by the Ka'akooa (tattoo) project, which is part of the exhibition "Tattoos—The Human Body as a work of Art" at the Eretz Israel Museum, sought to display "the growing tattoo scene throughout the country from October 2016 to October 2017."[8] All in all, tattooed Palestinians, including women, are excluded from the Israeli contemporary record making of history. Their exclusion is particularly critical, as body modifications have become important topics in Israeli discourses of modernity, which are significantly challenged by tattooed Palestinian women.

Instead, tattooed Palestinians are increasingly portrayed and referred to as "Arab hipsters" or, if they are based in Haifa "Haifsters," by Westerners and Israelis: "If you walk along Masada Street, Haifa's hipster quarter, you inevitably see fashionably dressed students with dreadlocks or flashy tattoos, looking for vintage furniture and second-hand clothes or you see them sitting in cafes, drinking beer at noon."[9] Such a portrayal is problematic not only for its assumption of a certain "Arab" appearance, behavior, and backwardness but also because there is simply no such self-identified group as "Haifsters." As a result, tattooed Palestinians are deprived of the opportunity to tell the stories behind their tattoos while the assimilationist rhetoric of a new "bubbling subculture" of Arab-Israelis who "dance through the culture clash" de-politicizes and distorts their lived realities.[10]

The hipster reference is particularly offensive to Palestinians because of the troubling historical antecedents of hipster culture back in its original homeland, another settler colonial state, the United States. While tattoo collectors often decorate their bodies with representations of other cultures or draw on ideas of heritage as a source of inspiration, cultural appropriation has always been at the heart of Western tattoo culture, as it was imported by sailors to the United States during the 1770s from indigenous communities in Fiji, Polynesia, and the Samoan Islands via Europe, which by then had lost its own tattoo tradition.[11] The normalization of cultural appropriation was revived by the white American hipster culture, as it was imported to Tel Aviv, often referred to as the "ultimate hipster destination."[12] Hipsters want to imitate the merchant and pioneering styles of the late eighteenth and nineteenth centuries, historical periods that coincided with both the largest waves of white European immigration to North America and the beginnings of the white appropriation of Native American tattoos. Similarly, hipsterism is established on a twisted notion of settler colonial nostalgia that revolves around the paradox of having erased a culture and then mourning it. Aesthetics expressed by hipster beards, shirts, and haircuts cannot be read as random, as they model themselves on times of thriving imperialism, settler colonialism, or, as is the case with the infamous Nazi Youth haircut, fascism.

Considering tattooed Palestinian women's bodies as part of (Israeli) hipster culture is problematic because Palestinian women are assumed to participate in a culture that is based on the cultural appropriation of colonized indigenous peoples. While, historically, native women's tattoos were forbidden in countries such as North America as they were seen as signs of nonassimilation (Mifflin 2001, 45), today, Zionist discourses seek to absorb tattooed Palestinian women into Israeli hipster subculture in order to strengthen its modernist myth of civilizing and liberating Palestinian women's bodies from their oppressive society.

Gender, race, and settler colonialism have always been closely entangled throughout the history of tattooing. Male European sailors and colonizers learned during their travels that tattoos served to mark significant practices and events in the lives of native peoples and started to get tattooed themselves (van Dinter 2005, 10). Upon their return, however, the majority of European society considered the behavior inappropriate, not only because they interpreted it as a visible rejection of their own cultural values (White 2005) but also because of imaginings of race according to which native peoples were regarded as barbaric and backward. The first trend of tattooed women was instigated by sensationalist freak exhibitions and circuses in the United States that showed heavily tattooed white women who, so their stories went, were tattooed under Native American captivity. In these stories, the tattooed women were cast as captives of barbaric Native American tribes from which they had been rescued by Western white men. While these stories paved the way for the social acceptability of tattooed women, as well as their economic breakthrough (many of these women earned a lot of money), they also sustained imaginings of barbaric Indian tribes, thereby legitimizing their extinction.

Tattoos were also a very significant site for male colonizers to establish and extend their control over native women, thereby often disrupting important indigenous gender orders. There are many stories about colonizers who used tattoos to mark colonized women as their property. In 1886, for example, Burmese mistress Mah Gnee's face was tattooed with the phrase "memma shwin" ("market prostitute") at the order of a British officer as punishment for her infidelity with a lover of her own community (Bailkin 2005, 33). The incident happened in the same year that the British began their operation to occupy Burma, demonstrating the intimate links between colonial control over indigenous land and indigenous women's bodies. Even though Englishmen considered native women's traditional chin tattoos a "hideous form of body mutilation," they were on an obsessive mission to try to make sense of them. Eventually, they sexualized the meaning of women's facial tattoos, going as far as to interpret them as a sign of women wanting an Englishman for a husband (Bailkin 2005, 39). In Mandalay and Rangoon, tattooed women dramatized a crisis of British global dominance that was exemplified by the failures of British men to police, protect, and modernize women's bodies. Simultaneously, "back home" in London, in a craze for the exotic, British middle- and upper-class women began to adapt the tattoo for their own purposes in the late-nineteenth and early-twentieth-century, when it enjoyed a period of popularity as an Orientalist emblem of elitism rather than the radical outsider status it conferred elsewhere in Europe. Today, elitism continues to be reflected in today's practices of tattooing in the West, particularly in historical settler colonial states, where heritage hipsterism and New Age paganism continue to be particularly popular subcultures among the white middle and upper classes.

Palestinian women's decision to get inked must be read not as participation in Israeli hipster or tattoo subculture but as part of a wider development among young Arabs whose tattoos celebrate Arabic calligraphy art, poetry, or religious references and thereby help to define and express their identity. This trend includes Palestinian women in the West Bank, the women who have revived the henna tattoo tradition in Gaza, and Arabs in the United States.[13] While it cannot be denied that this trend has been influenced by the fashion that swept the United States during the 1970s, and then Europe and the Middle East, it also draws on Eastern Asian techniques and is specific in its art form, identity, and authenticity. By tattooing their bodies, Palestinian women transform them and also their social relations as they take control of and consciously change their bodies in order to feel more beautiful or comfortable in them. To the women, tattoos are more than badges of self-determination, as their permanence and exteriority makes them a perfect medium through which to demonstrate the permanence of their indigenous presence in their homeland as well as their refusal to let their bodies be controlled by the plan.

(UN-)DRESS TO TRANSGRESS

On one occasion, when I stayed in Laqiya, an interesting rumor was circulating among the younger women in the Bedouin township about a young black Bedouin girl who had managed to get a well-paid job as a sales assistant in a shopping mall in Bi'r as-Sab'. The shop was run by a Jewish Israeli manager who had employed the girl on the false assumption that she was Jewish Ethiopian. When I asked some of the chitchatting women how the girl had passed as Ethiopian, as her dress surely must have given away her Bedouin identity, one of the women replied, "Well, what do you think? She took off her headscarf of course!" This story, which was told for a long time, caused controversy about the moral and religious implications of the girl's dress choice, speculations about what would happen if the girl were to be caught by family members, as well as narratives of praise, as, to some women, it was clear that the girl had acted out of desperation and just wanted to work hard in order to make a living. While class played a role in these narratives, as the girl's poor background explained and legitimized her actions for some, this notion was almost solely based on her blackness rather than tribe membership, as the commonly agreed assumption was that "the majority of black Bedouins are poor so this girl must have been poor, too." I could not help but notice that the non-black Bedouin women telling and discussing the story had a relatively relaxed attitude toward the girl's removal of her headscarf. It was not the first time that I had observed that culturally imposed social orders were narrated by a'rāb Bedouins as somehow more nonchalant for black Bedouins than for fellow a'rāb Bedouin women. It appeared as though the taboo of taking off the headscarf could not harm the social status of a black girl as much as it could that of a nonblack girl.

Even though I never managed to be introduced to this mysterious girl (and at times, I had my doubts about whether she was real), the story made a lasting impression on me, as I started to puzzle over the role of dress (and race) in Palestinian women's access to certain spaces that are reserved for Jewish bodies. In contrast to skin tone or hair color (unless changed artificially), dress is consciously chosen. As a result, the colonizer believes that he or she can read important information about the colonized women by looking at the way in which she is dressed: What is her religion? Where does she work? And, most important, does she constitute a threat? Exploring how the dressed body enters spaces allows a complication of the binary opposition of settler and indigenous spaces by considering the interplay of manifold spatial relations (between both different spaces and different bodies)—particularly those that are constructed along the lines of race, gender, and class—in the production of those spaces. As will be shown, these relations and the identities that they produce can overlap, reinforce, or antagonize each other. While they are based on specific histories, they are far from static. In fact, there is a continuous and diversifying process during which Palestinian women time and again establish or draw on specific spatial relations in order to reclaim their belonging to specific spatial units or identities.

This section delves into the role of dress in Palestinian women's access to colonial spaces that are reserved for Jewish citizens. Settler colonialism is increasingly understood as a spatial project involving particular imagined and practiced spatialities (Veracini 2010a) among both settler and indigenous communities. The extent to which these imaginings and concomitant identities are in a continuous state of flux (rather than constant), however, remains largely understudied. I aim for a more nuanced reading of colonial space and spatial practices in settler colonial settings by taking into account the intimate relationship between body and space, because it is through the means of the body that we experience space and, in turn, constitute it or, as Lefebvre famously noted, "each living body is space and has its space: it produces itself in space and it also produces that space" (Lefebvre 1991, 170). In concrete terms, this section investigates how both the boundaries and the identities of colonial spaces and "normative bodies" (also referred to as "unmarked bodies") can be destabilized by the arrival of Palestinian women's bodies entering privileged spaces that are reserved for others and for which their bodies do not qualify as the "somatic norm" (Puwar 2004). One of the means through which Palestinian women access spaces or remain barred from them is the way in which they are dressed.

An analysis of Palestinian women's dress when they enter certain spaces not only reveals the contradictions and loopholes of settler colonial space but, what is more important, further contributes to complicating the binary opposition and fixed boundaries between settler colonial and indigenous space and spatial practices. It will be argued that processes of refusal and desire to enter certain spaces, the rejection and appropriation of spaces by Palestinian women, are ambiguous. Whether by entering spaces reserved for Jews as openly marked "space invaders" (Puwar 2004) or by donning "white masks" (Fanon 1967)—in other words, drawing on a specific set of civilized/white/settler looks and skills—Palestinian women enable themselves to access valuable sources of social capital (Bourdieu 1986), which, in turn, enable them to access further reserved spaces. As mentioned in the previous chapter, many women emphasized their fluency in Modern Hebrew or their "Israeli body language" and suchlike to me. All these skills were acquired within Jewish spaces such as kindergartens, schools, hospitals, universities, or work environments and through being in close contact with Israelis (classmates, neighbors, nurses, teachers, colleagues, etc.). Thus, rather than perceiving the entrance into these spaces as a goal in itself, Palestinian women, both consciously and unconsciously, frequently use and benefit from dwelling in Jewish spaces for specific purposes.

The assimilation of bodies with space is built, repeated, and contested over time, but spaces are not left blank and open to anybody to enter and occupy them. While, in theory, all bodies can enter spaces, certain kinds of bodies are tacitly or openly designated as being the natural occupants of specific spaces. Some bodies are deemed as having the right to belong and others are marked as trespassers; in accordance with the way both spaces and bodies are imagined (politically, historically, and conceptually), they are circumscribed as being out of place.

Political theorists Carole Pateman and Charles Mills emphasize the close connection between the political constructions of bodies that are marked as different and their access to political spaces, the body politic. Both Pateman's *Sexual Contract* (1988) and Mills's *Racial Contract* (1997) cast light on how racial, sexist, and colonial social contracts demarcate and reserve space for privileged citizen groups via the construction, normalization, and strategic use of impolitic (i.e., marked as different) and politic (unmarked) bodies. The latter comply with what Mill refers to as the "somatic norm": white male bodies capable of leaving the (hypothetical) state of nature. The subordination of women and nonwhite bodies as impolitic, in contrast, is based on their identification with nature, "incarnating wildness and wilderness in their person" (Mills 1997, 87). Such bodies "are judged incapable of forming or fully entering into a body politic" (53).

More recently, Nirmal Puwar has built on the work of both Pateman and Mills in her book *Space Invaders* (2004), which presents the body as a thoroughly politicized entity that may be both enabled and constrained through the social practices and public spaces that help constitute it. Taking up Mills's notion of the "somatic norm," Puwar's analysis of contemporary bodies that are out of place (here: black bodies and women's bodies in the British Parliament) shows "the ways in which bodies have been coupled with and decoupled from specific occupational spaces" (Puwar 2004, 78), that is, the ways in which the specificity of raced and sexed embodiment constrain one's ability to occupy putatively neutral public space.

While Puwar's work supports Pateman and Mills's claim that neutral space does not exist, by making whiteness and masculinity visible, my research aims to debunk the myth of political neutral spaces in Israel. This myth is closely linked to Zionist discourses about equal citizenship in Israel, such as the celebrations of Palestinian women running for election to the Knesset. In considering the political structures of settler colonialism in which the Israeli parliament is embedded, we argue here that the demonstration of an inclusion of indigenous female bodies into Jewish spaces is possible and, in fact, serves the Zionist myth of the neutral space. Furthermore, by constructing and taming Palestinian women's bodies as assimilated bodies—the Arab-Israeli women— their inclusion can, in fact, serve the maintenance of Palestinian women's marginalized political existence as settler colonial citizens. This body is constructed as less different (than other female indigenous bodies) yet different enough from the somatic norm to remain readable and to not constitute a threat to the hegemonic body politic and its supremacy of political power in Israel.

The spatial internal frontiers that are established as a result construct the settler colonialist boundaries of both bodies and spaces in Israel and come into being via both imaginings and practices. A significant amount of power rests in some of these imposed boundaries, which aim to normalize Israel as a settler colonial space through strategies such as coexistence and mapping Palestine as somewhere outside the 1948 boundaries, but acts of defiance are found in particular among Palestinian women, who, for various reasons, frequently cross, and thereby destabilize, Israel's internal frontiers (Foucault 1984, 94–95) through their dress.

Throughout my fieldwork, I observed that Israel's efforts to present coexistence spatially become more difficult in spaces where the distance between indigenous and settler bodies decreases, where encounters between their impolitic and politic bodies are more frequent, and where impolitic bodies are less equipped with the skills required to don the white mask and, as a result, are easier to read as strangers by settlers. One of the spaces where I was able to observe this phenomenon, in particular, was the main post office in Bi'r as-Sab', which I visited regularly with the Bedouin women whom I lived with.

The purpose of this regular visit was for the important purposes of checking bank account balances and seeing whether social benefits had arrived. Sometimes the women would also take their monthly cash out. We usually entered the post office as a small group of up to five women after a security check, in which our bags were searched and we were asked to walk through an electronic metal detector. I quickly noticed that the women whom I accompanied were searched much more narrowly and asked more questions than Jewish Israelis (and so was I when accompanying them). The Bedouin women's bodies were particularly easy to read as members of Israel's group of suspected citizens, mainly from their dress in long, dark, dresses, sometimes decorated with traditional colorful embroidery, a black *abaya* (thin overcoat), and black, tight *mandeel* (headscarves). Women my age often wore a *jilbāb*, while older women would wear a white, loose scarf to cover their mouths.

Entering this public space, where all the staff members were non-Bedouins, clearly caused the women to receive many gazes, particularly from Jewish Israelis, some of whom looked concerned (possibly for their safety?). An older Jewish Israeli woman even changed seats after we sat down in her row (the only place where we could all sit next to each other), to wait for our numbers to be called. The cause of the Jewish Israelis' concern, it seemed, was linked to multiple factors, including the fact that the Bedouin women would always enter in a group, dressed in what they may have perceived as dark, unfamiliar, strange, traditional dress and speaking Arabic. Whenever one of the women stepped up to one of the cashiers, the cashier would usually speak to her very loudly as though she were unable to understand Hebrew properly (which some of them were). Sometimes one of the younger women would accompany an older one to help her translate throughout the conversation. An older Bedouin woman without much knowledge of Hebrew (as she was born and raised in an unrecognized village in al-Naqab with no school) described her regular experiences at the post office to me as follows:

There is a lot of racism ... when I go to the post office, or the bank ... to take out money there. I can always hear the office lady talking to Jewish women really nicely but if I forget to sign something they will talk to me rudely "Come here!" If it's a Jewish woman they will say "*Sliḥa* (Excuse me), come here please." ... I go there to sign for the government to claim and receive benefits. When I go to sign there is a lot of police and security and the security staff really focus on us Bedouin women. They think we are hiding something. So they always search Bedouin women and men much more than others.

As many scholars have pointed out, dress, particularly the veil, has played a central role in the way in which Muslim women have been perceived by Western audiences; it represents both inscrutability and mysteriousness, the imagined sensuality of Eastern women (in the harem), and the emblematic barbarity of Muslim society toward them (Lowe 1991; Yegenoglu 1998; Kahf 1999). Imbued with such power within the Orientalist imaginary, the veil has, in turn, emerged as a weighty symbol in anticolonial struggles, nationalist ideologies, and state-building projects in the Middle East (Ahmed 1992; Moghadam 1994).

Scholars such as Anna Secor (2002) have highlighted the ways in which dress, and more specifically veiling, can function as a form of spatial practice that can enable and constrain women's mobility. In Secor's context, urban Istanbul, veiling or not veiling marks an ideological fault line and power struggle between the secular state and resurgent Islamic politics, whereas in Israel the spatial practice of dress is structured by wider relations of power such as the struggle between religious (rather, religious and secular) groups. This is particularly the case, as Palestinian citizens are categorized into sectarian subcategories by the state and large parts of the society, most commonly Muslim, Christian, or Druze in official listings such as the Israeli census.[14]

Indeed, this struggle between religious groups is also expressed spatially in various spatial practices like dress. Whereas some forms of dress are deemed invisible (mainly Western forms of dress), some religious forms of dress are more accepted within settler society than others. For instance, the religious dress worn by Christian nuns or Haredi women and men is long and dark in appearance, at times even covering the faces of the people. These forms of dress are not perceived as threatening as much as, for instance, Bedouin women's dress. The veiling of Muslim women, and particularly traditional face covers like those common among Bedouin women, continues to be perceived as particularly threatening and is also narrated as backward and uncivilized, although less so than full coverings by other religious groups in Israel, such as the *shal* (a face veil) or *frumka* (a long garment that covers the entire body) worn by some Haredi women.

Thus, in many ways, notions of morality are linked to public spaces and the spatial practices that take place within them, including dress. While different spaces operate by different sets of rules that determine the norms of self-presentation encountered by individuals as they move into and between everyday spaces of activity (Entwistle 2000), these rules can be contested. In the case of the Bedouin women's visits to the post office—a space very much constructed as an Israeli public space—their entrance into this space challenged the geography of settler colonialism, Israel's project of Judaization, on multiple levels: They contested the very boundaries of this space by entering it with their bodies while also challenging the public morality of the space through the spatial practice of dress. Most important, however, the women challenged the boundaries of participation in a space that is very much linked to Israel's body politic by accessing the space in order to claim their benefits as Israeli citizens (in front of a mostly Jewish Israeli audience, both staff and other customers). Their regular visits to the post office challenge the ways in which Jewish embodiment, space, and identity provide a much broader scope of rights irrespective of formal citizenship and simultaneously transgress a Zionist spatial order, which facilitates direct experiences of racialized and gendered spatiality that are intended to keep them out.

Drawing on a very different strategy to access space through dress, Violet, a devout Muslim woman born in Kafr Qasim, decided to wear a headscarf in order to move more comfortably around Tel Aviv, "It happened when I spent a lot of time in Tel Aviv. I would go there for work and men would just look at me and say, 'Hey, you're beautiful, you look so nice'—I just didn't like it. I wanted to focus on my work, but it made me feel uncomfortable. It was not only a religious decision, you see, it was also a political one." Violet chose to wear her Otherness demonstratively by wearing symbols that indicated that she was a Muslim and not an Ethiopian Jewish woman in order to feel safer and protect herself from sexual harassment and sexist catcalling. But Violet's choice of dress also hindered her access to certain spaces, as was illustrated in her earlier story about how—because of her headscarf—northern (largely secular, middle-class) women's rights activists excluded her from their women's activism, arguing that feminism was incompatible with her religious identity.

Violet's decision to wear a headscarf not only transgressed the order of Israeli and Palestinian feminist spaces, it also took on an additional meaning in light of her rebellion against what she referred to as her father's "feminist upbringing." Violet's father, a black, radical Palestinian communist resistance fighter, insisted that his daughters should not wear the *hijab* in school even when the Islamic Movement dictated that the village residents should do so at the peak of its power. Israeli forces killed Violet's grandmother during the 1956 Kafr Qasim massacre when her father was only eleven years old. Adding to the emotional hardship of being an orphan, Violet's father had a tough time finding work, not least because of the color of his skin. His politics were very much, as Violet stated, "antireligious," which she explained was based on his strong feelings about the Arab racism that he experienced. One specific event that affected him was his release from jail after six years as a political prisoner, something that is usually celebrated greatly within the local community; yet he did not gain the same kind of social respect that white resistance fighters received. The link that Violet's father made between Islam and Arab racism led to his strong opposition to Violet's decision to wear a *hijab* in 1998.

NOTES

1. A. Nieuwhof, "Palestinian Women Testify about Ill-Treatment and Torture during Their Arrest and Interrogation," *Electronic Intifada*, March 8, 2012, https://electronicintifada.net/blogs/adri-nieuwhof/palestinian -women-testify-about-ill-treatment-and-torture-during-their-arrest.

2. Y. Bendaas, "Algeria's Tattoos: Myths and Truths," *Al Jazeera English*, August 11, 2013, http://www.aljazeera.com/indepth/features/2013/08 /201386134439936719.html.

3. C. Dukehart, "The Last Tattooed Women of Kobane," *National Geographic*, January 21, 2015, http://proof.nationalgeographic.com/2015/01/21 /the-last-tattooed-women-of-kobane/.

4. See, for example, "Israeli Tattoo Convention 2017," *Secret Tel Aviv*, October 20, 2016, https://www.secrettelaviv.com/tickets/israeli-tattoo-convention/.

5. See, for example, J. Rudoren, "Proudly Bearing Elders' Scars, Their Skin Says 'Never Forget,'" *New York Times*, September 30, 2012, http://www.nytimes .com/2012/10/01/world/middleeast/with-tattoos-young-israelis-bear-holocaust -scars-of-relatives.html?pagewanted=all&_r=0.

6. See, for example, Y. Schwartz, "Tattoos Rule in Israel—Despite Jewish Law and Holocaust Taboo," *Haaretz*, February 17, 2014, last updated April 10, 2018, http://www.haaretz.com/israel-news/culture/leisure/.premium-1.574672.

7. See "Guest Tattoo Artists," Israeli Tattoo Convention, https://www .israeltattoocon.co.il/מקעקעים/.

8. Tattoos—the Human Body as a Work of Art, exhibition October 16, 2016, to October 15, 2017, http://www.eretzmuseum.org.il/e/363/.

9. K. Brandstedt, "Haifa—the Capital of Palestinian Culture in Israel," *Al Sharq*, June 2015, http://www.alsharq.de/wp-content/uploads/2015/06/Haifsters -English3.pdf.

10. R. Arad, "Israel's Palestinian Citizens Dance through the Culture Clash," *Haaretz*, November 30, 2013, https://www.haaretz.com/.premium-how-do-you-say-hipster-in-arabic-1.5295748.

11. Cultural appropriation refers to the practice of a privileged group (usually white and Western) who take cultural practices or symbols without permission from an oppressed or marginalized group. This differs from a cultural exchange, in which the trading between groups is mutual. Instead, the power to appropriate another people's culture lies in the hands of the majority group that acts as the sole beneficiary of the appropriation, and its accessorizing trivializes and erases the oppression experienced by the dominated minority group.

It is important to note that, at the same time, settlers banned native American tattoo traditions on reservations across the country. Similarly, when white Christian missionaries followed in the footsteps of the first Western voyages, they violently stamped out native practices in order to force their own religious practices on the indigenous population.

12. H. Ofman, "Why Tel Aviv Is the Ultimate Hipster Destination," *Culture Trip*, November 2, 2016, https://theculturetrip.com/middle-east/israel/articles/8-reasons-tel-aviv-is-the-ultimate-hipster-destination/.

13. "Popularity of Tattoos on Rise in West Bank," *Group 194 Net*, May 14, 2015, https://group194.net/english/article/41425; Rasha Abou Jalal, "Gaza Women Revive Henna Tattoo Tradition," *Al Monitor*, April 10, 2016, http://www.al-monitor.com/pulse/originals/2016/04/henna-palestine-gaza-painting-women-tradition.html; H. Khalife, "Arab Ink: Locals Honor Their Culture, Individuality through Tattoos," *Arab American News*, June 18–24, 2016, https://www.arabamericannews.com/2016/06/17/Arab-Ink-Locals-honor-their-culture-individuality-through-tattoos/.

14. "2008 Population Census," Central Bureau of Statistics, accessed May 15, 2021, http://www.cbs.gov.il/census/census/main_mifkad08_e.html (Hebrew).

FOUR

—៱៱៱—

DEFYING DESIRE

THE STRUGGLE "BETWEEN THE SHEETS"

During an unusually hot afternoon, my friend Jalilah and I missed our bus back to her Bedouin township by a hair's breadth. Still out of breath from running and knowing that we were going to be stuck waiting for at least twenty minutes in the heat, I jokingly suggested that we could go inside the sex shop next to the bus stop just to take advantage of its *mizgan* (air conditioner). Jalilah turned her face away from an elderly Jewish lady who sat in the corner of the bus stop shelter, the only other person waiting, and smirked at me. "Let's go and wait over there!" Jalilah said in her typical soft but decisive tone, pointing to the other side of the shelter. While I was still a bit vexed that we always waited next to bus stop shelters, rather than underneath them, where our heads would be protected from the sun, she suddenly asked me, "So, have you ever been in one?" "In what?" I inquired, puzzled, while wiping the sweat off my forehead with my scarf. "Well, in one of those?" Jalilah asked while pointing to the sex shop with her eyes. "Oh. Yes, but ages ago. There are loads in Berlin and London. I went with some girlfriends for a laugh when we were young," I replied, casually leaving out the handful of times I went with a boyfriend, but Jalilah stayed on task, "So never with a boyfriend?" "Yes," I admitted. "But only like two or three times." "Ah, OK. What did you get?" she asked, and I tried to reactivate my memory while being totally drained and sweaty. "I honestly cannot remember, Jalilah. Nothing major, I don't think. Why?" "Just wondering." She played down her curiosity but mine was stirred up. "Do you want to get something?" I asked her, regretting my cheeky tone as soon as I had asked the question. "You know," Jalilah responded, "Just because we don't go in there doesn't mean

we don't know about these things." The following fifteen minutes flew by as
she told me about how she knew a lot of married women who use sex toys to
"please" their husbands, and sometimes themselves, too. "We know about
this," she frequently repeated, referring also to unmarried girls, who, as I
learned, know a lot about sexual practices from information on the internet
or, though to a lesser extent, from talking with each other. Even though
Jalilah indicated several times that unmarried Bedouin women acquire "sex
knowledge" in order to prepare themselves for married life, I could not help
but read this knowledge as something that is not strictly limited to pleasuring
husbands. There were only two other passengers on the big bus that took
us back, who were sitting on the other end, but we continued our talk in
whispers. She told me about sexual practices that are known to help women
conceive a son or a daughter and how she knew that her love interest was still
"untouched" because he had a birthmark on his earlobe. (October 24, 2013)

Undoubtedly, the kind of knowledge that Jalilah spoke about can be sneered at
as pseudoscience or superstition rather than factual knowledge. Nevertheless,
narratives like hers are, beyond doubt, fundamental to Bedouin women's talk
about sex. They signify that not only is sex inquired into and talked about but
also that Bedouin women seek to handle and have sex in their own ways. Despite
the fact that such discourse takes place among girlfriends in whispers on the bus
or behind the closed doors of their bedrooms, it is real and meaningful. Women's
talk about sex—just as their silence about sex—is expressive of their sexual interests and desires. This is particularly the case in an environment in which they
are often deprived of adequate sexual education from both conservative families
and state schools that are insufficiently funded and whose syllabi frequently fall
prey to the struggle between settler and colonized, especially to the detriment
of sexual education of indigenous Palestinian youth. Moreover, the plan for
Bedouin women, as for Palestinian women more generally, does not construct
them as sexual agents who desire, inquire into, and fantasize about sex or, still
less, lead and enjoy fulfilled sex lives. As a result, Palestinian women's bodies are
the object of the disciplining power of Zionist and patriarchal regimes, which,
in a seemingly paradoxical twist, by sexualizing indigenous women's bodies and
using indigenous women's sexuality as a battleground, essentially desexualize
them and deprive them of the ownership of their own sexuality.

This chapter aims to unpack and assess Palestinian women's sex lives in
Israel and the many ways in which they defy the plan. Sex lives, as they are
considered here, amount not only to personal stories about sexual encounters
and practices but also to current discourses about sex, sex identities, and sex
education where and how they are articulated and where they are kept quiet.

The regulation and control of the sexuality of indigenous peoples, particularly indigenous women, is intrinsic to maintaining the settler colonial order, as it serves two main purposes. First, as pointed out by Ann Stoler's (1989, 2002) comprehensive work on race and intimacy in the colonial context, the management of sexuality is central to the relationship between colonizer and colonized, acting not only as a metaphor for colonial domination but also as a marker of both racial and class identities. With a similar line of argument, Nira Yuval-Davies wrote, "it is not incidental, therefore, that those who are preoccupied with the 'purity' of the race would also be preoccupied with the sexual relationships between members of different collectivities" (1997, 27). In sum, settler colonialist control over indigenous sexuality guards the very categories of settler and colonized in Israel (1989, 634)—Jew and Arab—which is necessary in order to assert the privilege and power of Jewish citizens as well as their indigenization.

As a second purpose, indigenous elimination manifestly proceeds through the settler colonialist regulation of sexual relations. Indeed, Scott Lauria Morgensen goes as far as to claim that without an analysis of gendered and sexual power relations, the processes of indigenous elimination and settler self-indigenization cannot be fully understood (2012, 10). In the context of Palestinian sex lives in Israel, settler colonial strategies of elimination become most clearly apparent in the Zionist promulgation of a "modern sexuality" and its legitimization and replacement of what is constructed as Arab primitive sexuality. As pointed out in Foucault's *History of Sexuality*, "sexuality is a result and an instrument of power's designs" (1990, 152), as "those in power dominate representations of sexuality and the experience of sexuality in order to regulate and control populations" (26). As a result, in many settler colonial contexts, control over and the management of indigenous sexuality assists in establishing and nurturing what Morgensen refers to as a settler "modern sexuality" (2011, 1), which is very closely linked to notions of moral superiority. Modern sexuality can be observed in other settler colonial contexts, such as Australia, where settler moral authority and power, particularly that held by white men, have been secured through Aboriginal sexuality (Evans 1982, 11).

Israel strives to erase and replace Palestinian sex lives with Zionist modern sexuality, a project that Morgensen defines as "attempting to replace indigenous kinship, embodiment, and desire with the hegemony of 'settler sexuality,' or the heteropatriarchal modern sexuality exemplary of white settler civilization" (2011, 23). Modern sexuality is conceptualized here as "the array of discourses, procedures, and institutions that arose in metropolitan and colonial societies to distinguish and link primitive and civilized gender and sexuality, while defining racial, national, gendered, and sexual subjects and populations in a biopolitical relationship" (2011, 23). Zionist discourses construct Palestinian women's sexuality from their need for "Oriental sex" (Stoler 1995, 174–75). Like many other indigenous women living under settler colonial regimes, Palestinian women are represented both as sexually hyperactive (which according to this logic is reflected in their large number of offspring) and as sexually oppressed victims, deprived of any sexual pleasure or, worse, as targets of sexual abuse and exploitation. In sum, the Zionist assessment of Palestinian sexuality, whether as licentious or backward, is closely connected to Western Orientalist readings of sexuality as "one of the main axes by which civilization and barbarism can be classified," which emerged with the epoch of imperialism (Massad 2007, 6–7).

By nature, the Zionist encroachment on Palestinian sex lives has a destructive effect on Palestinian women's gender relations and sex lives. One of the most prevailing factors that disrupt and destroy women's sex lives is their widespread experience of sexual violence. Almost two out of three women I spoke with had experienced some form of sexual violence either personally or as witnesses within their families, communities, or circle of acquaintances. These narratives included stories of rape by family members or in dating or marriage relationships; sexual harassment by relatives, acquaintances, colleagues, and strangers; sexual slavery; obligatory inspections for virginity; femicide; and forced marriage. While it is important to stress that, of course, not all Palestinian women's sex lives are somehow doomed to have these experiences, narratives of sexual violence were pervasive whenever we discussed sex. A feminist activist in her late thirties, who explained to me how she had just discovered her own sexuality after years of being sexually active, described the significant impact of sexual violence on women's sexuality as follows: "How can we fall in love with sex? The first thing we find out about sex or the first way in which we experience sex is through sexual dominance, if not violence. 'Sex' is not about us or our pleasure. Nothing. For us to enjoy sex, to have fulfilled sex lives, that's special. It's nothing 'ordinary' for a Palestinian woman to have a healthy, fulfilled sex life, you see?"

But the centrality of sexuality in the struggle between settler and colonized also means that it carries great potential as a source of resistance against existing Zionist and patriarchal sex orders. In my conversations and observations throughout my fieldwork, I noticed two seemingly contradictory developments among Palestinian women in Israel. First, many of these women, particularly women's rights and feminist activists, made it their mission to break the taboo of talking about sexuality by improving and making more available sexual education within Palestinian society in Israel. They felt that their efforts were particularly needed in the face of the great frequency of sexual violence against Palestinian women and, as many told me, the difficulty for Palestinians in Israel to juggle both an increasing exposure to information about sex through a plethora of media and a widespread desire in Palestinian society to uphold traditional values in the face of Israeli modern sexuality. These feminist activists mostly target young students, teachers, and those women who lack access to education on matters of health and sexuality.

Second, discussions about women's sexuality, including an exchange of personal sexual experiences (as is common in some feminist movements in other places), were not a part of this mission. The more individual women opened up to me and the more we talked about sexuality on a personal level, the more I realized that the lack of public discussion about personal experiences of sex was not an indicator of a lack of vivid sexual lives and practices among the women. It is important to clarify that it was because the women *did not* decide to kiss and tell that they could continue living their sex lives without being coopted into Israeli modernist discourses (as Palestinian queer bodies frequently are) or intruded on or shut down by conservative members of Palestinian society. In other words, in light of the fact that even sexual violence against Palestinian women is not a topic that can be adequately discussed in public, how can women's sex lives be discussed publicly?

The goal of this chapter is to explore, through women's individual experiences and narratives, the emergence of a new set of strategies through which some women live their sexuality against the backdrop of patriarchal and settler colonialist sexual hegemonies. Because of the small sample size and the mostly middle- and upper-class backgrounds of the women who shared stories with me about their sex lives, it is impossible (and also not my goal) to make broad statements about Palestinian women's sex lives in Israel. Nevertheless, they are an important group of women to explore because, even though their activities do not become public, they take place in the contact zone between settler and colonized, where Zionist modern sexuality strives to establish and maintain itself. In their everyday lives in mixed spaces—at universities, in mixed cities, at schools, or in offices—Palestinian women come into regular contact with Jewish men, where opportunities for social and sexual contact can arise. When Palestinian women lead fulfilled sex lives, they are essentially acting on an "undesired desire" that destabilizes Zionist modern sexuality, which relies on Palestinian women's sexual oppression and the plan for them to remain chaste when unmarried, or, in the contrary case, active reproducers and nurturers when married. It is exactly because they remain unexposed that these women's sex lives are able to continue and thrive. Their sexual experiences not only have significant effects and reverberations for wider social relationships between settler and colonized but also transform gender relations within Palestinian society in Israel, as women become increasingly sexually experienced and reclaim active ownership over their sex lives.

When Palestinian women have sex, even if only for one night, it is more than a passing amusement because it threatens the social and moral order affecting all aspects of Palestinian women's lives; it also poses significant risks. Palestinian women's sexual desires and practices transgress gendered, racial, and class boundaries and, overall, remain embedded in a highly politically charged daily environment. As will be demonstrated here, a one-night stand, a sexual affair, or a relationship, whether with a Palestinian or a Jewish man (or woman), is not an ephemeral event but has meaning and significance to wider relationships, as Palestinian women reclaim access to and control over sexual pleasure and satisfaction. As a result, they transform themselves into autonomous sexual agents by defying, rewriting, and sticking to a new plan for their sex lives, whether or not they desire premarital sex or wish to wait until their wedding to have sex.

Like young Iranians of the same generation, many of these Palestinian women frequently find it easier to renegotiate some of their politics within the sphere of the intimate instead of negotiating changes in the state (Mahdavi 2009, 19–20). They frequently responded to questions relating to citizenship through intimate relations, which is how this research ended up delving into Palestinian women's sexuality in the first place. While, at times, the women expressed notions of modernity as transformations of gender and sex relations, their constructions of modernity challenge Zionist modern sexuality rather than echo it. Palestinian women, both in their personal sexual lives and in their public lives, are striving to break the silence on sexual violence and improve sexual education. They are contributing to a new national subjectivity; one that entails a vital improvement in sexual education, health, and awareness among Palestinians, as well as respect for, and the fulfillment of, women's sex lives, without buying into Israeli modernist discourses and strategic efforts to bargain opportunities for sexual control.

THE SOUND OF SILENCE

From early in my research, many participants—mostly feminists from middle- and upper-class backgrounds throughout the Galilee (northern Israel)—began to share personal stories, both positive and negative, about sexuality with me.

I felt privileged by their trust in me, which was perhaps partially based on my openness about my own sexuality and sexual experience, which allowed us to have several thrilling discussions (and giggles) when talking about sex, especially if the women were about my own age. Nevertheless, I was struck by the fact that, as they told me, their stories were seldom, if ever, shared among themselves as friends, colleagues, or fellow activists. I found that fact puzzling; almost all the women were actively involved in improving sexual education and fighting sexual violence in Palestinian society in Israel through manifold organizations such as *Women Against Violence* (WAV) in Nazareth, *Assiwar* (the Arab Feminist Movement in Support of Victims of Sexual Abuse), *Muntada* (the Arab Forum for Sexual Education and Health), and the Rape Crisis Center in Haifa. Moreover, in light of the significant influence of Israeli feminist groups such as Isha L'Isha[1] on Palestinian women activists from the 1970s onward, I began to wonder whether the intensive personal discussions and reflections about experiences of sexuality and sexual violence within those Jewish Israeli groups constituted something that Palestinian feminist groups may have somehow sidestepped or dismissed. Was there a mismatch between official Palestinian feminist discourses, which aim to break the silence on sex and sexual violence against Palestinian women in Israel, and feminists' actual practices? And, if so, what were the reasons for the mismatch?

It is argued here that in order to understand why Palestinian women choose to silence personal experiences of sex and sexual violence in Israel, we need to grasp the intersectional nature and quality of their experiences as indigenous women living under oppressive settler colonial and patriarchal structures. Thus, there would be little point in looking for an answer by making comparisons between Palestinian women's approaches to fighting sexual violence and those of Jewish women in Israel. This is not to say that Jewish Israeli women confront sexual violence *less* in any way, but that their experiences of sexual violence are simply qualitatively different (Smith 2003, 71). The quality or nature of sexual violence experienced by Palestinian women in Israel is rooted in a very specific history that continues to affect women's sexuality today. Any feminist exploration of Palestinian women's sexuality needs to consider the *nakba*, the forceful expulsion and displacement of 750,000 Palestinians from their homeland in 1948, as an analytical starting point. Recognizing settler colonialism as a structure, not an event (Wolfe 2006, 388), the *nakba* will not be understood here as a historical incident but as the ongoing Zionist "logic of elimination," which aims to remove the Palestinian people from their land in order to replace them with Jewish settlers. Today, Palestinian women's experiences of sexuality in Israel have become deeply embedded within the intertwined masculinist, hetero-patriarchal, and nationalist structures of settler colonialist occupation and patriarchal control.

Accordingly, Palestinian women experience sex in contradictory and complex ways (as do Palestinian men). Apparent safe spaces can emerge in the openings between the two oppressive layers, which frequently turn out to be not safe at all. This interplay of different kinds of oppression significantly limits and complicates the availability of safe opportunities for women to speak openly about their personal experiences of sex or sexual violence. For instance, state violence against Palestinian women, coupled with the state's failure to implement social reforms to provide a decent level of services, including the protection of women from violence (Shalhoub-Kevorkian 2004), allows social institutions such as the family, community, or tribe to take on powerful roles in women's lives. Such social units may provide spaces for protection from state violence and control, but they can also use their resultant great power over women to produce violence and reinforce patriarchal gender relations, once again silencing Palestinian women's experiences and narratives of sexual violence.

Despite the increasing number of male Palestinian activists who identify themselves as feminists, Palestinian civil society is not insensitive to its hetero-patriarchal power and its (ab-)use thereof to abuse women. As a result, reinforced gender relations continue to stigmatize personal experiences of sexual violence and render it difficult to speak out about it, even within activist circles. A particularly noteworthy case of sexual violence, which was silenced among feminist groups, took place during a demonstration of Palestinian activists against the Prawer Plan in November 2013.[2] On separate occasions, female activists described to me, individually, how fellow male demonstrators had sexually harassed them during the demonstrations. Several of these women also shared the frustrations they experienced when trying to bring this issue up for discussion among the feminist groups of which they were members. All the groups refused to discuss the subject, as an activist named Maryam testified when she explained the dilemma of many feminist activists to continue their activism while having to put up with sexism in the ranks of Palestinian activist groups: "It was marginalized. It was not discussed at all. . . . It might prevent women from participating in such demonstrations once their families find out. . . . That's what a lot of so-called feminists said. It's a clash between national and women's liberation and while I don't see it as a contradiction, other people disagree. They say the national struggle is prioritized over the women's struggle in the West Bank. I tell you it's the same here!"

It would be inaccurate to interpret feminists' silence on personal experiences of sexual violence as an expression of simply giving into patriarchal power. There is no doubt, however, that the relationship between the struggles for Palestinian national and women's liberation has been complicated at best. While the majority of Palestinian men had prioritized the defense of women against rape over the defense of their homes before and during the *nakba*, post-1948 nationalists chose the slogan *al'ard qabl al'ird* (land before honor) to promulgate the importance of the preservation of national territory at any cost (Warnock 1990; Hasso 2000). This prioritization increasingly led to an association between narratives of sexual violence and guilt about losing the land (or failing to hold onto the land), while women's memories of the atrocities committed against them were, once again, marginalized and silenced (Humphries and Khalili 2007, 213). Today, personal narratives of Palestinian feminists' experiences of sexual violence pose a powerful threat to the nationalist movement because they can contest official nationalist narratives and destabilize gendered meanings of honor.

On the basis of the intersectional nature of the sexual violence they experience, Palestinian feminists adhere to their struggle against sexual violence as an intersectional struggle. In practice and daily life, however, the deep entanglement and interplay of these intersectional structures of oppression has meant that speaking up about sexual violence usually comes at a high price. Sexual violence against Palestinian women is far from being silenced by Palestinian feminists as a matter of course, as is demonstrated by the great number of feminist initiatives that aim to raise awareness and launch a discussion about the topic. Speaking up about sexual violence on a personal level, however, usually involves paying a personal price, whether the perpetrators are Israeli or Palestinian. This price may entail social exclusion through gendered and nationalized stigmatizing as a betrayal of Palestinian society or the strategic gendered and racialized neglect of Palestinian citizenship rights by the Israeli state. Considering the ongoing Zionist occupation, the resulting strains on Palestinian patriarchy, and the lack of safe spaces for and effective protection of Palestinian women in Israel, the majority of women who speak up—feminists being no exception—are unable or unwilling to pay the price at present. The silencing of personal experiences of sexual violence among Palestinian feminists in Israel and, therefore, the absence of congruity between the personal and the political in feminist practices as concerns sexual violence, is unquestionably an intersectional product of both settler colonialist and patriarchal oppressive structures.

Because they know about and have experienced social and political punishment, many Palestinian women feel little incentive to engage in public conversations about their personal experiences of sex. As Maryam, a self-identified feminist, described it, "I call it 'sex-phobia,' which means I cannot go out in public and say, 'I believe in sex before marriage,' It's impossible to talk about this. It's the place where you need to be silent. That's not because these are 'private' issues but because they are so central to patriarchal power."

Besides the public, the family too remains a space in which women remain largely silent about their sex lives. Hajar, for instance, a young student in Jaffa, explained to me that while she can talk to her mother about sexuality, their talks remain by and large theoretical as, overall, she is required to "stick to the plan." As a result, she does not talk to her mother about her personal experiences or the fact that she is a lesbian. Nevertheless, her silence about these issues does not affect her actual sexuality: "I had conversations about homosexuality and gender with my mother but it's all theoretical. When it comes to the deeds, she would say, 'Don't go to demonstrations, don't participate in any political things, don't date anyone who is not an Arab, a man, and a Muslim.' She was very clear. Nevertheless, I went against all of her recommendations, and I broke all of the rules she gave to me. She doesn't know about it. My mother knows little about my activities."

Hajar's experience also testifies to how the silence about sex takes on gendered forms, as women can be active agents of maintaining the silence about sex. I observed this phenomenon in various communities and families. A Bedouin friend, for example, once asked me via WhatsApp what kind of contraception I could recommend to her. We started to have an in-depth chat about the pros and cons of condoms, vaginal contraceptive rings, and coils, during which it emerged that she and her husband had already discussed contraception in detail. My lack of knowledge about the accessibility and cost of contraceptives in Israel and awareness of her closeness with her sisters, I asked her why she had not asked any of them for their advice. I was astonished that, even though they were all married and had several children, contraception was something that they would not broach with each other as women, but instead often speak more about with their husbands.

Generally, it appeared that women were extremely careful about choosing whom they spoke to about issues of sexuality. Sina, a young researcher in Jerusalem, for example, told me that while she was open about her sexual experiences with her feminist friends, she felt that she had to act in a very conservative manner among the friends of her current boyfriend. She shared how she felt that she would have to be immensely careful about choosing the right time to tell her boyfriend about her sexual life before their relationship. Even though she was proud of her sexual experience and regretted no part of it, it was clear that she preferred not to speak to her partner about it in order not to risk the relationship. She was cautious because she was fully convinced that if he found out she was sexually experienced, it would lead not only to the end of their relationship but also to her social condemnation:

> I've had a boyfriend for years and we even lived together in Jaffa, which my family didn't know. We had a normal sex life. . . . Now that I have a new boyfriend here in Jerusalem, I face a dilemma. Can I tell him about the fact that I had sex in my previous relationship? Guess what my feminist friends are telling me?! They all say "Sina, don't touch this issue!" Even my Jewish friends say that because they know how sensitive this topic is with Palestinian men. I've had nightmares because this situation really doesn't reflect me. At the same time, it will take a really long time for me to trust him enough to tell him the truth. We've spoken about literally everything, including all of the "forbidden things" so far, but sex, no way! Before this, I was surrounded by a very small group who declared themselves "feminist" and we were all on the same page about sex, we were all open-minded, all doing the same things. And now, all of a sudden, I'm acting like a conservative because I have to, not because I am.

LET'S TALK ABOUT SEX

> I believe that sexual rights are very important, especially in our conservative community. When I say "freedom" and talk about wanting to live in a liberal society, I also want to talk about women's rights and their sexual freedom as well as freedom from this racist and discriminatory state. You can't separate this and I'm working on both. I need freedom as a nation from the occupation and I need women to have equal rights. (Asma, November 16, 2011)

Even though there was a clear absence of discussion about personal sexual experiences among Palestinian women, many of them were campaigning to enhance the current state of sexual education for Palestinians in Israel. In particular within the framework of both new and established organizations in Palestinian civil society, activists, social workers, and educators are striving to lift the taboo on talking about sex. One such organization is Muntada, the Arab Forum for Sexuality, Education, and Health, that envisions "a free Palestinian society where human rights are respected for all; where social and national justice prevails; where both men and women have equal personal and collective rights (including sexual rights at an early age); and where every individual has the right to freely choose the lifestyle and intimate relationship best suited for her/him."[3] It is important to take into account the overall context in which initiatives such as Muntada emerge, as there have been manifold developments sweeping through Palestinian society in the last decade that have emphasized the increasingly urgent need for sexual education, particularly among the Palestinian youth.

In Palestinian society at large, various reasons are advanced about the need for sexual education. There are those who argue that sexual education in Palestinian society is needed in order to prevent what are understood to be perverse sexual practices (for example, premarital sex, homosexuality and bisexuality, masturbation) and the sexually transmitted diseases and social taboos linked to those practices. These sexual practices are perceived as particularly threatening, as is exposure to various forms of media that distribute ideas about sexuality imported from the West and Israeli society. A part of this group of people who strive to ensure conjugal heterosexuality and legitimate children advocate sexual education to improve the sex lives of married couples and prevent divorce and adultery in order to stabilize the traditional family model. Children's constant exposure and easy access to a wide array of information about sex has emerged as a major cause for concern among parents, particularly in light of the increasingly public scandals about sexual abuse and violence that have taken place.

When I spoke to Rania, a woman in her mid-forties who founded an organization that aims to enhance the education of Palestinians about sexuality and sexual health, she emphasized the significance and challenges of external influences and stimuli among Palestinians in Israel, which she referred to as "internal socialization." She particularly underlined the speed with which new developments have occurred among younger generations in recent years and the inadequacy of existing education and the lack of preparation for parents and educators to react to those changes. She told me about some dramatic events, such as a twelve-year-old Palestinian girl who became pregnant from being raped by her classmates before the heyday of social media, and she also described how she felt that Palestinians are in the process of becoming more open to talking about sexuality, but on their own terms rather than those imposed by the State of Israel:

> I finished my BA in nursing (in 1988) and I wanted to work in a "normal setting" because I got so sick and tired of Israeli hospitals and remember that 1988 was only one year after the breakout of the First Intifada and I lived in Jerusalem and for me it was a totally painful experience. And so, I worked in a village in Galilee as a school nurse and there was a case of a twelve-year-old girl who was taken to a doctor. She was pregnant—in the eighth month. Six male students from the school had raped her and they had convinced

her that they were just "playing." I arrived two days after the news. There was no media as it is today, but there was total panic. When I challenged the principal and said that we have to meet and discuss this and invite the parents, he said that the parents wouldn't come, that we're a conservative society and so on, and I said, "well, I'm sorry, apparently this conservative society allows for twelve-year-old pregnant girls and rapists." And, actually, many of the parents came—more than forty came. And they said, "you talk," and I said, "okay, let's talk about sex." I was a fresh graduate and only twenty-two. And my grandmother said, "Why are you doing this? I got married when I was thirteen and your grandfather was sixteen and we had nine children and we did fine and could cope with the issue of puberty." "But today," I told her, "children have a long time between puberty and when they get married and so they have a lot of questions for their parents. So, this is something you need to think about as parents. You cannot ignore this." And then parents realized the necessity but they didn't want to talk and they said, "Why don't you do it?!" So, I did it and spoke to the students and sat in a circle. And then one of them asked, "If we masturbate will we get hairy hands?" And I said, "Of course not. Otherwise, all of you would have hairy hands." (She laughs.) Then they looked at each other's hands and asked, "How many times a week is normal?" and I said, "I don't know but I will check." That was when I realized that I'm actually not that shy, and so I started to check out where I could study sexuality and I realized that it was only at NYU that I could do a master's degree in human sexuality. And, at the beginning, nobody wanted to employ me because I was seen as "bad," someone who wanted to bring something "bad" from the West, and then I started to do workshops here and there.

As Rania's story testifies, the state of knowledge and conversations about sexuality among Palestinian children and grown-ups alike was poor in the 1980s and led many Palestinians, particularly parents, to demand better sex education not from the state but from within Palestinian society. The demand was rather specific: on one hand, parents asked for more and better sex education but, on the other hand, with the proviso that this education would keep some distance from information imported from the West.

In order to account for the lack of sexual education, one has to take into consideration the institutionalized discrimination against Palestinians in Israel in the area of education more generally. Schools intended for Palestinian children in Israel are, according to a special report by Human Rights Watch, "a world apart in quality from the public schools serving Israel's majority Jewish population."[4] Racial segregation runs throughout the educational path of Palestinians from nursery up to the university and includes a lack of access to the proper resources and training necessary for sexual education. This lack of access is not accidental but a strategic necessity in order to maintain the "cyclical and cumulative" nature of the discrimination that takes place within education available to Palestinians in Israel[5]: "When one generation has fewer educational opportunities of poorer quality, their children grow up in families with lower incomes and learn from less well-educated teachers."[6]

Sexual education plays an important role in legitimizing the general segregation of education imposed by Israel's Ministry of Education, as Israeli government officials and educators argue that—because of their traditional background and upbringing—Palestinian children cannot be taught about sexuality in the same way as Jewish Israeli children. "Out of respect," exceptional arrangements are also granted by Israel's Ministry of Education for religious Jews, who, in contrast to Palestinians, have a direct say about what should be included in the curriculum of and teaching material on sexual education.[7] The rhetorical cloak of cultural sensitivity used to legitimize a special approach to Palestinian students, however, differs, as it is underpinned by an explicitly racial approach that tends to conflate and Other all Palestinians as backward Arabs. They are presented as being in urgent need of basic lessons on how to control what is constructed as a licentious drive for reproduction, particularly in order to prevent the spread of sexual diseases.

The attitude is not restricted to a small right-wing nationalist Israeli minority but permeates official educational bodies and teacher training facilities in Israel. Moreover, the need for a "special approach for working with a traditional population" (Oz 2008) in sexual education for Israel's Arab sector is normalized and scientificized, as Israeli scholarship produces more and more papers that serve to scientifically prove the need for a special approach to Arabs because of their backwardness. Without accounting for the racialized structures of education that are currently in place in Israel, a study about the knowledge of Arab men about sexually transmitted diseases published in 2016, for instance, contributed to the construction of Arab men as ignorant of, or indifferent to, sexual health matters (because they have more unprotected anal sex) and as generally more sexually promiscuous than Jewish men: "The knowledge of AMSM (Arab men who have sex with men) regarding HIV transmission and their attitudes towards condom use were less favorable than those of JMSM (Jewish men who have sex with men), and they performed more UAI (unprotected anal sex). AMSM may benefit from targeted interventions, including reconciling their same-sex attraction in positive terms. Same-sex attraction and gay identity may provide common ground to strengthen Arab-Jew communication in Israel" (Mor, Grayeb, and Beany 2016).

In this context, initiatives for sexual education, such as the organization founded by Rania, aim to work independently of Zionist frameworks, not least in order to be authentic and trustworthy with Palestinians. They are faced with several challenges, such as the decades-long absence of good quality education on sexual education and health in Arab schools and the increasingly firm and legitimized Zionist constructions of Arab backwardness and special needs that derives from this lack of education, which allow poor standards to continue under the cloak of cultural sensitivity. Both Rania and her colleague Asma emphasized the difficulty of lifting what they referred to as the "occupation of the mind" among Palestinian women and men, by which the two meant the decades of Zionist indoctrination that resulted in the internalization of feeling subordinate and backward and the tendency to hold onto traditional values in an effort to protect one's identity—resulting in what they referred to as a "closed society." Both women emphasized that sexuality is a central site where such restrictiveness takes place.

For women like Asma, who grew up as part of the third *nakba* generation, such developments have a particularly significant impact, as the lives of Palestinian citizens who were born and raised in Israel are marked by complex and contradictory structures of being "in" and "out" at the same time through education, their largely fluent Hebrew, their access to social media, and the ease with which they are increasingly able to move between communities and spaces, both Jewish and Palestinian. Even though their social abilities open up new opportunities for Palestinian women to fulfill their sexual desires, at the same time, both the state's and society's social expectations of them are becoming stricter. According to Asma, the way out of this dilemma lies within Palestinian women, in that they need to ask themselves how they imagine their ideal sex lives. She explained that often women do not know what they actually desire sexually and that they make decisions based on what is expected from them according to the plan, which has emerged from the internalization of both the patriarchal and settler colonial hegemonic social orders.

> We don't give lectures about homosexuality, sexual practices, and so on; we work on the thinking and we try to change the way children are brought up and educated. My strategy is to put a mirror in front of everyone and ask them to reflect on how and what they think, how they are brought up to think, which thoughts are their own. Suddenly they discover many things. Some of them succeed at looking into the mirror honestly and they change, not only in the way they look at themselves but also in the way they look at others. There is no "right" and "wrong." If you don't want to have sex before marriage,

that's your thing but you shouldn't decide this for the wrong reasons. I don't tell people to think this or that. I want to teach them tolerance and basically say, if a woman decides differently, that does not make her a "prostitute." This is a problem of minorities. As a minority we have certain ways of thinking and certain norms and you're not meant to think outside of the box. We face daily discrimination and threats from the state, so we shut ourselves off and make our "own rules" and you will be punished if you don't act according to those rules. I wanted to write about how our thinking is linked to being an oppressed minority in this state at university but my professor at the time said that I shouldn't because "after all this is an Israeli university." Many Israelis explain things like honor killings as "cultural issues." Our norms and the way we think—those are all "cultural things." As "Arabs" we think like this. They don't see the full picture, the way the state treats us as a minority, of us growing up as a minority. . . . Of course, this has a critical impact. To grow up and to change, to be and feel democratic, we need to feel safe in order to grow up. The minority here doesn't feel safe, which is why they are very closed.

Throughout our conversations, both Rania and Asma made it clear that, before they could start their work and talk to participants of their courses about sexuality, the participants had to work on their ways of thinking about themselves and the people around them. While tolerance played an important role in their work mission, both women emphasized that there were some topics, such as homosexuality, that were better left untouched during the classes, as it was hoped that the participants would eventually conclude that all sexual orientations should be respected. School projects, mixed seminars, and couple therapy sessions all relied on the authenticity and Palestinian ownership of the education that was provided. These factors played an important role in gaining the trust of course participants, parents, and educators, but also for Rania and Asma themselves, as the former told me about the impossibility of her continuing to work under an Israeli umbrella. Sex education includes education about contraception, which, as Rania emphasized again, is a sensitive issue in the conflict between settler and colonized. Because she could not remind Palestinians to use condoms under the umbrella of an Israeli organization, Rania decided to continue her work independently, even though this meant that she was deprived of the penis model provided by the Israeli Ministry of Health, as she told me laughingly. She explained her decision as follows:

> I was approached by the Israeli family planning association. It's responsible for the Palestinian society within Israel while the Palestinian family planning association is responsible for the one in the West Bank and Gaza and East Jerusalem. So, I said I would take the position but on the condition that I

would only work within Palestinian society and that I would not work with
your society. And also, that I would not do anything with the Palestinians in
the West Bank under the umbrella of the Israeli government. When anybody
from Gaza comes and meets you in your office in Tel Aviv, then I will consider
it. So, we developed the idea of our organization until the year 2006 together.
We started as a project, but we had so many volunteers and every time we
finished a course, we had more people who wanted to get involved. . . . We
didn't have the capacity to turn into a full-blown Palestinian organization.
The other problem was that we had so many requests from the West Bank and
we couldn't go under an Israeli umbrella even though we wanted to. Also, I
simply could not meet with many Arab organizations—I simply could not
meet them under the Israeli umbrella.

While Rania and her team have to navigate their work within the rigid frames
of what is considered appropriate among the Palestinian parents, teachers, and
couples who attend their courses, one of the most critical outcomes of their activism is that it gets the ball rolling not only during the classes but also outside
of them. For instance, while homosexuality remains a taboo subject during the
classes, Rania has personally experienced how, for instance, parents have opened
up and talked about the issue with her. She told me a few anecdotes about cases
when individual course participants had come up to her or called her after classes
to ask questions that they felt could not be discussed during the sessions. To
both Rania and Asma, the emergence of and ability to have those conversations
as parents, family members, or friends plays a substantial role in their mission, in
how they are striving for their society to behave and look in the future.

> They finally talk to their children about sex and sexuality. The parents here
> are not the main source of information about sex and sexuality for their kids.
> The kids get the information from the internet and so on. Finally, they sit
> down with their kids, give their questions space, and answer them. This is
> amazing. This is really amazing because if we keep working on this, we can
> become a really healthy community. This essentially means that the children
> will grow up to choose partners, girlfriends, and boyfriends and live with
> them in a more aware and healthy way. So yes, this is one aspect of it. . . .
> Now things are much more open. People have to live with these changes very
> quickly in practical ways outside of the home. I spoke to my parents about
> LGBT rights and my mother is 69 and my father is 74, and ten years ago this
> was a topic that I could not even touch with them. And now it's okay.

The combination of Zionist control over Palestinian sex lives, particularly sexual education, and what Rania and Asma called ongoing Palestinian "sexual
closed-ness" has a serious impact on Palestinian women. The lack of discussion

about sexual consent, the myth and ongoing importance of virginity and the ongoing sexual violence committed against Palestinian women attest to the fact that women's sexuality continues to be significantly managed and controlled by Zionist and patriarchal social orders. As a result, for many feminist activists like Rania and Asma, sexual education constitutes an essential strategy of both their anticolonial and their women's liberation struggles. In many ways, their narratives of women's liberation, including their sexual liberation, were not only connected to their imaginings of the nation but also constituted the very first steppingstone toward national liberation.

"LIKE" A VIRGIN

Jalilah: Have you lost your virginity yet?
Kim: Yes.
Jalilah: Did you bleed?
Kim: No.
Jalilah: So you didn't lose it.
Kim: I guess not then. (sarcastically)
Jalilah: No, you don't understand. You *didn't*. I would be in serious trouble if I didn't bleed on my wedding night. (February 12, 2014)

The custom of verifying newlywed women's bleeding during their wedding night as an indication of virginity remains of significant importance to some Bedouins. While the Bedouin women I spoke to were all keen on entering their married lives not only as virgins but as sexually chaste more generally, they were also concerned about how to demonstrate this sexual chastity to their husbands. My first reaction—though on reflection it was a very white, Western reaction—was to inquire the point of this demonstration with them as I kept pointing out that the first sexual intercourse is not always accompanied by bleeding. The biological facts did not matter to the women. Eventually, I realized that they knew all about the biological facts (a few of them worked as nurses) and still it seemed as though those facts were irrelevant to their concerns. During their wedding night, the anatomy did not matter. All that mattered was for them to demonstrate their virginity through bloodstains. Even though I never managed to find out the details about their tricks, some women assured me that "there are ways to make sure you show that you're a virgin." I never inquired further into these ways, knowing that they were kept secret for a crucial reason, and being very much aware of the price that these women would have to pay if they did not manage to prove their virginity, or if men (or some women for that matter) were to find out how they helped make their virginity evident.

Nizreen, a feminist social worker and sexual health educator, pointed out to me that the idea of saving one's virginity for marriage continues to be prevalent among not only Bedouin women but Palestinian women from all kinds of educational, regional, and class backgrounds. Moreover, she emphasized the sharp contrast between the tenacious and ongoing social expectation for women to remain sexually chaste before marriage while, frequently, the opposite is expected of men:

> I have noticed that young girls, however educated and open-minded ...
> believe that they should save themselves (their virginity) for marriage even
> if that means that the boyfriend will wander off and sleep with someone
> else for the time being. It's not the girl I'm criticizing here, it's the fact that
> she has been spoon-fed a certain type of mindset about her own sexuality.
> It is all in here [points to her head]; it is very deep and, no matter what you
> learn at university, even when you study social work or psychology, there is
> something stuck in your way of thinking.

Nizreen further described how many of the men who participated in her sexual education classes prided themselves on their assumed ability to tell whether their wives were virgins or not at the time when they got married: "Actually, there is no evidence about whether a woman is still a virgin or not, and I told my course participants that I would challenge any man who said that he was sure that his wife was a virgin when they married!" Nevertheless, she told me, the men often insisted that they knew regardless of a clear lack of biological evidence. Overall, men's adherence to standard that their wives enter marriage as virgins, coupled with their own expertise in assessing women's sexual experience, demonstrate the central role that women's virginity continues to play for Palestinian men as well, whether in regard to their honor and (sexual) masculinity as husbands and men or as a reflection of their own knowledge and experience about sex.

Being an outsider also enabled me to talk to some men about their sexual experiences before marriage. These not only outweighed those of women by a great margin but were also often supported by parents, who believed that it was not only acceptable but even advisable for young men to collect sexual experiences before entering marriage. The acquisition of sexual experience was sometimes even actively helped along by their parents, who paid for sex workers to deflower their sons. An often-mentioned scandal was the opposition of religious leaders to the sex work that took place in the rather conservative village of Kafr Kana (near Nazareth), where, within the suburbs, numerous cars lined up, bringing in sex workers to deflower young men, among other purposes. In my own encounters, out of twelve young and unmarried Palestinian men whom I spoke to casually about their sexual experiences, more than half of the men had slept with a sex worker at least once in their lives. All of them had lost their virginity before marriage.

Even though in some other parts of Palestinian society proving women's virginity from bleeding has largely become regarded as archaic, virginity as a cultural concept and social expectation of women at the time of marriage is very much maintained. In other words, while bleeding as the key indication of the loss of virginity during the wedding night has become increasingly regarded as (scientifically) inaccurate or primitive (see also Sa'ar 2004, 7), particularly among families who bestow on themselves a reputation for being modern and educated, women's sexual abstinence often continues to be expected. While, in the past, a woman's virginity had to be demonstrated to family members (or sometimes even to the public) for instance through the so-called "sheet of the bride" (the blood-stained sheet) in Bedouin communities, practices of virginity and sexual chastity take place increasingly elsewhere today.

Matrimony remains the only publicly accepted context for sexual activity among Palestinian women in Israel or, as a friend of mine from Haifa put it casually but earnestly, "for women in our society, marriage is the only permit to fuck." While a small number of women found it natural to have premarital sex and believed that, just like men, they had a right to have sex, the majority of them nevertheless continued to carefully negotiate performances of virginity in front of their parents, friends, and (current) boyfriends. The performance of virginity could be observed within all religious, class, and ethnic groups, regardless of whether the women had actually had sex. The conversations I had during my fieldwork, however, revealed only women from socioeconomically stable and supportive families who had had premarital sexual relations, usually with their current long-term boyfriends. Because they desired an active sex life, some women maintained sexual relations with ex-boyfriends, which, they argued, meant sleeping with somebody they trusted while also not having to kiss and tell.

Moreover, alternative sexual practices were frequently chosen by women who preferred to avoid vaginal sex before marriage and preserve their virginity but still wanted to be intimate with their partners (or "please" them). The alternatives chosen included sexual activities without penetration, oral sex, "outercourse" (heavy rubbing over clothed bodies), and anal sex. A friend of a friend assured me over coffee that "we are Arabs, we turn really creative if we want to have sex. So many people just do it the other way around because they don't want to risk too much." A few young women referred to anal sex as the "Arab way." I could not figure out whether they referred to it as such in opposition to vaginal sex constructed as some kind of "Jewish way" or were referring to the popularity of anal sex in other Middle Eastern countries like Egypt (El Feki 2013, 68) or Iran (Mahdavi 2009, 148).

Overall, all kinds of physically intimate relations were kept quiet in front of family members and, often, also among friends. Among the reasons for concealing their sexual experiences were the fear of ruining their social reputations (Abu-Baker 2002, 97) and offending or disappointing their parents but, more important, the fear that their current partners might reject them if they found out about their sexual experience. The latter fear was a predominant concern even among outspoken feminists, who, I observed, often advised each other not to tell their current partner anything about their previous sexual experiences. Maryam, a feminist activist in her twenties, for instance, said, "I cannot talk about my sexual experiences with my boyfriend. . . . You should write about this. This is how messed up we 'feminists' are."

Throughout our conversations, it emerged that, to the women, more important than virginity as a biological fact was the performance of virginity, especially in front of their parents, who rarely approved of premarital sexual contact. Naturally, the attitude and opinions of parents have a major influence on how women's behavior is judged or supported when marital problems occur. One woman emphasized to me that women whose parents knew of and tolerated premarital sexual contact tended to be less supportive of their daughters during times of conflict with their husbands, whereas parents who believed that their daughters entered their marriages as virgins supported their daughters more during such times.

"ISRAEL IN MY BEDROOM"

During my fieldwork, a gay male friend of mine told me that between mixed male homosexual couples, Arab-Palestinian and Jewish, the Israeli man usually expects his Arab sex partner to take on the active role because of an apparently rather common sexual fantasy among Jewish Israeli homosexual men that draws on gendered and racialized stereotypes and a historical fetishization of Arab hypermasculinity and machoism, asserting Jewish men's moral authority and power in a classic settler colonial fashion. Apps such as Grindr, Scruff, and

Tinder are very popular among homosexual men in Israel and are frequently used in order to arrange dates or meet potential sex partners. A very common tagline on the online profiles of Jewish Israeli men reads "Please be manly, I'm manly," which, according to my friend, should be read as "I want a masculine man, a dominant man." Together we observed that new Jewish members of these sex and dating apps frequently put the Star of David as a badge on their profile photographs as some kind of enhancer of their masculinity. They quickly remove it, however, as soon as they realize that it does not help to arouse the interest of gay Arab-Palestinian men they feel attracted to. Sexual fantasies, particularly when they are common within specific groups of people, say a lot about how political and social circumstances, including strong political tensions and conflict, have the power to intimately influence and inflame sexual desires that are based on deep-seated sexual stereotypes of the Other.

Even though sexual intermingling between Palestinian women and Jewish men was not as common as that between Palestinian men and Jewish men, a significant number of my female research participants talked about their sexual experiences with Jewish Israeli men. This section explores one-night stands or sexual affairs between Palestinian women and Jewish Israeli men rather than serious long-term relationships (which will be discussed in chapter 5). The women I spoke with often narrated their decision to sleep with an Israeli Jewish man in terms of their sexual desire for that person or their desire to "get what they want or feel like having"—as many reminded me—"just as men do." Another common reason why women chose Jewish Israeli sex partners was that they felt it was easier to have short affairs or one-night stands with Jewish Israeli men because they are members of a separate society, meaning once the affair ended, so did their contact. Simultaneously, the chances of the affair or fling being revealed were significantly smaller than with a Palestinian man. Like a few other women, a psychology student based in Tel Aviv named Leen followed a similar reasoning but also emphasized that I should keep in mind that the options for Palestinian women to have sex flings are generally limited. Because of the taboo on Palestinian women's premarital sex within their own society and the price that they pay if premarital sex is revealed, some Palestinian women prefer to have sexual relations with Jewish Israeli men, especially if these relations are intended to be short-lived: "It's easier to have an affair with an Israeli guy. I'm not trying to say that they're nicer human beings and I really don't want to marry one in the future. It's just easier to have an affair with them because we're a fucked-up society. I'm not saying that they're more attractive or more 'feminist,' but it's easier because I don't need to be so careful all the time. I can be more straightforward and just get what I want."

Even though sexual flings are one-off events by nature, they do not constitute mere ephemeral pleasures as a break from everyday life for Palestinian
women. Instead, it is argued here, they disrupt the plan for Palestinian women
to have unfulfilling or non-existent sex lives. Furthermore, they disrupt the
discourse and strategy of Zionist modern sexuality according to which Palestinian women are constructed as sexually oppressed by Arab men and sexually
liberated by Jewish Israeli men. By acting on their own personal sexual desires
and having just plain sex, Palestinian women defy the hegemonic sex orders imposed on them. This is not to neglect the power relationship of sexual relations
between colonizing men and colonized women in general but to say that they
do not always succeed in reinscribing white male Jewish privilege in Palestinian women's sex lives. By keeping their affairs secret, women who have such
affairs enable their sex lives to continue without being revealed, interrupted,
or cut short by conservative family members or exploited by Israeli modernist
rhetoric. Unlike a few Palestinian men I spoke with about their sexual experiences with Jewish women, none of the Palestinian women showed off their
sexual experiences with Jewish men as trophies or achievements. To me, the
difference seemed to indicate that they did not enter sexual encounters for any
reason other than their own pleasure and satisfaction, which they dealt with
very privately.

Nevertheless, I noticed that women' talk about their sexual encounters with
Jewish men frequently had political connotations. For instance, one of my
interviewees talked jokingly about her current sexual affair: "Really, I'm just
sexually occupying them back if you like." Another woman described how she
felt that she was at the more powerful end during sex with a Jewish Israeli man
because of her non-Jewish uterus. The idea that sex could result in a Jewish
man producing non-Jewish offspring made her feel superior, but this notion
of power also informed her own sexual fantasy. "We should all get married
to Jewish men, so there won't be any more Jews in the future," she laughingly
told me, even though she had emphasized several times before that she would
never consider being in a serious relationship with, let alone consider marrying,
a Jewish Israeli man. When I spoke with a feminist scholar from Haifa about
these narratives, she did not appear to be surprised by them at all. Instead,
she emphasized the ways in which Zionist settler colonialism aims to inscribe
its power over all aspects of women's everyday intimate lives: "Israel is in my
bedroom, you see? It's everywhere. That's its goal for me, to feel that I cannot
breathe, that every part of my body, every part of my life is occupied."

In the context of Palestinian women in Israel, to conceive of sexual relations with Jewish Israeli men as political is nothing farfetched or irrational.

The management of interracial sex is critical to the Zionist project, and sexual relations between Jewish men and Palestinian women (like sexual relations between Palestinian men and Jewish women, or mixed queer sexual relations) have always been central to the Zionist discourse and strategy, albeit in ever-changing ways. Rabbi Meir Kahane, the founder of the Jewish Defense League in the United States and its counterpart, the Kach movement, is one of the most outspoken opponents of Arab-Jewish sexual relations, which he perceived as part of his proposed ethnic cleansing solution to rid Israel of its Palestinian citizens. During the Israeli parliamentary elections in 1981, Kahane prosed laws that would forbid any kind of intimate relations between Jews and Arabs and punish any Arab scofflaws with a five-year prison sentence. In the same year, Kahane's Kach followers distributed posters all over the campus of Hebrew University in Jerusalem to warn Jewish female students to "Beware of Arabs, who seek only to shame you and take advantage of you" (Masalha 2012, 151). Even though Kach rhetoric is brushed aside by Israeli centrists and leftists as religious fundamentalist or right-wing radicalism, the idea of Arab-Jewish sexual relations is nowhere near being tolerated by mainstream Israeli society.

An emerging series of local initiatives led by organized groups of Jewish Israeli residents, rabbis, religious organizations such as Yad L'Achim, and organizations such as Lehava have made it their mission to expose Jewish-Arab relationships in order to "rescue" Jewish Israeli women who are dating Arab men. Impromptu teams of youth counselors and psychologists have been set up in Petah Tikva near Tel Aviv in order to identify and proselytize Jewish women who are dating Arab men. Special telephone hotlines have been created, which parents and friends of Jewish women who are in relationships with non-Jewish men can use to inform the municipality about them, and websites, known as shame pages, which feature the photographs of such women.[8] In Bat Yam, religious nationalists rallied under the banner of "Jewish girls for the Jewish people."[9] An interesting sidenote is that Russian girls are regarded as particularly vulnerable to the attention of Arab men, as many of them "did not undergo the religious and Zionist education."[10]

Kahane's vision has been realized to some extent as, for instance, Sabbar Kashur, a thirty-year-old Palestinian man, was sentenced to eighteen months in prison in 2010 for having sexual intercourse with a Jewish woman who believed him to be Jewish. The woman filed a complaint, and the court ruled that he was guilty of rape, even though there was strong evidence that the sex was consensual.[11] The myth of the colonized male or black rapist that continues to linger in settler society is not unique to Zionist politics but has been commonly drawn on in other colonial regimes and their societies in the form of colonial rape scares.

"Because in the colonial imagination it was unthinkable that all but the most degenerate white women would willingly engage in sexual relationships with colonized/enslaved men, rape became the primary paradigm through which such relationships were understood. Popularly known as the 'black peril,' hysteria over the rape of white women gave way to draconian legislation. In early twentieth-century colonial contexts such as Papua New Guinea and Southern Rhodesia, native men were put to death for the rape, attempted rape, or even suspected rape of white women" (Ray 2013, 194). A typical characteristic of colonial rape scares is that they are usually vastly exaggerated, such as the allegations made in the December 2016 session of the Knesset's Status of Women Committee. During the opening of the session, Yulia Malinovsky, a representative of the far-right Yisrael Beiteinu party, claimed that throughout the previous nine years, there had been eight hundred cases of Jewish Israeli women being sexually assaulted or harassed by Palestinian men in the Jerusalem area. Other legislators from parties of the ruling coalition agreed that there was a "suspicious pattern" of Palestinian men and boys preying on Jewish women and girls in Israel without pointing out any specific facts.[12] As famously noted by Ann Stoler, frequently there is no correlation between the colonialist rhetoric of sexual assault and the actual incidence of rape of white women by colonized men: "Just the contrary: there was often no evidence, ex post facto or at the time, that rapes were committed or that rape attempts were made. This is not to suggest that sexual assaults never occurred, but that their incidence had little to do with the fluctuations in anxiety about them" (Stoler 1989, 641).

As Ann Stoler illuminates in her work on Southern Rhodesia, Kenya, New Guinea, and the Solomon Islands in the 1920s and 1930s, "political and sexual subversion of the colonial system went hand in hand" as rape charges frequently resulted from a perceived transgression of colonial space (1989, 641). She illustrates how in her studied regions the declared danger of sexual assault on white women by black men led to the emergence of citizens' militias, ladies' rifle clubs, a preference for female colonial domestic servants, and death and public flogging penalties for rape or the attempted rape of European women and girls by black men. Stoler underlines two issues that are relevant to the context of Israel: First, the centrality of race within colonial discourses and legal practices, as sexual abuse of colonized black women was not classified as rape, nor were white rapists prosecuted for raping black women. Second, the colonial imaginings of space and sexuality are intimately linked to each other, as the colonial concern over the protection of white women intensified during real and perceived times of crisis when the colonial borders and internal cohesion were threatened.

Sexual relationships between Palestinians and Jews are also managed in subtler ways, particularly under the rubric of Israeli modern sexuality, which frequently communicates through a modernist rhetoric of sexual liberalism. Liberal or left-wing Zionists narrate sexual relations between Jews and Palestinians as something that ought to be encouraged or celebrated. One example is the video "Jews and Arabs Kiss" launched by *Time Out Tel Aviv* in September 2016.[13] The video was released in protest against the Israeli Ministry of Education high school curriculum's omission of *Borderlife*, a novel written by Dorit Rabinyan, which tells a love story between a Jewish Israeli woman and a Palestinian man. During the video, six Palestinian-Jewish couples kiss in front of the camera. The sensationalist effect is magnified by the inclusion of both hetero- and homosexual couples, relationship partners, and people who have never met before. The video caused a public uproar and was removed from *Time Out Tel Aviv*'s homepage. Intended as a statement and call for peace through the means of free love, the video is problematic, as it took for granted the power relationships between Jewish Israeli and Palestinian participants. According to this logic, peace between Jews and Arabs relies on the sexual availability of indigenous Palestinians to settler colonialists. While Palestinians and Jews kissing each other is exoticized as a forbidden deed, interreligious marriage and family formation remain sacrosanct.

While heterosexual Palestinian bodies are exoticized, racialized, and absorbed into Zionist discourses of modern sexuality and queer bodies are frequently cohabitated into pinkwashing discourses, intersexual indigenous bodies constitute a real threat to the stability of the sexual order of the binary Zionist gender regime. Like many of the women who shared stories about their sexual experiences with me, Nabilah, who identified as an intersexual woman, related how the key to a fulfilling sex life for her lay first and foremost with the liberation of the self.

> I was raised a woman but I'm not only a woman. All these search for gender identity in the catalogues of gender.... I think they're closer to making us stupid than smart. If there is an empty men's toilet, we'd rather queue in a massively long queue with other women than go and use the men's toilet. Unless there is a bad smell, I don't see the point of that. The biological system is not just female and male. My weight should not be calculated according to solely female and male. All of this happens out of fear not out of knowledge. My papers, really, say nothing about me. They're just to relieve the anxiety

of the state. Friends of my family voted for a communist Christian mayor in Nazareth just because they were afraid of what could happen if there was a mayor with a Muslim family background. We group out of fear, not out of knowledge, but I refuse to do so. I should liberate myself first, then my papers—they don't say anything. State vaginal examination—if the Nazis come back into the picture and ask who is a man and who is a woman then this question of "what" I am could become a problem but otherwise it is not important to know. If you are liberated in your fantasy, then it doesn't matter what your papers say. What would you do if you woke up next to a woman after a one-night stand? You met her, a beautiful woman in a bar. And then you are informed that she was a man in the past. Most people would be shocked. And why? It all comes from fear. It's not about whether Israel gives a third gender, it is about me making love like a woman if I want to and me making love like a man if I want to. Whether there are more masculinities or femininities doesn't matter. We all have both anyway.

The prioritization of the "liberation of the self" narrated by Nabilah is very similar to the sexual educators that I spoke to. Rania's narrative is representative of that of many other activists who regard the "occupation of the soul" to be a result of the internalization of inferiority imposed on Palestinians by the state. Like many other feminist activists involved in my research, Rania understood the colonial and patriarchal oppression experienced by Palestinian women as inextricably linked. As a result, she argued, any liberation process of Palestinian women has to start within themselves, an often much greater challenge, or, as she put it, "Challenging yourself is more difficult than challenging the occupier... because we're not used to thinking like that."

NOTES

1. Hebrew for "Woman to Woman," a mainly Jewish Israeli feminist organization based in Haifa.

2. The Prawer Plan or Prawer-Begin Bill was approved by the Knesset in 2013. It called for the destruction of thirty-five Bedouin villages that are unrecognized by the State of Israel and the mass expulsion of seventy thousand Bedouin citizens in al-Naqab. Palestinians managed to bring down the Prawer Plan in 2013, but new Jewish settlement plans for al-Naqab were approved in December 2021.

3. Muntada, "Our Vision," https://www.jensaneya.org/welcome (accessed January 17, 2022).

4. Human Rights Watch, "Second Class: Discrimination against Palestinian Arab Children in Israel's Schools," Special Report, September 20, 2001,

https://www.hrw.org/report/2001/09/30/second-class/discrimination
-against-palestinian-arab-children-israels-schools.

5. Ibid., 3.

6. Ibid.

7. H. Sherwood, "Israel Orders School Textbook Publishers to Remove Sex Education Material," *Guardian*, September 3, 2013, https://www.theguardian .com/world/2013/sep/03/israel-school-textbook-sex-education.

8. N. Sheizaf, "The Holy War against Arab-Jewish Relations and the Jerusalem Lynch," +972 *Magazine*, August 21, 2012, http://972mag.com /the-holy-war-against-arab-jewish-relations-and-the-jerusalem-lynch/54198/.

9. M. Guarnieri, "Don't Take Our Girls . . . - Jewish-Palestinian Couples in Israel Face Increasing Pressure as Racism Becomes More Open," *Al Jazeera*, January 29, 2011, http://www.aljazeera.com/indepth/features/2011/01 /201112912322207901.html.

10. M. Zonszein, "Jewish Women Can't Volunteer at Night—to Avoid 'Contact with Arabs,'" +972 *Magazine*, October 17, 2013, http://972mag.com /jewish-women-cant-volunteer-at-night-to-avoid-contact-with-arabs/80527/.

11. J. Adetunji and H. Sherwood, "Arab Guilty of Rape after Consensual Sex with Jew," *Guardian*, July 20, 2010, https://www.theguardian.com/world /2010/jul/21/arab-guilty-rape-consensual-sex-jew.

12. D. Sheen, "Israel Weaponizes Rape Culture against Palestinians," *Electronic Intifada*, January 31, 2017, https://electronicintifada.net/content /israel-weaponizes-rape-culture-against-palestinians/19386.

13. "Jews and Arabs Kiss," *Time Out Tel Aviv*, January 6, 2016, https://www .youtube.com/watch?v=N8DMGaeDXE4.

FIVE

—〰—

DEFYING INTIMATE RELATIONS

INTRODUCTION

During one of my stays in Laqiya in December 2013, I received the news that my sixteen-year-old cousin had just given birth to a healthy baby girl back in my German hometown. The news was shocking to me, not only because of her youth but also because nobody knew that she had been pregnant, including herself, apparently. Despite the fact that she was a slim girl, there were no visible signs of her pregnancy until her water broke. I told Jalilah the news when I had finished talking on the telephone with my mom, as it was just too perplexing for me not to share. We were sitting in Jalilah's childhood bedroom with two of her sisters who, at the time, were already mothers themselves, and discussed whether one could go through a whole pregnancy without knowing. While Jalilah's sister could not believe that my cousin's own mother did not notice anything unusual about her, I was more disturbed by thoughts relating to her future: What would she do if the relationship she was currently in did not work out and she was left to raise her daughter as a single mother? What about finishing school? "She might end up being a sixteen-year-old single mom one day," I said, emphasizing that she wasn't married to her boyfriend. The older of Jalilah's sisters quickly responded, "What is your problem with this? So, she is not married. She's German, it'll be fine." The other sister added, "Yes, your family is supportive and that's all that matters. She'll be fine. Don't worry so much!" All of a sudden, I felt a little embarrassed about my rather conservative reaction.

I noticed that all the norms and values of family formation that I had observed within the Bedouin community were not presented by Jalilah's sisters as somehow universally valid or of superior morality to norms and values else-where. Instead, they were, to many women, as Jalilah once phrased it, "just the way things work here." I did not understand this statement as downplaying the reality that the plan of affective relationship and family formation usually entails sexist and racialized expectations of Palestinian women in Israel. In-stead, I understood it as pointing out the fact that women could still navigate and realize some of their personal wishes either despite, or exactly because of, playing by the rules of these expectations, by defying them altogether, or by carefully navigating around them.

Family and monogamous marriage have come under significant criticism, if not attack, by feminists and, still today, they continue to be explosive topics for some. In particular during the 1960s, white radical feminists in Western countries launched the harshest critiques of biological families as the root of the sexist oppression of women, "the sex class," thereby demanding their aboli-tion and claiming that otherwise—so feminists such as Shulamith Firestone (1970) argued—women's pregnancy and motherhood would prevent women's liberation. I encountered various versions of this idea among some Jewish Is-raeli feminists, but, interestingly, I did not come across it among their Palestin-ian counterparts in Israel. Instead, their concept of family resembled more the black feminist thought of Patricia Collins or bell hooks, who have pointed out that while patriarchal regulations and structures of effective relationships have, no doubt, frequently oppressed, exploited, and silenced women, families can also serve as safe and empowering spaces within wider oppressive structures (Collins 2000, 52; hooks 2004, 110).

Whom they live with in intimacy plays an especially important role for in-digenous women living in settler colonial states such as Israel, where Zionist policies have actively shaped and reshaped the conditions and possible frame-works of affective relations, family formation, and married life among Palestin-ian women. The lingering effects of the *nakba*, such as displacement, economic marginalization, restricted mobility, and limited access to education, health services, and job opportunities, have had a significant effect on Palestinian women's ongoing reliance and dependence on male family members, as well as the maintenance of traditional gender roles within families. The Zionist state has increasingly focused on including new bodies to fulfill its project, particularly as regards marriage and family formation, and is in the process of gradually extending equal rights to Jewish Israeli lesbians, gay men, and bisexuals. In order to boost the Zionist demographic war against its Palestin-ian citizens, Jewish Israeli gay citizens have been increasingly included in the state's obsessive search for ways to boost the Jewish population, for instance

through adoption, artificial insemination, or surrogacy.[1] Simultaneously, Palestinian family life has come under stricter regulations through laws actively
prohibiting family unification, public campaigns to prevent mixed relationships between Jews and Palestinians, and even direct attacks when Palestinians' intimate relations have somehow been perceived to be crossing a line.

While the majority of Palestinian women in Israel are under great pressure
to stick to the plan of leading the love (i.e., married) and family lives envisioned
by their family members, they are also pressured by the state not only to stick to
their own kind but also not to threaten the stability of the Zionist project, which
strives for Jewish demographic superiority and firm control over its non-Jewish
population. Overall, the majority of women I interviewed spoke of families,
long-term relationships, and marriages as a source of stability, continuity, and
support. I found that these women, often by sticking to the rules of the plan,
sought to build up their families in new ways within the family's potential in
the face of women's discrimination and oppression. Other women—a minority of younger women in their twenties or early thirties, but also some older
individuals—sought new ways to live their intimate relations outside the social
parameters. Some of them did not care for having children of their own; some
did not care for marriage and had come up with new ways of building alternative families. Even though the latter group can be regarded as being in a clearer
or more direct confrontation with the patriarchal and settler colonialist order
of intimate relations, both groups demonstrated the potential to challenge or
transgress social orders.

LOVE UNDER OCCUPATION

"Israel occupied our land, but it can't occupy our hearts. I am free to love who I
want as any man is free to love who he wants. My happiness is with that person.
Not a single racist or fascist law, or separation wall, can separate a boy and girl
who love each other" (Meissa from Jenin).

It is important to underline that not only do traditional family and community values strive to regulate Palestinian women's intimate relationships, in
a great variety of ways, but so does the State of Israel. Even though a detailed
outline of the ways in which the Zionist state interferes with Palestinian family
formation goes beyond the scope of this book, I would like to touch on a few
areas of family formation that commonly came up during my conversations.

One is the state's control over women's intimate relations by constraining
marriage to religious marriage only, its tolerance of polygamy in the Bedouin community, and the separation of Palestinian families. I came across an

example of the latter during the early stages of my fieldwork when I was introduced to Amin from Haifa and his wife Meissa from Jenin. The two had met
during the Second Intifada when Amin was conducting research in refugee
camps in the West Bank, soon after the Israeli military demolished the Jenin
refugee camp during Operation Defensive Shield. When I met them in 2013,
Amin and Meissa had been married for seven years and were parents of two
daughters. Meissa had not been granted citizenship, nor could she begin an
application for citizenship after their marriage, which meant that she had to
reapply for a permit to stay in Israel every year. The permit provided her with
no rights, as she told me: "I don't have health insurance, I'm not allowed to drive
here, I can't go to university, and I can't work. I'm just here for my husband and
children." The case of Laila, a feminist activist working in the field of sexual
education, demonstrates that even women with good relationships with official
state bodies do not receive special treatment when it comes to family unification: "When I was married, I was married to a Palestinian, so every month
my husband was threatened with being thrown out of the country—that's
discrimination only because he's not Israeli. It took me ages to get him a work
permit and so on. I worked with the Ministry of Health. I was the director of a
health program in Jerusalem, and I represented the office all over the country,
but I was denied the right to bring my husband. The discrimination affects all
parts of our lives, including our love lives."

The Nationality and Entry into Israel Law was passed in 2003 as a temporary
law banning residents from the Occupied Territories from becoming Israeli
citizens after marrying spouses with Israeli citizenship. Although the order
was initially temporary, the Knesset has repeatedly extended it.[2] Today, Adalah
estimates that between twenty and thirty thousand persons inside Israel live in
relationships similar to Amin and Meissa's;[3] they are forced to live apart, move
abroad, or live in Israel in constant fear of deportation.[4] The Nationality and
Entry into Israel Law and Israel's Citizenship Law serve to police Palestinians'
love and familial lives for the purpose of cultivating the Zionist racial order
in Israel and denying land claims that would emerge as a result of recognizing Palestinian familial ties and descent. This kind of law, establishing Jewish
privileges to enjoy citizenship and the right to live in Israel, can also be found
in other settler colonial contexts. Canada, for instance, where the Indian Act of
1876 imposed a form of patrilineal inheritance that denied status to the children
of indigenous women with legal status if they married or bore children with a
person without status. As a result of the loss of recognition of their indigenous
heritage, more than twenty-five thousand indigenous women lost access to
reserve land and community between 1876 and 1985 (Morgensen 2012, 10). Just

as the Indian Act defined indigenous status, Israel aims to define and regulate racial identity and indigenous rights through gendered and sexualized legislature. Depriving indigenous people of the right to citizenship is one method, and another is granting citizenship or recognition of the right to citizenship so as to contain indigenous people as a domesticated difference (Coulthard 2007).

Relationships and marriages between Palestinians with Israeli citizenship and residents of the West Bank are not rare. The fact that a residency permit, even if provided, offers no rights impinges on women's lives if they happen to be the spouse without Israeli citizenship. I observed some of the most extreme experiences of this situation among the Bedouin community in Laqiya. One woman who shared her story with me was Sarah, a woman in her sixties with three children. She came from the West Bank to get married to a Bedouin man as his second wife. I met her by coincidence when she was cleaning the floor of a women's rights organization, and we casually got into a conversation. She seemed surprised that somebody would talk to her, and the first thing she said about her experiences of life in Israel was "I'm deaf and cannot speak to her (the researcher). I have nothing to say. I just breathe and be here for my children." Her life took a turn for the worse when her husband died and the sons of his first wife started to make decisions about her. According to Sarah, they "terrorized her daily life." The only reason that she continued to stay in Israel without either citizenship or a permit was for her children to receive an education and citizenship. The only way for her to make a tiny living was by cleaning the floor of the women's organization.

According to a befriended lawyer, the phenomenon of polygamy going hand in hand with lack of citizenship is common, particularly in the Bedouin community, where a significant number of men continue to marry a second wife from Gaza or the West Bank. As my friend put it, "They are screwed both ways: they don't get a status from the state because polygamy is a criminal offence, even though it is tolerated by the state, and they don't have any real rights because their husbands can easily kick them out of the house without any repercussions if they get tired of them." Polygamy in Israel is possible because marriage remains strictly in the hands of religious courts. As a result, a first wife will be registered by the state and a second wife is married by *shari'a* law while the state remains uninformed. The second wife usually agrees to the arrangement. If there is a dispute with the second wife, provided she has Israeli citizenship, she can address the *shari'a* court with the help of two male witnesses and evidence (such as photographs of the wedding ceremony, their families, etc.), and the *shari'a* court can legally recognize the marriage. Women frequently get compensation of around one hundred thousand shekels, and ex-husbands rarely go to jail even though the maximum penalty for polygamy in Israel is five years imprisonment. Unlike women with Israeli citizenship, however, women like Sarah cannot address the *shari'a* court and therefore end up with no rights whatsoever.[5]

MIXED RELATIONSHIPS

Palestinian women's intimate relationships in Israel are inextricably entangled with the politics of women's liberation, settler colonialism, and patriarchy. Palestinian feminists, in particular, often narrated their desires for their love lives as closely linked to, or influenced by, their political beliefs. It was not uncommon for feminists to describe to me how they felt that their imagined ideal relationships stood in sharp contrast to the patriarchal and settler colonialist social orders, which are based on clear and firm social categories. Zionist, but also Palestinian, assessments of modernity and civility, on which racial and social memberships draw, are measured less by what people do in public than by how they conduct their private lives (Stoler 1989, 634). In other words, I will address questions such as, With whom do Palestinian women live together? Where and how do they live? Do they want families of their own and, if so, what families do they desire? This section explores how mixed relationships function to stabilize or destabilize racial and social memberships. It is argued here that the personal must be considered political by involving a set of associations held by Palestinian women about sexual and political morality, racial membership, national identity, social acceptability, and feminist principles. Because of the personal sensitivity and intimacy of these issues, discrepancies between women's associations and practices are not uncommon.

I was taken aback by the number of Palestinian women who revealed to me that they were in serious long-term relationships with Jewish Israeli men, though these remain a rare occurrence in Israel overall. The Palestinian women with Jewish partners usually lived in shared flats in mixed urban localities such as Jaffa. They often kept their relationships secret from their families. My astonishment was not so much about Palestinian and Jewish Israeli people falling in love, but about them building a life together in the face of a large number of powerful structural, social, and religious obstacles, as well as the increasing hostility in Jewish Israeli society to mixed relationships, much of which is expressed through violent attacks on mixed couples.[6] I began to puzzle over why there were more Palestinian women dating Jewish Israeli men than there were Jewish women dating Palestinian men and soon sought to find answers while cautiously keeping in mind the Orientalist modernization rhetoric of the state. Instead, drawing on Ann Stoler's work, I conceptualized sexual asymmetries as "tropes to depict other centers of power" (Stoler 2002, 44; see also 1989, 635). Throughout my conversations with Palestinian women who were in relationships with Jewish men, gender and feminism emerged as important core factors in explaining their experiences.

Feminism was frequently cited as playing an important role for women's relationship choices and imagining of what their ideal relationships and partners should be like. Notably, feminism was linked to both women's choices to be and not to be in relationships with Jewish Israeli men. One young woman explained the former choice, for instance, by saying she "honestly had enough of the Arab chauvinism." In a similar vein, Zarah, a student and feminist activist based in Tel Aviv, explained to me that she simply found it easier to be with her Jewish Israeli boyfriend, whom she had met at the university, because "he understands feminism . . . because he was raised like that." Similar to women who had one-night stands and sexual affairs with Jewish men, some women perceived particularly left-wing Jewish Israeli men as more "women friendly," "feminist," or "modern" than Palestinian men. Of course, the existence of miscegenation and mixed relationships signaled neither the presence nor the absence of an unequal distribution of power, sexist, and racist elements among the couples. In contrast to women who had only had fleeting sexual affairs with Jewish men, Palestinian women in ongoing relationships with them emphasized the "modern man" aspect much more. In sum, their prime motivation for building long-term relationships with Jewish men, despite all the difficulties and challenges that it entailed, was their belief that they could be more comfortable with them and act more like themselves than if they were with Arab men.

Palestinian women also expressed their personal rejection and opposition to mixed relationships, and some whom emphasized their concerns about the power relationships in mixed couples. Again, interestingly, such sentiments were often linked to their feminist beliefs. Nazirah, for instance, a young law student from the Galilee, explained why she could never be with a Jewish Israeli man: "I could never really truly trust him. So how could I love him? I don't understand these women. If he doesn't respect my Palestinian identity, he does not respect me as a woman. I am both and I cannot separate the two, you see?" Another young feminist from Haifa voiced a similar opinion closely linked to national identity and imaginations of the nation: "As a Palestinian woman, I can only be with a Palestinian man. There is no question about that. I know you might think this is silly, but that's how it is." Although they were tiny in number, other women went as far as accusing Palestinian women with Jewish Israeli boyfriends or husbands of turning a blind eye to the fact that even left-wing Jewish Israeli men have served in the army and, thus, really, they were dating the enemy. They often echoed the hostile rhetoric about mixed relationships being national treason, as both the Palestinian and Zionist nationalist camps maintain. It is important to note, however, that they also added that they would, in theory, be tolerant of mixed relationships once the occupation came to an end. Until then, Arab-Jewish relationships were perceived by most as a paramount danger to both Palestinian national and women's liberation.

Palestinian feminists' opposition to mixed relationships in Israel did not appear out of nowhere but is rooted in their knowledge of the history and endurance of rape, sexual harassment, and sexual control experienced by Palestinian women in Israel since the early days of the Zionist invasion of Palestinian land. As in other settler colonial countries around the world, both consensual sexual relations and rape between colonizing men and indigenous women have figured prominently in Israel. As Stoler points out, "the regulation of sexual relations was central to the development of particular kinds of colonial settlements and to the economic activity within them" (1989, 637). Because of the centrality of Jewishness to the Israeli state-building process, to the project of Hebrew labor, and the Jewish family unit as such, intermarriage was discouraged even before 1948. Historically, the construction of *goyim* (Gentiles) is directly linked to enemies, hate crimes, and opposition to mixed marriages.[7]

Marriage in Israel is under the jurisdiction of religious courts in Israel. Marriage between Jews and Palestinians in Israel, as is marriage between people who are members of different religious communities, is illegal. The legal prohibition of mixed marriages is not only a religious matter but also a political one that defines and maintains the social and racial supremacy of Jewish citizenry. Within a framework of legal and administrative measures of segregation in work, education, and housing systems and spaces, the possibilities of close relationships developing between Jewish and Arab citizens are very limited even within mixed cities. As a result, mixed marriages remain scarce and, because they are legally prohibited, have to take place outside Israel. Even though interfaith marriages are recognized upon the return of the newlyweds, not being able to marry within Israel confronts many people with challenges, including financing a wedding abroad and the ongoing social stigma attached to mixed marriages, even among friends and family members. Despite the fact that interfaith weddings remain scarce, numerous Israeli politicians have publicly attacked initiatives promoting miscegenation, as it is widely perceived as undermining the Jewishness of the state.

One of the most public counterinitiatives was the government's launch of a television and online video campaign in 2009, which urged Israelis to inform Jewish friends and relatives abroad who were "at risk" of marrying non-Jewish partners.[8] Hostility toward mixed relationships of this kind is common, not only among high-ranking officials, but also among the mainstream Israeli public, of which, in 2007, more than half believed that intermarriage was equivalent to national treason.[9] The biggest counterinitiative is Birthright Israel—a program that covers all expenses in bringing to Israel every Jewish boy and girl outside Israel with the explicit goal of encouraging their Aliyah and settling in the country. Central to the program is the idea of matchmaking in order to bolster the Jewish Israeli birthrate in the demographic race between Arabs and Jews.

In Jaffa, I met Sabiha, a feminist scholar who proudly identified as Muslim. She told me her incredible life story and how she had met a Jewish American man, David, who, in order to live with her in Israel, had made Aliyah. Upon his return to the country as a new citizen, however, he converted to Islam so they could get married and, as Sabiha phrased it, "be closer together." The couple had made use of the Law of Return in order to naturalize Sabiha's boyfriend as quickly and smoothly as possible and, shortly afterward, undermined its very goal (that of a Jewish demographic majority) through David's conversion, which ultimately meant that any of their children would be Muslim too. The fact that I did not come across any stories comparable to Sabiha and David's does not diminish the size of the loophole in the plan and couples' ability to bend the rules to their own advantage.

Zionist anxiety about Arab-Jewish relationships has a significant impact on Jewish Israeli women too. Their role as transferrers of Jewish blood and identity causes them to be regarded as particularly threatened by and in need of protection from Arab men. As a result of the taboo against Jewish women dating Palestinian men, most such couples keep their relationships hidden even from their closest friends and family members. The only married couple of this kind that I met throughout my fieldwork decided to move abroad after they had their first child.

This hostility of Jewish Israeli citizens to mixed relationships is widely shared throughout Israel and the settlements. In Pisgat Zeev, for example, a large Jewish settlement in the midst of Palestinian neighborhoods in East Jerusalem, settlers have gone as far as forming a vigilante-style patrol named "Fire for Judaism" to stop Arab men from mixing with local Jewish girls. Schools actively participate in the demonizing of mixed relationships: In Kiryat Gat, the municipality has launched a program in schools to warn Jewish girls of the dangers of dating local Bedouin men. The girls are shown a video titled "Sleeping with the Enemy," which describes mixed couples as an "unnatural phenomenon." Notably, Kiryat Gat's antimiscegenation program is state-sanctioned and operates in collaboration with the Israeli police.[10] As mentioned earlier,

Zionist activities to prevent romantic interest between Jews and Palestinians also target school curriculums, which was demonstrated in the Ministry of Education's banning of Dorit Rabinyan's novel *Borderlife*, a love story about a Palestinian man and a Jewish woman (see chapter 4). Ministry official Dalia Fenig's statement highlights the idea of protecting the Jewish nation and Zionist notions of assimilation of the indigenous as central to the ministry's decision to bar the book from Israeli high schools: "Adolescent youth tend to romanticize and don't have, in many cases, the systematic point of view that includes considerations about preserving the identity of the nation and the significance of assimilation."[11]

The Zionist hysteria about protecting Jewish women from Arab men has led the government to prohibit Jewish women from volunteering as part of their national service at hospitals at night, when they might be more vulnerable to Arab workers and doctors.[12] The fear of the "black rapist" is a classic colonial strategy that many other colonial contexts have drawn on, and in which colonizers' accusations of rape have not matched the actual number of sexual assaults on white women.

As mentioned previously, black Palestinian women in particular are discriminated against in the context of marriage, and even more so in the context of mixed marriage. Many black women shared stories with me about how they were tolerated as girlfriends of white Palestinians only as long as their boyfriend's mothers thought the relationship was not serious. Perhaps coincidentally, all the black women I interviewed happened to be between their late thirties and midforties and single. Violet, a successful social worker who was widely known for her work in the black community in Palestine, had been in a relationship with a nonblack Palestinian from her local community who was significantly younger than she. Her story illustrates the central role that race continues to play in the context of marriage:

> At the same time, a white man asked for my hand in marriage. And his family was very angry . . . and I understood. It was not the age . . . it is quite common for us to have two partners who get married with a big age gap. The mother of this person was a very religious woman and she gave lectures at the deaf center. She had two deaf children and I translated there, too. She was talking all the time about prophet Mohammad and Hadija and I thought, "Okay she won't disagree because of the age gap." So, it was clear for me that it was not only the issue of the age gap. It was a gap of twenty years . . . and one of her children asked her, "But what do you think about the age gap (between Hadija and Mohammad)?" and she said, "Nooo, Hadija was a special woman . . . she was beautiful, she was rich, she was intelligent."

And I translated the conversation. . . . Then I understood why she was against our marriage. We loved each other and were together for three years. Then he ran away to the US because he has family there. He was there for two years, and his mother also went there to talk to him that it couldn't be and we broke up.

Expressions and notions of Othering through sexual control, which takes places along real and imagined social and racial identities, is very common among people from all religious, education, and class backgrounds. Importantly, they include imaginaries of identities that are constructed along the lines of north and south, according to which Palestinian women from the north, particularly feminists, are constructed as nontraditional, if not slutty by people from the south. Conversely, I noticed that some Palestinians refer to people from the north as more modern and less traditional or less backward than people from the "wild south." Inas, a young teacher from the Galilee who had moved to Bi'r as-Sab' for a new teaching position, explained:

I was in a relationship with a guy from Jerusalem for seven years. We met each other's families. At some point, I was refused (rejected) by his sisters and his mother. They probably didn't expect it to become so serious. I asked him later, "Why was I really rejected by your mother?" and he said, "Because you're from the north." His mother is educated, she is a teacher, and his sisters work for the UN. They are all really feminist in a way. . . . He said, "Honestly, my mother never really felt comfortable with people from the north—it's very complicated." His mother had a very big impact on him. Maybe he got tired of fighting at some point?

Both stories illustrate the central roles that mothers play as gatekeepers of marriage who serve to maintain social order. Nevertheless, social order has its cracks, and mixed marriages, despite the big array of challenges that they commonly entail, do take place. Even though my insights are too limited to say whether the number of mixed marriages is increasing or decreasing, I met mixed couples in all kinds of circumstances: Palestinian women married to or in relationships with Jewish men, Bedouins from different families marrying each other, a Bedouin woman who had married a non-Bedouin, a Jewish woman who had married a Palestinian man, a Muslim woman who had married a Druze man, and many others. Such mixed relationships not only challenge the plan made for Palestinian women by their ethnic or religious communities but also disturb the Zionist sectarian strategy of dividing and conquering the Palestinian population in Israel, which fundamentally relies on the ongoing separation of Palestinian communities.

"FREE LIKE A BUTTERFLY":
ALTERNATIVE FAMILY MODELS

While in other settler societies, such as Australia, the call for the settler community has also been to populate or perish (de Lepervance 1989), Israeli pronatalist policies are closely linked not only to the settler colonial strategy but also specifically—often in problematic ways—as some kind of compensation for the Nazi holocaust (Kanaaneh 2002, 45). The sentiment is reflected in the state's celebration of Israel's Jewish population passing the 6 million mark for the first time in 2013 and also in the construction of Jews who do not have children, or who have non-Jewish children, as contributing to a demographic Holocaust (Yuval-Davis 1997, 30–31).[13] There is also a crucial eugenicist discourse, which is concerned not only with the size of the nation but also its quality. That is, Israeli pronatalism is also marked by a logic of racial hierarchy that is reflected in its history and strategic use of adoption not only as a means of maintaining and increasing the Jewish population but also to construct a certain kind of Jewish population. During the so-called Yemenite Children Affair in the 1950s, for instance, thousands of babies of newly immigrated Jews from Arab countries were taken away from their parents (who were told that they had died) shortly after their birth and given to wealthy Ashkenazi Holocaust survivors.[14]

As mentioned earlier, the institutionalized and legalized prohibition of mixed relationships, and thereby mixed offspring, in Israel serves the purpose of preserving the Jewishness of the state and the Jewish identity of its people. According to Judaism, this identity materializes in the blood of Jewish women through which Jewishness is passed on to biological offspring. The pivotal role played by Jewish women's bodies, that is, the Jewish womb, as an instrument of religious conversion is demonstrated, for instance, in the fact that an increasing number of Jewish couples in Israel, particularly Haredi couples, use artificial insemination from a non-Jew donor abroad.[15]

In order to reproduce the Jewish population and privilege, the State of Israel strives to control its demographics by explicitly favoring traditional family units and sexual normalcy. In their widely cited essay, "The Politics of Reproduction," Faye Ginsburg and Rayna Rapp write, "concerns over the eugenic control of the individual and social body long precede the development of modern reproductive technologies. Nineteenth century Euro-American Victorian mores at home and imperialism abroad helped to construct and maintain racial and class categories through the control of reproduction" (1991, 315–16). Because alternative—nonbiological—family planning in Israel constitutes a threat to the Zionist settler colonial order, it is subject to strict laws and regulations. Israel's adoption law of

1971, for instance, made interreligious adoption illegal by requiring that (heterosexual and legally married) adoptive parents be of the same religious group as the biological mother. It then follows that surrogate mothers must be of the same religion as the contracting couple (Kahn 2000, 190). Artificial insemination in Israel was initially used primarily by heterosexual couples when the man was sterile. Today, it is increasingly used by lesbian couples and single women, who make up 85 percent of Israeli sperm bank clients.[16]

While new medical technologies can enhance family planning, particularly women's and children's health, and cure infertility, they are also methods of surveillance and regulation (Ginsburg and Rapp 1991, 314). Israel's desire to win the demographic race is reflected in its having more fertility clinics per capita than any other country (Kahn 2000, 2) and as a result performing the largest number of in vitro fertilization (IVF) cycles per capita in the world.[17] As the main competitors in this race, Palestinians' access to fertility clinics (like access to any other medical facilities) remains restricted, as health care and reproductive state services in Israel have long been organized along the racial lines of Arab and Jew. While, for Israelis, religious identity, the premise of membership in its imagined national community, is passed on through the mother, Arab identity is passed on through the father (Massad 1995, 472). In a mixed relationship, however, paternity is considered more dominant and determinative of ethnic identity than maternity. Thus, while the marriage of a Palestinian man to a non-Palestinian woman is often regarded as adding her to the nation, the marriage of a Palestinian woman to a man of another nationality is seen as a loss for the nation, if not treason (Kanaaneh 2002, 71). In a similar vein, the adoption of a non-Arab child or artificial insemination with non-Arab sperm is often regarded with suspicion because of its potential mixing of offspring, as well as religious concerns about adultery if the sperm is from a man other than the husband (Kanaaneh 2002, 222).

In line with Yuval-Davis's argument, it will be shown here that "whether women are encouraged, discouraged or sometimes forced to have or not to have children . . . depends on the hegemonic discourses which construct nationalist projects at specific historical moments" (Yuval-Davies 1997, 29). Palestinian women in Israel both participate in the Palestinian nationalist project of birthing the nation and appropriate Israel's reproductive modernization (Kanaaneh 2002). This section of my book will illuminate a few cases in which women's desired forms of family planning have taken on alternative routes, essentially conflicting with and often resisting both patriarchal nationalist and Zionist expectations for them. Huda's story, for instance, illuminates the perfect interplay between the patriarchal and settler colonial regulation of family planning to the detriment of Palestinian women, making it nearly impossible for her to adopt a child. Over lunch, Huda, a Druze women's rights activist in Jerusalem, told me about her wish and protracted struggle to become a mother. For a long time, she sought information about alternative family planning, she explained, but the odds were against her because of her religious membership, the fact that she was unmarried, and her age:

> I'm not keen on marriage, but I want to be a mother . . . so I tried to adopt so I started to ask people how can I adopt. . . . And I discovered that I had many problems . . . first of all because I would be a single [parent]. . . . This is very much a problem . . . because Israel is very much a conservative state. Second, I discovered that I cannot adopt because I am Druze. . . . By the law of the state, each family can adopt only children from their own religion, so I am a Druze and I have to adopt from my religion. But, in our religion adoption is also forbidden, okay? So, in Israel's eyes (it's) "Okay, you want to adopt? Fine, but just Druze children!" And according to our, my, religion (it's) "You want to adopt? Fine, but *not* Druze children!" So, I cannot adopt a child. . . . After that, I decided to be a foster mom. I did . . . all the procedures, but it was also a problem. They told me it is not a problem for the state, just for my society. If you want to foster a Druze child, you need to live in your community and be married. So, legally, I could not foster a Druze child. So, they told me the only option they have is a child that is defined as "not religious" like some Russian children. So, my chances are very small.

Months later, Huda still had not received any new or positive information from the adoption agencies that she had contacted years earlier. Her protracted struggle for a child eventually meant that she, too, was worried about the age she would reach by the time adoption became a real possibility. The continual lengthening of the process demonstrates the neat interplay of heteronormative hegemonic orders, which, in the end, act to the detriment of single Palestinian women and to the advantage of the Zionist social order, which aims to restrict Palestinian reproduction in Israel.

Nadia, a woman born to a Palestinian mother and an African father, had done what many other Palestinian women in Israel would regard as the impossible, as she decided to start a family out of wedlock with a close male friend, Assad, with whom, she stressed, she had never been in any kind of romantic relationship. Even though she told me about her story with joy and lightness over lunch, she also emphasized the many difficulties and the antagonism that they had encountered, stemming from both the Palestinian society and the Israeli state.

My mother's legacy was always "Be free like a butterfly." I always knew that I
never wanted to get married, but I wanted to become a mom. I was thirty-six
and had returned from the US and I thought about going to a sperm bank.
So, I talked to everybody around asking them . . . [and] everybody supported
me. I felt it. By coincidence, Assad started working in the company I worked
in, and we became good friends, and one day I told him about it. He said,
you know any woman who wants to have a child without getting married? I
said I know many Jewish girls but no Arab women. And I started talking to
my mom, and she said that it would be better for my child to have a father
than not to have a father. We have a parenthood agreement signed by a
judge. We are a family. We go out together, we travel together, sometimes
he sleeps in our house. We call ourselves an alternative family. He has a big
responsibility. He lives in a difficult situation. I worked while pregnant in
the Wadi Nisnas (an Arab neighborhood in Haifa), I went to an Arab doctor,
we were very open about everything. My family supported me until the end.
Without them, I couldn't have done it. It's a single family in a way. Because
on a daily basis, I'm the one dealing with most things. I was pregnant, my
dad was here, my mom was in Africa. Then she came and supported me too.
My friends supported me, my work supported me. My society doesn't owe
me anything. They don't put food on my table. I do. But it was hard on his
family. He had big problems, not me. But he did it. The day after I delivered,
his mother came and said, "Mabruk" (Congrats). And she looks after our
son a lot. That's feminism. For me, feminism is that I can do whatever I want
without anybody asking me, "What are you doing?" while, of course, I am
responsible for my choices, but I don't have to defend myself. When I had my
son, I was thirty-nine, now I'm forty-five. We said that if it's working, we have
to do the same thing [have a child the same way]. We didn't do anything
for a couple of years because Assad was going through a rough period. We
tried again but with no success. And last year I got pregnant, but it didn't
[survive]. . . . So, after that, I was pumped with hormones. . . . Very nervous
and so on and so I decided "That's it, I will only have one child." We thought
about adoption, but things happened to us, the forces from above are
stronger than us and we cannot adopt because to adopt a baby the age gap
has to be forty-three years maximum, so we're too old. . . . I'm an open book.
What's going to happen to me? They will kill me? No, they won't kill me.
They say I'm a whore? So what?! Let them talk. It's so cool to be a feminist in
Haifa. . . . It's "in" to say things like "I'm a feminist and I work with all these
feminist organizations" and "It's the occupation here and there," and I think
that's not right. Everything is the occupation. No, it's not! It's us! It's very
"in" to talk about feminism, but practice it? Nothing. I don't get along very
well with these feminists. I can't stand them. . . . Can you do what I did? No!

They are still waiting for Prince Charming to come along and save them
from the occupation. Come on!

While notions of feminism are entangled in Nadia's story, her relationship to
feminism is complex and contradictory: On the one hand, she rejected feminism during our conversations as it has been advocated by the feminists whom
she knows, while, on the other hand, she demanded some of her own actions to
be recognized as "practices of feminism." Overall, feminist ideology is not as
much of a driving force in women's choices for their family formation as is their
pursuit of personal fulfillment. Nevertheless, it is argued here that while Nadia
resisted feminism as it is advocated by the mainstream feminist discourse, she
did challenge and contribute to altering the meanings of Palestinian feminism
more generally.

Nadia's choice to give birth to a child out of wedlock and raise it within an
alternative family setting resists the imposed gendered roles offered to Palestinian women by both Israeli modernist promises and Palestinian nationalist
recognition of women as the reproducers of the nation. Even though Nadia had
given birth to a child whose father was Palestinian, and thereby added to the
nation, the fact that the child was born out of wedlock defied the patriarchal and
heteronormative nationalist social order on at least two levels: Single motherhood and alternative parenting. Similarly, having chosen artificial insemination, she went against the mainstream sensitivity and antagonism to alternative
reproduction that continues to be regarded as undermining the very foundation of the Arab family even if she is navigating within a framework of social
acceptability (artificial insemination means, technically, her virginity remains
intact). Nevertheless, the risks Nadia took are serious, as having children out of
wedlock, and therefore outside the proper religious and national boundaries,
is frequently regarded as bringing shame on the family, while women who are
suspected of undermining their duty to "birth the nation" are punished in all
kinds of ways (Yuval-Davies 1997, 36).

Nadia therefore resisted what Yuval-Davies has referred to as the "people
as power" discourse, which entails the demographic race between Arab and
Jewish citizens in Israel. Most notably, she did so by choosing a nationality
other than Arab for her son. Instead of providing her son with an Arab status
on his identity card, she decided, along with her child's father, to provide the
child, Minem, with a Portuguese nationality. The option arose because Nadia's father originally immigrated from Guinea-Bissau, a former Portuguese
colony (she herself is also identified as "Portuguese" in her passport): "When
we registered Minem, they asked us, "What do you want us to write?"

I was shocked. . . . I left Assad to decide . . . and he is very nationalist and has his own beliefs. . . . But he said, "You know what, let us make his life easier and write down 'Portuguese.'"

By choosing a nationality other than the father's in order to obtain more rights and future prospects for their child growing up in Israel, Nadia and her partner, in a way, circumvented settler colonial citizenship. The fact that their decision will grant Minem more rights and privileges underlines the specificity of Israeli settler colonial citizenship, which strives to eliminate indigenous identity and land claims. The specificity is that Minem will have more rights and privileges from being non-Jewish "Portuguese" than being a non-Jewish "Arab." Nadia contributed to the blurring of the Zionist categories of settler and colonized.

Moreover, by choosing to select the sperm of a friend rather than acquiring sperm from an Israeli sperm bank, Nadia circumvented participating in Israeli-assisted conception and modernist reproductive discourses. On the downside, raising a child out of wedlock, primarily as a single mother, Nadia had to face additional challenges such as the vivid racist stereotypes of black women as sexually promiscuous. Moreover, by raising a mixed-race child, she defied the racist nationalist eugenicist discourse about the quality of the nation, according to which mixed-raced children are regarded as being of lesser quality. Overall, it can be said that Nadia's family formation defies the racial logic of blood quantum of both Israeli settler colonialism and Palestinian nationalism.

"I COULDN'T BE WITH A FEMINIST": RELATIONSHIPS AND SELF-DETERMINATION

As mentioned earlier, relationships are an aspect of women's personal lives that was reported by Palestinian women as significantly influenced by their feminism. Many feminist and women's rights activists, for instance, described to me the experience of what they referred to as "losing partners to feminism," which they explained as "a price to pay" for being feminists. The price was the cost of their refusal to make certain compromises with their partners, such as the traditional constructions of husband and wife roles, which their partners clearly expressed through expectations of a gendered division of labor. Many women had gone through painful breakups and divorces because they had refused to make compromises contrary to their feminist principles and others stated that once they had chosen to go down the feminist road, they considered it very unlikely to find an understanding and supportive partner with whom to start a family.

Abir, a very active and well-known feminist activist and local politician in her midsixties, for example, reflected on her path as a single woman with dry sarcasm, "That is the price to pay in our society. They all adore and praise a strong woman but nobody wants to marry one. I am done with that. I have moved on and focus on my work." Abir's sentiment was common among the women I met, especially those who, as activists or local or national politicians, frequently appeared in public and worked in environments dominated by (both Palestinian and Jewish Israeli) men.

Several feminist activists of the third *nakba* generation whom I spoke with had gotten married before getting involved in women's and feminist groups. A large number of them told me that they had decided to get a divorce when they felt that the gap between their feminist ideology and what they described as a rather traditional married life was getting too large for them to bear. Many of them emphasized that their decisions were not only based on feminist ideology but closely linked to decreasing affection for their partners, which raises the question (which they frequently asked themselves) of the extent to which feminism influences women's emotional attachment, relationships, and love. Marie, a twice-married director of a feminist organization, for example, explained her divorce to me as based on several factors, including her feminism, the continuous stigma of feminists within society, and the decreasing affection she felt for her husband, which, in her experience, all worked in an interwoven manner:

It's part of being at this place [the feminist organization]. Maybe the age . . . maybe the age . . . and, of course, you pay. It opens up questions. Not because I was Arab, but because I was raised in a traditional way in which your aspirations are clear . . . and then it opens up. I mean my understanding was much more open than (that of) my husband's family and I felt it was not the place for me. That the gap between who I am at [name of the feminist organization] and whenever I was with that family was getting bigger. . . . It was getting very difficult to harmonize between these two levels. And maybe . . . I just didn't love him enough. Even then, because of a lack of love, these forces become even stronger. . . . My husband once told me that somebody asked him what I was doing and he told him, "She works in a feminist center," and that guy said, "Wow, I couldn't be with a feminist." And this guy is educated, he works as a lawyer. He's a guy who went to university and in a way, he is exposed to different values and I believe that many men would find it hard to live with a feminist. I think that men, of course, gather their confidence from "being men" and power. It gives them confidence and security. If a woman comes along and does the same thing they do, they are scared. And they very much care about their image. And to be married to a

strong woman sometimes gives you a different image. It looks like you are
being "dominated" by a strong woman.

It is interesting that Marie also raised the issue of her husband's masculinity,
which, she described as somehow threatened by her feminism. It was particularly fragile when exposed to other Palestinian men, not only because they
expressed common negative stereotypes of feminists as "hard work" (for men)
but also when the presence of other men reemphasized the convenience and
comfortableness, if not "naturalness," of the traditional social order of husband
and wife. One of Marie's fellow feminist activists, Khitam, also linked her
divorce directly to her feminism, as she acknowledged that, upon reflection,
at the time of her marriage, she was going through what she called an "angry
feminist phase." It is worthwhile to note that she compared the ways in which
she communicated her feminist principles to her ex-husband to the militant
Zionist rhetoric, which, eventually, turned into oppression:

> I would go to abroad for a week to do some work.... My suitcase would
> always be close to the door. I didn't need any permission from my family, so
> I didn't wait for permission (laughs). He was much more traditional, Arab,
> sexist, chauvinist, which I didn't understand. I'm not doing the shopping
> alone ... we're doing it together. And, of course, we're cleaning the house
> together.... So, I was oppressing him actually. With all my feminism and
> orders. These just weren't questions for me. And he would say to me, "You're
> the Israeli. You're my Israeli army. You're oppressing me. And all this
> feminism of yours, you can shove up your ass. I won't be doing the laundry.
> I won't let you turn me into the woman of the house just because you want
> to feel the power." So, yes, feminism can kill relations. In my case, it actually
> killed it. Because I was fighting. And I know how to fight and I know how to
> win the fight. And this was the only fight I didn't win. So, we would have all
> these mountains of laundry all over in the living room and the kitchen. We
> had mountains of dishes. We had dirty dishes lying around for three weeks.
> And, in the end, I did them because I couldn't stand the sight of it all. I was
> just disgusted by it. So, I was losing my wars there. And it didn't occur to me
> to change the tactics of my fight. I was so into this feminist war because I felt
> that I was right. I realized that we had some deep intimacy problems and so
> we did family therapy, cooking courses, massage courses, communication
> courses ... because "education is your weapon." But it got worse and worse.
> And I didn't feel loved most of the time. I felt rejected and neglected most
> of the time. Nagging and demanding ... and not really noticed. And he was
> a very gentle and delicate man. He wasn't macho by nature. Eventually, he
> stopped talking about his feelings. I had a mummy sitting in my house. Blind.

Deaf. Speechless. And it was torture for me not being able to communicate. In this phase, I was an angry feminist. The anger can kill us and our relationships. Angry feminism is a phase we go through, but we shouldn't get stuck in this. Feminism really killed my marriage. I really loved the man and I still love him somehow and it was very painful to leave. And at the moment he said, "I don't love you anymore," he couldn't bear it anymore. I just left. It was shocking. We were together for twelve years. Even though in the end he did the shopping, he did the housework, he massaged, and everything. But something was broken. I realize now I was too young to get married, too young to be with someone like this. It takes a lot of guts to take your things and go. My family said, "Why can't you keep the man? You're smart, you can fix it," but it wasn't our marriage it was my marriage . . . and this is what I understand now . . . that it was my "angry feminist phase." It was all of my anger I put into my relationship. Like "Boom!!—I bombed everything. Then I had more space to take the softened side from it. It was really, really hard.

Feminist principles, if defined as women's pursuit of personal self-determination, affect more than just the relationship making and breaking of middle-class feminists from the north such as Maria and Khitam. A young female Bedouin soccer player who rejected the idea of feminism, for instance, told me about how she had broken up with her boyfriend when he asked her to stop playing football. What differed among the women was the price to pay for acting on their desire for self-determination, which was largely determined by the extent of their socioeconomic independence, their physical safety, and their net of supportive social relations. Druze feminist activist Huda, for instance, emphasized to me that, despite the firmness of her feminist ideas, she still chose not to act on her personal desire: "I do not want to marry a non-Druze and spend my life running away. Also, I don't really believe in marriage. So even if I could marry a non-Druze, I wouldn't do that because I'm a feminist. I was in relationships with non-Druze men and I could not go all the way with them. I'm less afraid today but I still need to hide so much. There are so many obstacles."

NOTES

1. It is worth noting that Israel is still far from achieving equal rights for gay Jewish Israelis. In terms of adoption, for example, although same-sex couples have been legally allowed to adopt since 2008, heterosexual couples continue to receive preferential treatment by Israel adoption agencies. As a result, as of today, only a handful of same-sex families have successfully adopted children in Israel.

2. In 2005, minor exceptions were introduced for special medical or work cases and for children under the age of 14.

3. C. Silver, "Palestinian Families Denied Rights by Israel's Racist Marriage Laws," *Electronic Intifada*, January 27, 2012, https://electronicintifada.net /content/palestinian-families-denied-rights-israels-racist-marriage-laws/10866.

4. "Ban on Family Unification: Citizenship and Entry into Israel Law," *Adalah Newsletter*, October 2003, https://www.adalah.org/en/law/view/511; The Citizenship and Entry into Israel Law, Law 5763, 2003, Knesset of Israel, unofficial translation, http://www.knesset.gov.il/laws/special/eng/citizenship _law.htm.

5. Conversation with befriended lawyer who specializes in family law in Israel, Haifa, March 17, 2014.

6. N. Canetti, "Jewish-Muslim Couples Tell Their Stories," *Al-Monitor*, October 26, 2015, http://www.al-monitor.com/originals/2015/10/israel-jewish -muslim-mixed-couples-violence-acceptance-media.html.

7. N. Hasson, "Vandals Slash Tires of 34 Cars in Hate Crime in East Jerusalem," *Haaretz*, March 24, 2014, http://www.haaretz.com/israel-news /.premium-1.581633; V. Lee, "Love in the Time of Racism: The New, Dangerous Low in the Campaign to Stop Interracial Relationships," *Haaretz*, April 25, 2013, http://www.haaretz.com/israel-news/love-in-the-time-of-racism -the-new-dangerous-low-in-the-campaign-to-stop-interracial-relationships .premium-1.517545.

8. "Israeli Ads Warn against Marrying non-Jews," uploaded May 21, 2012, accessed May 15, 2021, https://www.youtube.com/watch?v=XQ1ru59M8BA.

9. J. Cook, "In Israel, Intermarriage Viewed as Treason," *Electronic Intifada*, September 25, 2009, https://electronicintifada.net/content/israel-intermarriage -viewed-treason/8459.

10. S. Freedman, "Israel's Vile Anti-miscegenation Squads," *Guardian*, September 29, 2009, https://www.theguardian.com/commentisfree/2009 /sep/29/israel-jewish-arab-couples.

11. *Guardian*, "Novel about Jewish-Palestinian Love Affair Is Barred from Israeli Curriculum," January 1,2016, https://www.theguardian.com/world/2016/jan/01 novel-about-jewish-palestinian-love-affair-is-barred-from-israeli-curriculum.

12. M. Zonszein, "Jewish Women Can't Volunteer at Night—to Avoid 'Contact with Arabs,'" +972 *Magazine*, October 17, 2013, http://972mag.com /jewish-women-cant-volunteer-at-night-to-avoid-contact-with-arabs/80527/.

13. H. Sherwood, "Israel's Jewish Population Passes 6 Million Mark," *Guardian*, January 1, 2013, https://www.theguardian.com/world/2013/jan/01 /israel-jewish-population-six-million.

14. J. Cook, "The Shocking Story of Israel's Disappeared Babies," *Al Jazeera*, August 5, 2016, http://www.aljazeera.com/news/2016/08/shocking-story-israel -disappeared-babies-160803081117881.html.

15. D. Even, "Sperm from Foreign Donors Generates More Pregnancies than Israeli Sperm, Study Finds," *Haaretz*, June 19, 2012, http://www.haaretz.com /israel-news/sperm-from-foreign-donors-generates-more-pregnancies-than -israeli-sperm-study-finds-1.437198.

16. Y. Avivi, "Israeli Sperm Donor Crisis," *Al-Monitor*, February 26, 2014, http://www.al-monitor.com/pulse/originals/2014/02/israel-sperm-donation -judaism-pregnancy-fertility.html.

17. See "IVF Israel," https://ivf.co.il (accessed January 19, 2022).

SIX

—ᗯᘉ—

DEFYING THE PLAN

Feminist Selves?

This chapter explores the role of feminism and the emergence of a new Palestinian national subjectivity of women's intimate politics and the decision making about the form they should take. The exploration includes questions such as whether to participate in collective or individual practices. In order to shed light on how and whether women construct themselves as feminist selves, I will discuss personal narratives of feminism expressed by individual women rather than drawing on official discourses produced by women's organizations and political groups. Is there a Palestinian women's or feminist movement in Israel? Is there such a thing as a Palestinian feminism in Israel? And, if so, how does it differ from that of Palestinian women in Gaza, in the West Bank, or in exile? These questions came up consistently throughout my research, often brought up by research participants themselves, indicating not only feminist activists' preoccupation with them but also a wider relevance to Palestinian women more generally.

At the time of my fieldwork, there were fifteen actively operating Palestinian women's rights organizations in the country. While not all of them openly identified as feminist, many of their members and much of their staff did. In addition, a large number of individual women whom I encountered outside such organized channels self-identified as feminists. Voices of women who reject the label feminist are also of particular significance, as they unveil many of the underlying social and political particularities of Palestinian women in Israel. The diversity and complexity of Palestinian women's everyday experiences and the notions and narratives of feminism that I collected are manifold.

It is important to understand the historical and political context in which narratives emerge; Palestinian women's activism and feminist thought in Israel neither emerged out of nowhere nor did they ever operate in isolation. In fact, as will be argued here, the Palestinian women's struggle in Israel remains in many ways closely connected to the historical processes that took place before the creation of the State of Israel. While, outside the 1948 boundaries, the women's movement does not define itself as explicitly feminist (Peteet 1991) as it continues to be inextricably embedded within the wider Palestinian national movement, the situation in Israel is slightly more intricate: more than seventy years of settler colonial citizenship have had an undeniably determinative impact not only on Palestinian women's relationship to Palestinians outside the green line but also internally, where Zionist divide-and-rule strategies have buttressed the separatist and sectarian segmentation and isolation of Palestinian communities from each other. Various ethnic and religious communities have always been part of the Palestinian population, but the new extent of Israeli segmentation policies is reflected in the growing disparities between the social and economic needs as well as the political interests of Palestinian women activists throughout the country.

Not much recent research has been dedicated to the accumulation of an in-depth historical account of the Palestinian women's movement as it evolved within the State of Israel since 1948. Remedying the research gap is far beyond the scope of this chapter, but it is vital to at least historically contextualize the current developments of Palestinian women's contemporary intimate politics in Israel. The sociologist Nahla Abdo wrote, in her profound analysis of women's citizenship in Israel, "The history of the Palestinian women's struggle and resistance since the 1920s, including the 1936 revolt, the First Intifada and up to the present time, provides sample evidence to the fact that women's national identity has always been prioritized over their individual or gender identity" (Abdo 2011, 60–61). Assuming that Abdo was referring to women themselves (rather than men or national bodies) who prioritized their national identity over their individual or gender identity, I venture to disagree slightly.

Most of my interviews left me with the overall picture that, while in the Occupied Territories women's liberation was ancillary to national liberation according to classic two-stage liberation theory ("national liberation now, women's liberation later"), the women whom I spoke with inside the green line conceived of their liberation as women as an essential part of national liberation. They frequently presented this notion as being in contrast to the notion of their counterparts in the West Bank. It would certainly be necessary to conduct more in-depth research on the precise concepts of national and women's

liberation, as the meanings attached to both differ significantly not only between Palestinian women in the Occupied Territories and Palestinian women
in Israel but also among the latter themselves. In fact, it is likely to be a grave
mistake to distinguish notions of liberation among Palestinian women in Israel
from those of other Palestinian women, as, in many ways, they develop more in
a reciprocal relationship with each other than in isolation from or in contrast
to each other. For now, however, I think it can be said that the history of the
women's struggle from the 1920s until today offers valuable insights into the diversity and complexity of a rather augmented discourse on Palestinian women's
social and political position, national liberation, anticolonialism, and feminism.

This book takes the view that the women's movement from the 1920s until
today is marked by both change and continuity, and the movement in Israel
from 1948 onward shows both differences and similarities with the movement
outside Israel. One of many continuities in Israel is the protracted and deep-
seated tension that permeates the relationship between the women's struggle
and nationalism. Second, and despite that, under the rule of a settler colonial
state, the struggle for national liberation remains at the heart of the women's
movement. While there has been a tremendous amount of change (much of it
is part of the legacy of the women's struggle) in the achievement of higher levels
of education and the organizational and networking skills of women, a third
continuity that I have observed, and one of the major obstacles to becoming a
fully-fledged movement, is the ongoing internal division and power hierarchy
according to class, race, and religion (even though, throughout the decades,
these have been subject to various levels of change, too).

Notwithstanding internal divisions, there is an important continuity in the
way that a women's movement appears and mobilizes on a large scale and on an
ad hoc basis when it comes to the big themes of the women's struggle. At present, these themes include forced displacement (e.g., demonstrations against
the Prawer Plan; see chapter 4) and violence against women. While the lines
between political, social, and charitable work often remain blurry today (even
though there is a tendency, particularly by women's organizations, to refer
to their work as political), the blurring does not automatically constitute a
disadvantage when spontaneous gatherings and demonstrations are needed.
Already back in the 1980s, Rosemary Sayigh observed that a great deal of Palestinian women's political action is spontaneous and individual, taking place
outside any organization (1987, 14). It appears that this continues to be the
case in Israel, particularly whenever a movement does come to the fore; it is
usually made up of women mobilizing from individual motivation rather than
under the umbrella of an organization. Even though living in Israel hinders a

lot of possibilities for cooperation with other Arab women's movements, a large number of Palestinian women activists continue to see their struggle today as part of wider regional (and today also a global) women's movement. Finally, women's organizations continue to address the state (and international bodies such as the United Nations) in their efforts to fulfill the needs of women that the state has failed to address. In many ways, the situation is very similar to that of the movement as it emerged and developed under Ottoman Empire, the British Mandate government, and immediately after the creation of the State of Israel.

Traces of Defiance? Palestinian Women's Activism, 1920–90

Throughout Palestinian history, Palestinian women have constituted an integral part of the resistance. Their activism in the late nineteenth century was predominantly led by rural women who, in contrast to their urban middle- and upper-class counterparts, enjoyed more freedom, did not veil, and whose economic productivity gave women, especially older women, significant power over their households (Fleischmann 2003, 28). Because of the economic hardship and challenges stemming from the urbanization (internal immigration from the village to the city) of Palestinians at the time, women's organizations founded between 1910 and 1947 mainly concentrated on charitable or religious interests, education, sports, scouting, and labor unions. Nevertheless, in many ways, social work did not take place in a vacuum but can be regarded as a "form of political activity" (Peteet 1991, 55) as nationalism increasingly became a driving force behind the mobilization of women, with the first women's demonstration against the British taking place in 1919. Throughout these early stages of conflict with British imperialist and Zionist forces, Palestinian women's political organization flowed directly from this conflict rather than from organizations led by men (Sayigh 1979).

The Arab Ladies Club was already established in 1921, but the real turning point in the transformation of women's political organization came with the 1929 foundation of the Arab Women's Association (AWA; later Arab Women's Union, PAWU), which established a national framework and served as an umbrella organization for the local branches of the Arab Women's Executive Committee (AWE), which was established in Jerusalem with the aim of founding a women's movement in Palestine and which was intended to act as the coordinating and administrative committee for affiliates. The AWE included women from various social strata and religious and regional backgrounds, yet most of the leading women lived in cities and were educated and wealthy. The AWE was not active much beyond the early 1930s, but before then it played a central role in how women began to initiate a movement that allowed them to seamlessly appropriate nationalism and politicize their experiences of working within the framework of charitable societies and other association structures. The project largely failed from inner tensions about its agenda (charitable versus political), identity (religious versus secular), and continual complaints from rural women, who felt that they were not seen as potential and equal members but, rather, as clients and objects of charity (Daoud 2009, 50).

Palestinian women's actions turned more radical and militant during the revolt of 1936–39, especially so in the case of peasant women who were arrested in large numbers for arms smuggling, the possession of weapons, hiding rebels, writing threatening letters to police forces, and also for physically defending their villages from Zionist attacks. Despite urban elite women's reluctance to transgress the prevailing social norms at the time and a less public expression of their actions, these actions were nevertheless politically significant. They included the collection funds for the revolt, the enforcement of the strike, the coordination of resources throughout the country, the writing and mailing of printed protest and condemnation letters to the government and to international observers, and networking with other women's groups in the region via the press and the telegraph (Fleischmann 2003, 128). The AWA concentrated its efforts on reaching out and connecting the villages. It initiated numerous demonstrations and intervened on behalf of women who were arrested, often getting their sentences reduced. One of the most striking means of women's defiance at the time was through the strategic exploitation of British fears about world perception of the way they got women's demonstrations under control. British attempts to use Palestinian patriarchy to restrain the women's militancy very much failed, and they often found themselves embarrassed by the public perception that they were attacking peacefully demonstrating women (Fleischmann 2003, 161).

The legacy of Palestinian women's activism before 1948 was shockingly severed by the *nakba*, the aftermath of the 1948 war and the establishment of the State of Israel, when vast material losses caused the decay of social and political institutions, and Palestinians in Israel devoted their efforts to survival under a Zionist military rule. Palestinian women's groups were active at the forefront of survival efforts by providing aid to internal refugees. In many ways, Palestinian women constituted the primary victims of the war, as their lives became increasingly controlled by male family members, while at the same time strategic assaults of women's *ird* (women's honor) and attacks on their families ensured that Palestinians would flee their homeland (Peteet 1991, 59). The Zionist strategy of targeting and isolating women also aimed to put a halt to their active role in the national resistance by pressuring families to oppose their women's involvement, a strategy that French colonialists, for example, used in Algiers but that Zionists also deployed during the first Intifada in 1987.

Already in 1948, Al-Nahda al-Nesa'yya (Women's Renaissance Association, WRA), an organization focusing on legal issues, was established in Nazareth. Its specialness lay in its ability to mobilize women in order to publicly demonstrate against the military government and its discriminatory treatment of Palestinians at a time of insecurity and fear. In 1951, WRA was the first Palestinian women's organization to merge with a Zionist women's organization, Progressive Women, an organization associated with the Israeli Communist Party, which in 1973 was renamed Democratic Women's Movement (DWM; TANDI in its Hebrew acronym). At its heart, DWM raised political awareness and actively worked to fight domestic violence and improve women's access to education. Remarkably, Palestinian women also participated early on in meetings provided by Na'amat, the largest Zionist women's organization in Israel at the time. Again, it is noteworthy that the main goal of the organization was to fight violence against women (Daoud 2009, 56).

In the 1970s and 1980s, Palestinian women entered university education in vast numbers, which translated into their growing participation in Israel's labor force, as well as into increasing personal freedom, movement, lifestyles, and mobilization (Daoud 2009, 69). The First Intifada sparked an outstanding amount of national awareness and caused the second generation of Palestinians living in Israel to raise questions about their heritage that many families had stopped communicating about. Palestinian women were particularly active but also increasingly cautious to raise their voices and demand gender equality within a national resistance movement that continued to be led and dominated by men. The active roles played by Palestinian women in the Occupied Territories had a particular impact on Palestinian women in Israel. In a new complex reality marked by unrest and upheaval, their contact with Jewish women intensified; while discussions of patriarchy and sexual violence brought the two closer, particularly within feminist environments such as Isha L'Isha (1983) in Haifa, or Women Against Violence (WAV, 1988) in Nazareth, controversial debates about politics and peace movements often demonstrated a prioritization of national over gender interests. Overall, the spread of feminist discourses among Jewish Israeli women and organizations had an undeniable and significant influence on Palestinian women, even though discussions of feminism, nationalism, occupation, and war brought the two groups together even when it separated them.

Palestinian women's political activities in Israel have flourished from the 1990s until today within the framework of women's organizations, Palestinian civil society, and also conventional political bodies, as well as in the Islamic movement. Among the three hundred active registered Palestinian associations in Israel, about twenty focus on women or include gender issues in their objectives (Daoud 2009). Openly feminist Palestinian organizations remain few—the first being established with al-Fanar in 1992—and their main target remains fighting sexual violence and femicide within the Palestinian society. They continue to struggle with external and internal tensions over funds, personal politics and competition, ideologies, and agendas—something that very much echoes earlier challenges of the women's movement and can be led back to its persistent reproduction of inner power hierarchies and forms of oppression along the intersecting lines of gender, class, and religion but also region and race. As Rosemary Sayigh notes, "a great deal of women's political action is spontaneous and individual, taking place outside an organization" (Sayigh 1987, 14). Her observation remains particularly true in the case of the many women who reside in the rural north, Bedouin women in the south, women from weaker socioeconomic backgrounds but also black and sometimes religious women, whose activities to fight gender injustice remain disconnected and excluded from organized discourses on feminism.

Organized Feminism: The Absence of a Movement (for All)?

Since the 1990s, Palestinian women have set out to seek their own feminism on several levels, the most important ones being organization and ideology. The aspiration for something of their own is based on their specific identity, experiences, and struggle as indigenous women, who, many felt, cannot talk with or mobilize with Jewish Israeli feminists (regardless of some of the latter's antioccupation rhetoric) as if they were at eye level with each other. The emergence of many new Palestinian women's organizations in Israel can also be linked to women's increasing dissatisfaction with the Palestinian nationalist movement, in which many women became actively involved after the First Intifada. Increasingly outraged about the ongoing sexual violence within their own society and the sexism that permeates Palestinian political ranks, the Palestinian art scene, and civil society in Israel, the emergence of organized Palestinian feminisms in Israel must be understood to be seeking something of their own, on the one hand, and a dissociation from hegemonic discourses of both Jewish-Israeli feminism and Palestinian national liberation, on the other.

In Israel, Palestinian women's narratives of feminism take place within the borders of a settler colonial state, in which the women were born and grew up. As was the case before 1948, the core of the feminist movement in Israel primarily consists of middle- and upper-class women who are educated and live in cities. These women initiated the materialization and organization of Palestinian feminist thought and interests by establishing several organizations that popped up throughout the 1990s, most of which were based in the Galilee. Founding members characterized the emergence of Palestinian organizations that worked for the improvement of women's status and access as natural and somewhat inevitable. Many women became exposed to Western feminist ideas through their entry into Israeli academia and Jewish Israeli feminist organizations. Frequently, the latter organizations, which are primarily led by Ashkenazi feminists, provided Palestinian women with a first safe space, particularly in the case of lesbian, transgender, and divorced women, single parents, and abused women. According to one of its founding members, a felt need for Palestinian ownership played a central role in the establishment of Kayan-Feminist Organization, a Palestinian-led women's organization that branched off the Jewish Israeli feminist Organization Isha L'Isha in 1998: "It was about 'ownership' of a space in which Palestinian women only could speak freely, feel safe to come out of the closet, etc. So far, they could only do so in Isha L'Isha. They still do . . . feminists prefer to stay in their safe space and avoid the ego battles of Palestinian spaces." What is interesting is that, within the Bedouin community, the need for Bedouin women's organizations was explained to me not so much in terms of "ownership" but in terms of taking the wheel of an already ongoing historical process. Among the Bedouins, many women linked Palestinian feminism in Israel not to that of Ashkenazi, Mizrahi, or Sephardi Israeli women (in fact, none of them did) but to wider developments in the Arab world and globally.

Nevertheless, whether to cooperate with Jewish Israeli feminists and Israeli civil society more generally remains a matter of much debate and significance, but most of the women I interviewed prefer not to work with them. The reasons revolve to a great extent around the roles of organizations, funding, and ownership of those organizations, but, above all, the very common sentiment that Palestinian women do not feel as if they could cooperate as equals—despite the fact that Jewish Israeli women call out to them in order to "fight nationalism together." Within Jewish Israeli women's organizations, global sisterhood rhetoric of a united struggle against patriarchy and all nationalisms is still very much present. This rhetoric is problematic in that it remains ahistorical. By putting Zionism and Palestinian nationalism on a par and assuming that Jewish Israeli and Palestinian women are equally threatened, it fails to acknowledge the ongoing *nakba*. "For now, I cannot work together with Jewish women as 'equals.' We are not equals. We are not equals among Palestinian women either. This civil society is all about 'fusion' and 'coexistence'—that is what is perceived as sexy. Fusion of Palestinian or Arab-Israeli and Israeli citizens.

But it cannot work," explained one feminist lawyer to me. Another woman mentioned that, while she hoped that one day there would be more collaboration with Jewish Israeli feminist groups, she also openly admitted that working with Israeli activists is an emotional challenge. "We try to compensate a lot— we don't want Israelis to participate in the Prawer Plan demonstrations because we have been humiliated too much by Israelis. So, we take revenge that way . . . on the activists."

Among Palestinian feminists, the longing for a Palestinian feminist movement was frequently expressed. One of the most recent initiatives to create such is the Palestinian Feminist Forum, which works to unite individual feminists rather than organizations under one umbrella in order to make Palestinian feminist thought and activism more accessible throughout the country. To accomplish that, the forum does not function as an organization but almost like a club or association of individuals who have to agree with its principles and manifesto and formally apply for membership. The forum has no fixed physical space, but meetings take place in a different location each time all over the country to allow a greater variety of women to participate. It serves as a platform in which individuals can initiate projects such as the flash mob against violence against women in Nazareth in early March 2014.

As the former coordinator of the forum explained to me, the Feminist Forum was initiated in the early 2010s under the umbrella of Shatil, the New Israel Fund's Initiative for Social Change, which had asked the prominent Palestinian feminist A. H. to ask around within Palestinian civil society about the practical and organizational needs of Palestinian feminists in Israel. Initially, the forum sought to coordinate between the Palestinian women's rights and feminist organizations in Israel but, after a year of discussions, members of the forum decided that more important issues needed attention. Throughout the first three years, about fifty women discussed what the forum should look like, who would be allowed to apply for membership, whether membership would be strictly offered to women only, and whether it would be a Palestinian-only space. It was agreed in the end that only Palestinian women could apply and also that the forum should lose its attachment to the Israeli umbrella organization. The central need that was identified was having a space in which the feminists could speak about the things for which there was not time during the daily life of organizations, what one of the forum members referred to as "higher questions":

> We felt that there was no feminist movement inside of Israel and it was a big question for us, "Why don't we have a feminist movement?" So, this forum is trying to start [to] give a push for a feminist movement inside of Israel.

You know the UNSC 1325? If you want to apply UNCSC 1325 we asked ourselves . . . where do you put Palestinian women? Are we on the Israeli or the Palestinian side? And we needed a say on this. Other NGOs are busy . . . working on different projects. Instead of having and practicing an ideology, you are a social worker or a project coordinator. You work from 9 a.m. until 6 p.m. The forum tries to speak about things that are not spoken about . . . and sometimes the feminist organizations are very limited in terms of their audiences, for example, the lesbians. I know that many feminist and women's organizations want to raise this issue, but they hesitate and now they can still speak about this, but under the umbrella and in the name of the forum rather than "this organization said that." After two years of gatherings and discussions we wanted to open it to feminist activists not only NGOs.

The forum functions well (noting that most of the communication takes place online), has maintained a relatively stable membership (today there are more than 120 members, though the active members number no more than thirty), and has a noticeably very specific character: While at the opening of the forum women from all over the country were present, including a rather large group of religious women from rural areas, the size of the group decreased sharply over the following two years. The regular meetings, which occur about every two months, increasingly took place in Haifa (where most of the prominent voices of the forum live), and access to the forum remains difficult for women who lack mobility, access to the internet, and the finances needed to participate (transport, time, food, and—when the travel time to the location is long—accommodation). Two members who I interviewed criticized what they referred to as the forum's "white, privileged, liberal and secular feminist politics." One of them said,

I was very disappointed, I felt like it was just another NGO rather than a Palestinian feminist forum. There was a time when many women were marginalized, at the beginning there were many women who were religious, you saw many women wearing a hijab. Today you hardly see any woman wearing a headscarf. The biggest problem is that the so-called feminist movement is controlled by the NGOs, the influence of foreign money and professionalized and competitive neoliberal dynamics. So only privileged women—who has a laptop, who has internet access, who has a mobile phone? Most of the members are middle-class, are aware of the theoretical feminism, first, second, third wave, many are single, many are divorced, most have private rented flats not at home but in mixed cities, most drive a car, so they are independent and mobile, it's pretty white "i.e., privileged." Many times, they get into the "white mind"—secular, privileged, very liberal—and these women are a minority if you talk representation. They do not represent the majority of Palestinian women in Israel. But they control the forum. We control the forum.

As has been noted by feminist theorist bell hooks, women can and do participate in a politics of domination as perpetrators as well as victims (2004, 109). Feminist spaces are not immune from privileges and exploitation. The fact that the forum is dominated by a certain group of women does not come as a surprise when considering the identity categories along whose lines various communities are imagined by Palestinians in Israel more generally. The categories are usually binary, which include

North—South
city—village
white—black
religious—secular
educated—uneducated
Christian—Muslim
wealthy—poor

Many feminists criticize the ways in which communities continue to uphold various stereotypes about each other; for instance, I was told that many residents of Christian villages think of themselves as more modern and open-minded than Muslim villages, which they consider backward; Palestinian mothers in the south sometimes oppose their sons marrying a woman from the north, as they are considered promiscuous. That does not mean, however, that they themselves did not draw on such binary categories throughout our conversations. Criticism of the forum, which evolved around its neglect of true intersectionality and its elitism, but also around the discrimination against black and religious women, can be regarded as a reflection of power feminism among Palestinian women activists more generally. Some members shook off this criticism in an effort to underscore the benefits of a core elite: "Listen, I thought a lot about elites, and I don't think *elite* is a negative word. I think in context of settler colonized society, elites can play a positive role, especially women. Still, we need to be close to the field and include the voices of these women. It's not a negative thing. I cannot say that the forum represents all of the women. We tried. We have some women who communicate with us less, I know that the lesser education, the less the women can participate."

Another issue was generational, as young women did not always feel they were really taken seriously, but also, again, ownership and, more important, the independence from Israeli and Zionist organizations. A young woman, Fiddah, criticized the forum as follows:

> I didn't like the vibe at the forum. This forum was organized by Shatil (the New Israel Fund's empowerment and training center), [which] takes money from the New Israel Fund. . . . Why can Palestinian feminists not organize without this help? Why do we need Shatil to organize ourselves . . . that was the question I had in my mind. But then, I didn't stay long enough to find out more about the reasons behind that. I really appreciate their efforts and achievements though, . . . but you could see the hierarchy. It was a hierarchy of age. And, besides that, it was also a hierarchy of dialects. By saying that, I meant that villagers were alone, Bedouins were alone, and urban Palestinians were alone. . . . It was all about "think global, but act local." . . . With all due respect, talking about LGBT is important, but . . . I think we have more fundamental and pressing issues than advocating LGBT rights. It was a global agenda. The discourse was global. But it was very much detached from what was going on in reality. I'm being very honest here. . . . I think that some of the women had international experiences here and they wanted to embrace this global feminist agenda. And LGBT is so attractive today, so that's why they advocated this. But we still have women who are circumcised, we have honor killings and child marriages—and I'm not underestimating the importance of LGBT, but I think that maybe we should reconsider the agenda. In such a forum, there was an ego war going on about which political parties you work with, so we would take that into the forum. . . . Something else I found annoying, . . . representation: they made sure that there would be a fair representation of the different segments of the Palestinian community. While let's say not always could this add value. Some representatives—the way they presented themselves, they spoke and behaved, even body language-wise—I could tell they weren't on the same page. So, in a way, there were some things that were not coherent. It was also age. Some of the women were pushing their forties or fifties. . . . Some of these figures founded the organization to deal with sexual victims, . . . so you cannot compare someone like this with someone who is twenty years old. It just created another hierarchy, and you could tell.

A leading Bedouin women's rights activist also pointed out the challenge of the disparity of interests and needs, linking that to the notion that there is no such thing as one Palestinian feminism in Israel:

> I will tell you one joke. There is a forum for Arab feminism from the north to the south, where I met all of the feminists you know and we started to speak about women's issues, and so they started to talk about the gays and the lesbians and the sexual rights and the "woman and her body," and I thought

to myself OMG, I'm still fighting to be able to sit in a meeting with men, to be able to decide whether I want to cover my head or not, I struggle with the fact that our villages are still unrecognized, and you are talking about these things! So, after a while, I started to understand that feminist needs come from different contexts. I think my mother is a feminist. She never stopped struggling and she took what she needed. And not only encourages me to study but she said all of the time. . . . I think that every woman who wanted to do something and does it no matter what is a feminist. I don't think that there are some sort of levels of feminism. If you talk about lesbian rights, you are not more feminist than the woman that fights to go to work and her rights to work. It's the same thing, I believe.

The lack of intersectionality inherent in many Palestinian feminist spaces hits women the hardest, and they have to face discrimination on several levels. A black religious Bedouin activist from the south, for example, told me how she traveled to the north for a study day offered by a feminist organization. Two of the organization's members told her that she cannot call herself feminist if she is religious and that she needs to decide. The black women's narrative was very important for her to bring to the table, but, even though many Palestinian feminists are cognizant of the racism that black Palestinians experience, race is still not included in the agendas of women's organizations.

NARRATIVES OF FEMINISM: WHAT KIND OF LIBERATION?

Even though during our conversations women proudly identified as Palestinian, their disappointment with the national movement was apparent at all times and was most clearly expressed in their rejection of nationalism and all the negative associations they had with nationalism. I found that the central agenda of Palestinian feminists—as expressed in their personal narratives—is not so much to make space for women in the movement for national liberation, but, instead, to create a national subjectivity of their own making, a movement that is by its very nature feminist. One interviewee expressed the sentiment as "To be 'Palestinian' is to be free as a woman." In other words, for a Palestinian woman in Israel to identify as feminist entails not only the struggle against gender inequality and sexism within the national movement but also the struggle to resist Zionist settler colonialism on Palestinian women's own terms. Still at an early stage, this Palestinian feminist discourse provides a space in which women are able to imagine the nation as indigenous women on their own terms—independent of both Jewish Israeli feminist and Palestinian nationalist discourses.

Many Palestinian women whom I met identified as feminists from a position of privilege in comparison with other Palestinian women. For instance, they were born into wealthy families that enjoy a high socioeconomic standing. They were provided with opportunities such as higher education and the freedom to choose their own paths in regard to work, the choice of a partner, and choices of how to build their own families. Most of these women have been exposed to Western feminist ideas and are very familiar with gender and feminist theory, having extensively studied or worked in the field. Still, even while taking their privilege into account, I did not encounter a single woman who did not have to pay some kind of price for supporting the feminist project.

These women's definition of feminism had been significantly affected by their exposure to Western feminist thought, as they commonly divided themselves into liberal and radical camps. The former defined feminism using the terms *freedom, equality*, and *justice*, but the latter rejected the idea of *equality*, as they argued that the notion was fundamentally flawed and opposed to what they regarded as true justice and participation. In other words, rather than advocate an equal share of participation for women in existing systems, they called for a radical restructuring of the systems themselves. An important emphasis was that the nature of their ideology did not always translate into action. For instance, Ameer, a staff member of a women's rights organization and feminist activist, admitted that, while she supported radical feminist ideas, she was more of a liberal feminist in terms of how she lived her daily life. When asked about how she would define "feminism," she responded, "What does feminism mean to me? Equality and freedom. Freedom to do whatever you want regardless of the gender role that others suppose you should fulfill. But feminism is not only about a woman . . . it is also that the man feels free to put on lipstick or go out on the street doing whatever he wants. Feminism is not only for women but all of society."

Equality and freedom also played central roles in other women's definitions of feminism, such as Nabila's, a colleague of Ameer, who also stressed the importance of the freedom to abandon traditional gender roles.

> I think that feminism means to me that I want justice in the society and I
> want a society that treats women with respect and that treats women and men
> equally and that women can achieve whatever they would like achieve. I have
> one girl, she is two years and two months, I don't even look at her as a girl or a
> boy and I don't care. For me, she is a human being. Society tells her to be this
> as a girl or that. But, still, I see that she is a human being to me at the end of
> the day. Of course there is something very beautiful about men and women
> but I also think that everyone carries some parts of both within themselves.

And it's the same with the Arab-Jewish thing, I want to be treated not as an
Arab or a Jew but as a human being. Call me a romantic . . . but because of the
situation we're in, I don't have this privilege. Because of the situation I am a
female Arab Palestinian.

Nabila also linked the subordination of women within Palestinian society to
the subordination of Palestinian citizens in Israel. Similarly, Haneen, a social
worker in her mid-thirties in Nazareth, connected her ideas of radical change
for Palestinian women to those of Palestinian citizens in Israel more generally. Unlike Nabila and Ameer, however, she criticized the notion of equality
and, in its place, called for a fundamental restructuring of society. She sharply
criticized the mainstream equality rhetoric as a maintenance mechanism for
wider unequal, structured, and institutionalized power relationships. Discussing both citizenship and women's issues, she argued for a questioning of those
discussion frameworks and a radical restructuring thereof:

> I think it [feminism] is about not being content with only equal rights
> because it is not about equal rights or opportunities. It is about the whole
> structure, about how the whole society works. And radical feminism, as
> you know, doesn't want half of the cake for us to be equal. We want the
> whole cake, we want it all . . . to see the elements, evaluate each and every
> component, and maybe use another recipe, a different recipe. If you want to
> have equal rights what you say is "this community is working" and I want half
> of it. I want to define the rights because, right now, they are defined for me
> in patriarchal ways. And that is not radical, really, it makes a lot of sense. It
> cannot be any other way.

Contemporary Palestinian feminist discourse cannot be regarded as an offspring of Western and Israeli feminist discourse, despite their influences.
Instead, it is argued here that Palestinian feminism in Israel is considerably
engendered by the passing on of oral herstories of women's ancestors and their
experiences of the *nakba*. Palestinian women storytellers attribute feminist
qualities to ancestors and their acts of resistance, frequently bestowing feminist role model functions on them. While some women focused on dismissing
Western feminism as something irrelevant to Palestinian women's lives, others
appropriated the term according to their own experiences and the context in
which Palestinian feminisms, despite not having been referred to as such, date
back to well before the establishment of the State of Israel.

"To be Palestinian is to be free as a woman" captures the widely proclaimed
desire by Palestinian women for national and women's liberation to go hand in
hand. This desire is complicated by the fact that Palestinian women cannot be

treated as an undifferentiated category. Thus, a central goal of my research is to widen the discourse of Palestinian feminism in Israel in an effort to include some of the voices that have remained either marginalized or completely excluded from organized women's groups, such as black, poor, trans-, intersex-, and religious women. By considering these women's stories and experiences, internalized and reproduced power hierarchies will be identified, shedding light on the politics of domination that take place among Palestinian women.

A significant amount of the women interviewed for this research had a critical stance toward both the ideology and terminology of feminism. This critical point of view is frequently based on the fact that Palestinian feminism in Israel, as such, is dominated by a powerful group of individuals who are practically all from very educated, middle-class, secular backgrounds and who outspokenly support an ideology that is very similar to Western liberal feminism.

Women who have rejected feminism have mainly done so based on their claim that contemporary Palestinian feminism in Israel lacks an awareness of intersectionality, reproduces power hierarchies, and strives to represent some women without their consent nor their agreement with its principles.

FEMINISM AS NATURAL

Feminism as a Natural Reaction to the Subordination of Women in the Family

Bound to their descriptions of feminism as "natural," many women began their stories about how they became involved in feminism with early childhood memories. They often described how they first noticed and became increasingly aware of the unequal gender relations within their families. As a result, many, even though they did not know about the terminology at the time, said that they had acquired a feminist consciousness as young girls or teenagers. Although one might argue that, with the benefit of hindsight, it is easy for the women to look back and say that what they had obtained was a feminist consciousness (rather than a gender consciousness, or simply feelings of jealousy or injustice among siblings), family constitutes an important space where girls notice their subordination to boys. Palestinian girls go to school, socialize, experience friendship and their first crush, and grow up and long for independence from their families just as boys do. Women's experiences of being treated differently from their male relatives and the ways in which contemporary cultural expectations structure their lives chronologically from school, university, and work through to marriage and child raising all start from childhood.

There are long-standing gendered cultural customs that women have experienced, even those who claimed that they had enjoyed a generally feminist upbringing. For instance, Yaminah, who grew up with her grandmother in the Triangle area, described her upbringing as feminist because her grandmother supported all her boyish passions, such as playing soccer. She struggled, however, with other issues, such as the first son being named for her parents: "Of course, they named my brother after my mother and my father and not me even though I'm the oldest. And I asked my mother and she said, 'they name the boy after us and not the girl' and I remember thinking to myself, 'Okay' [rolls her eyes]. That was my first experience, but I cannot recall another experience like this until I was older."

Many women talked about how they had resisted or rebelled against what they perceived as their clear subordination as girls within their families, turning the family into a space where they first practiced their notions of feminism. Their memories of being treated and raised differently from boys were strong for the women, who often felt that they had been treated unfairly. They frequently constructed a feminist consciousness around those experiences and described how they had resisted this gendered upbringing, for instance, by speaking up or rebelling against family norms. Thus, consciousness and resistance were both part of their notions of feminisms as they emerged through their childhood memories, as another woman, Nizreen, described:

> I have had a big mouth since I was a child. I wanted to become a lawyer from an early age. Also, I felt like I was rebelling within my own society where I felt as a woman I'm not equal to men, especially in my own family. Within my own society I can tell you that the place I was born in there was a clear distinction between men and women: Women were not allowed to go out, to have sex, to have relationships with women. Even in my family, it was clear that if I wanted to do something that wasn't part of going to school or wasn't to do with a family event I would have to ask for permission, which was not always given to me, while my brother was allowed to go out on a Friday night at ten p.m. In fact, if he wouldn't go out, they would think that something was wrong with him.... So, he had rights for which I had to ask and fight and, when I wanted to leave the house at the age of twenty, twenty-one, there was a big struggle because for my parents it wasn't acceptable at all to leave the house without being married. So, the concept of a woman living outside her family frame was unacceptable. So, I had to fight. And in general, I know this from my own home—women are expected to stay at home. There are big expectations for women: they are supposed to be good mothers. If the kids aren't raised well, it is naturally her fault. She is supposed to be a good

cook, a good housekeeper, and if there is an economic crisis in the family, they will also blame the woman. This is often gossip but it is true. If the man cheats nobody will accuse him, if a woman cheats once everyone will talk about it and judge her. But I remember since the age of thirteen, I remember myself struggling all the time. I never accepted that discrimination between men and women. I remember being the only female child in the family who rebelled against this. Even my older sisters, did not rebel against this. They just accepted that.

As a result of these early experiences, the family can be regarded as the first space in which many of the women I spoke with not only started to notice and experience gendered barriers but also started to resist and struggle against them. It is within the family that the women realized that there was a plan for them as Palestinian girls: predominantly, this plan was for them to be "good," obedient girls who stay at home, focus on their education, and accept the privileges given to male relatives of the same age. As Nizreen described it, this consciousness also separates many women from their sisters or other girls who accepted and lived by their families' and community's expectations. The women described how empowering the moments were when they found out about other women who shared their experiences and desire for resistance. While many women described their discovery of feminist terminology, ideology, and organizations as empowering, it was mainly the contact with like-minded women, fellow pioneers, and women whom they could trust with their personal struggles that comforted them. For Afaf, who joined a group of feminist, postcolonial academic women, the realization that other women struggled with the same issues gave rise to an important collective identity, too: "And I was always a feminist . . . in the way that I was interested in women's issues, the way that I was in my family, the organizations I worked for and supported and so on . . . but to see that there are more women like me . . . was okay, it's not just your personal story, there is a collective thing going on . . . Maryam and I, for example, became really good friends."

The family constitutes a space in which the majority of Palestinian women first experience subordination as women and sexist treatment by both male and female relatives. Because families are sources of both suppression and care, they are particularly difficult spaces within which to practice resistance. The majority of the women I spoke with described patriarchal and sexist oppression within Palestinian society as "more immediately threatening" and more likely to cause immediate pain than colonial violence. The question about resisting conventional gendered hierarchies within families occurred in all my conversations, as ideas of women's self-fulfillment were closely coupled with notions

of resisting traditional family norms. The idea of family being the first level on
which to practice and train resistance was aptly captured by a young activist
when she asked the rhetorical question, "How can you explain to me that we
can stand up against the colonizer for years, but you cannot stand up against
your father? I don't want to believe that." bell hooks captured the family and the
sexist power relations that can exist within it in very similar ways in her essay
"Feminism: A Transformational Politic":

> Unlike other forms of domination, sexism directly shapes and determines
> relations of power in our private lives, in familiar social spaces, in that most
> intimate context—home—and in that most intimate sphere of relations—
> family. Usually it is within the family that we witness coercive domination
> and learn to accept it, whether it be domination of parent over child, male
> over female. Even though family relations may be, and most of them are,
> informed by acceptance of a politic of domination, they simultaneously
> relations of care and connection. It is this convergence of two contradictory
> impulses—the urge to promote growth and the urge to inhibit growth
> that provides a practical setting for feminist critique, resistance, and
> transformation. If we are unable to resist and end domination in relations
> where there is care, it seems totally unimaginable that we can resist and
> end it in other institutionalized relations of power—if we cannot convince
> the mothers and father who care not to humiliate and degrade us, how can
> we imagine convincing or resisting an employer, a lover, a stranger who
> systematically humiliates and degrades? (2004, 110–11)

Families also act as sources of support for women who struggle against gendered conventional norms and support many women in their struggle for self-
fulfillment, as Areen, the director of a Bedouin women's organization in al-
Naqab, told me:

> Sometimes my family, with all their expectations for women, do not consider
> my way of living as acceptable for me. For example, they want me to cover
> my head. All my family here—thousands—are all covering their head. But
> I—since I was a little kid—never felt like covering my head. I just didn't like
> it. All the time they push you to cover your head. Sometimes they even use
> emotional blackmail and say, "if you don't cover your head you're no longer
> part of this family." And, of course, I want to belong to this community, this
> is my family—this is who I belong to. I don't want to give up their love and
> their support—I need them. I need them! Especially when living in this
> community and state, and working with Laqiya. I need my family's support.
> So, all the time I needed to work hard to convince my family about what I'm
> doing. So, all the time I'm struggling for a solution that I feel comfortable with.

Class and privilege play important roles in determining the extent to which women can bend the barriers of contemporary cultural expectations. Whether they are from a poor Bedouin community or a member of a prestigious family in the Galilee can have a favorable effect in situations in which women act against these expectations. Such acts, which in other contexts would be categorized as unacceptable behavior, are often forgiven or tolerated by their families or the community because of their social status and power and otherwise good reputation. I came across several examples, such as a young feminist from Haifa, who, despite being unmarried, decided to live with her boyfriend in a shared flat and go out with him while holding hands or kissing each other in public. She said that even though her parents were not a hundred percent happy with the situation, they had made an agreement that she would inform them whenever they went out so that her parents could react in a way that was relaxed and knowing if a neighbor pointed out to them that they had seen their daughter in public with a man.

Another woman, from a prestigious Bedouin tribe, had run away with a Muslim Jerusalemite. While getting married without parental agreement to a non-Bedouin would usually be regarded as a social scandal, and punished with banishment, she was eventually forgiven and her parents even invited her and her husband into their house. A well-known feminist politician from Nazareth also emphasized the central influence that her family's status had had on her life: "I was privileged being born into my family, in comparison with other women in Nazareth. Not only in terms of economics but also to be raised in the Zoabi family, it's a symbolic status. I was always protected by a big family."

"Naturally, I'm a Feminist": Feminism as an Internalized Given

Whenever I discussed the meanings that women attached to feminism with urban middle-class women, I frequently came across statements such as "I was always a feminist," "I was born a feminist," or "feminism is a natural part of me." I came to understand that my interviewees drew on this kind of sweeping statement in order to emphasize two key assertions: first, how important feminism was to them and the way they perceived and lived their lives and, second, that their linking of feminism with naturalness was their way of stressing that they had not acquired some kind of fixed, ready-made feminism, but had *their own* feminism, or a feminism that was natural to them. Such was especially the case for women who claimed that a feminist way of thinking was such a fundamental part of themselves that the word *feminism* or their identification as feminists was, in fact, not important for them anymore. In other words, they perceived themselves as naturally feminist, meaning they did not require or rely on any

kind of schooling in feminism, feminist consciousness raising, or feminist identity in order to understand and struggle against the unequal gender relations
and sexism in their social environment.

It is important to stress that, as mentioned, I collected these narratives from
urban middle-class women, many of whom had entered higher education and
often completed degrees in gender studies and joined or even founded feminist and women's rights organizations. While, of course, they did not become
advocates of feminist politics simply by being born women, the fact that they
regarded themselves as feminists by nature gives succinct expression to a sentiment that was common and is significant in understanding the different ways
in which feminist consciousness comes into play for different women.

From attending several women's groups organized by a feminist organization in Palestinian villages throughout the Galilee, I noticed that there was
a significant class aspect to this sentiment. One of the central goals of these
women's groups is to raise a feminist consciousness among women who are
from poor socioeconomic backgrounds and lack access to education and
work opportunities, mobility, and health services. In these villages, feminist
social workers aim to raise awareness of gender inequality in order to boost
the women's self-confidence and initiate women-led projects. Their projects
take place within organization-led frameworks and are largely funded by an
international community of Western foundations who are currently keen on
promoting women's rights and gender equality at what they refer to as "the
grassroots." During my personal experiences as a fundraiser for a Palestinian
feminist organization, *empowerment* was the term that was commonly used
whenever women educated other women about their rights or feminism. While
the empowerment of women by other women, many feminists might argue,
is problematic, differences in power distribution were clearly reflected in the
language that the women used when describing their experiences of, and relationships to, feminism.

By claiming to be feminists by nature, many city-based feminist activists
clearly distinguished themselves from poorer and less educated women in rural
areas—the grassroots—who, unlike them, were not considered "born feminists"
but relied on more privileged women to empower them by raising their awareness and, eventually, foster a feminist identity and politics among them. In that
way, the claim of naturalness set middle-class women apart from, and essentially
on a higher level than, women whose consciousness, according to the middle-
class women, had to be raised through education. A feminist social worker from
Nazareth described to me the importance of language and identity in her work
with local women as follows: "At our first meetings, the women said that they

are not 'feminist,' but we worked on this. Sometimes the women don't understand the difference between 'feminine' and 'feminist.' Mostly they mean
'feminine' rather than 'feminist.'" Throughout my conversations with women
in the villages, I quickly noticed that even women who had been participating
in the feminist-organization-led groups for years did not use the term *naswiyy*
(feminist), but rather *nisa'iyy* (feminine), whenever they discussed the projects
that they were working on or the ideas that they had for the future.

As Julie Peteet points out in *Gender in Crisis* (1991), the distinction between
feminist and *female* in women's lexicon is telling. Peteet's ethnography about
Palestinian women in Lebanese refugee camps differentiates the "female consciousness" of "those who spoke of women's rights . . . (and) sought rights considered legitimately theirs within a division of labor that assigned to them
domesticity" (1991, 89) from the "feminist consciousness" of women who "advocate transformations in gender relations and meaning as ways to achieve
autonomy and equality rather than simply integrating women into extant
structures" (97). Peteet's interpretation attributes the difference in vocabulary
and ideology to different levels of women's politicization. I argue that in the
context of Palestinian women within the 1948 borders, the difference needs
to be read through the lens of an existing class struggle. I often observed how
rural women's usage of the word *feminine* was looked on (if not frowned on) by
feminist activists from elite backgrounds as a mistake, explained by their poor
educational backgrounds and language skills. But the use of *feminine* instead of
feminist cannot be explained simply as a result of poor women's lack of access
to education about feminism.

Throughout my conversations with rural women, I realized that notions
of feminists as power-grabbing women whose aim for self-fulfillment destabilizes the sanctity of domesticity were still widely held. Women from poor
rural areas are by no means ignorant of the meanings or official definitions
of feminism but often are simply not interested in taking part in any kind of
feminist project. Their interests and, more important, their needs often lie
elsewhere as they strive to attend schools, find work before marriage, and gain
the socioeconomic stability that many feminist activists were born into. As I
observed group meetings, workshops, and seminars about inheritance, health,
and mobility, it became clear that widening the access to and share of women in
these areas builds the foundations of what constitutes women's rights for rural
women. Despite the fact that feminists may argue that fulfilling these needs
is simply augmenting, rather than contravening, the normative consensus on
domesticity, it must be emphasized that, essentially, many rural women are
not interested in destabilizing the balance of domesticity, as domesticity often

constitutes the key space in which they are provided with stability, responsibility, and—as is important to note—self-fulfillment as wives, mothers, and
household managers.

Several long-term feminist activists mentioned during our conversations
that, over the years, *feminism* as a term and an identity had become less important to them. Marie, for instance, had been the director of a feminist organization for more than a decade at the time of our interview, during which I could
not help but get the impression that, perhaps as a result of her long and extensive
involvement with the cause, she was tired of talking about feminism. Even
though the meanings and content of feminism had been somewhat internalized in her way of life, the act of identifying as a feminist, she implied, had in
some way lost its importance as a motivation for her, making space for what she
perceived to be more important incentives, such as love. Marie had no children,
but life for her had become more complicated over the years, perhaps because
of that fact. It is still rather exceptional for Palestinian women to consciously
choose not to have children. Moreover, she had divorced her first husband
and remarried a Druze man—for a nonreligious Muslim like her, to do so is
rather unusual:

> You know ... when you've been involved with feminism for so many years,
> you don't really think of yourself as a feminist.... It's just part of you. Just
> part of how you perceive the reality, and so ... I would say today on a personal
> level I'm not concerned.... It's not that I think of feminist terms on a daily
> basis. Just ... I'm motivated, I behave based on other things ... based on love,
> on other values that I think are much more important to me than ideology.
> Feminism is an ideology. And I think that it is a great analytical tool to
> analyze the society and the structures critically, but sometimes practicalities
> and solutions that are offered in a way lack other values ... sometimes of love,
> sometimes of partnerships, sometimes of the complexity and subsidization
> of life. Feminism for me is a tool to see things, but I don't think it can be a
> comprehensive agenda to provide me with all skills that I need in my life.
> If I say that I'm a feminist, it means that I'm against oppressing women, I
> understand that women are oppressed because that is the widest kind of
> oppression of mankind—and womankind—you might say, and a woman
> should be economically and socially independent, you know? That kind of
> understanding of gender relations in society. But life is not only that—that's
> all I'm saying. I don't have children. Sometimes I talk to women who have
> children and their interest in improving the opportunities for their children.
> Their lives change so dramatically and you see them sacrifice their time and
> they don't question that because they do it out of love. I know a story of a

woman whose daughter was sick and was in the hospital and she was the one
who was spending the most time with the child, much more than the father.
And when I asked her about why she was doing that she said that she didn't
even question it because it was about her child. And in a way I understand
this. Sometimes people's motivations are so different and . . . in these extreme
examples especially . . . stronger than the ideology . . . you could say, "Why is
she sacrificing her time like that? She should be doing her job."

I also spoke to Yaminah, a Haifa-based researcher on land segregation,
whom I was put in touch with because of her background as a long-standing
feminist activist and founding member of one of the leading feminist organizations in Haifa. I was surprised by her dismissive tone about feminism and found
it somewhat similar to Marie's: she had been involved in feminist activism
for decades and, over the years, increasingly found that other struggles were
equally important or more so. Nevertheless, at the same time, one could argue
that she also emphasized the importance of feminism by demanding that we
should all "naturally be like this":

> Whenever people ask me, "Are you a feminist?" I say no, "I'm not a feminist,"
> because I think that, naturally, you have to be like this. This is how they
> educated me . . . being equal . . . that I can say whatever I wanted to say. . . . I
> think that my family and being with my grandmother really structured my
> life and mindset. My aunt is married to someone from Nazareth but lives in
> Tira next to my grandmother. Usually in Palestinian society boys live next to
> their mother, not girls. Also, her husband changed his family name to hers.
> So, when you see all these things . . . you see everything is possible.

FEMINISM AND FAMILY HISTORY

For many of my research participants, discussing their feminisms was inextricably linked to talking about their family history. Usually, women's stories about how they perceived and practiced feminism, or how they resisted
the occupation, would be linked to one specific family member, such as a
grandmother or grandfather. Most of the women had learned the histories of
their ancestors orally, either directly from their grandparents themselves or
indirectly through other family members. A lot of the time, it was clear that
I was not the only or first person to listen to their stories but that the stories
that they shared with me had been told on numerous occasions within and,
at times, outside the family. What stood out especially were the detailed ways
in which my interlocutors remembered and described their family members,
despite the fact that sometimes they had never met them in person. Their

descriptions most commonly included details of physical appearance, smell, touch, food preferences, laugh, dress, and humor but also politics (or lack of interest in conventional politics).

While I was aware of the central role that storytelling and oral history accounts play in the struggle of internally displaced Palestinian citizens who are struggling to return to their home villages, I quickly realized that I had underestimated the significance of oral history both in the struggle of Palestinian women to resist Israeli memoricide and in women's decentering of masculinist nationalist narratives. In particular in the absence of a Palestinian state, which could be expected to devote material and cultural resources to commemorative events, memorialization projects, archives and museums, Palestinian communities have actively promoted commemoration and collective memory as a form of cultural resistance, liberation, and nation building (Khalili 2007). Also, in the face of Israel's obsessive building of museums and archaeological theme parks, together with the mountains of collections of archival sources, Palestinian oral history has proven to be a particularly useful method of decolonization, "not only for the construction of an alternative, counter-hegemonic history of the *nakba* and memories of the lost historic Palestine but also for an ongoing indigenous life, living Palestinian practices and sustained human ecology and liberation" (Masalha 2012, 212).

As in other subaltern narratives, such as those of refugees, peasants, the urban poor, and Bedouin tribes, Palestinian women's memoirs were effectively marginalized until the 1960s and 1970s by the PLO's efforts to articulate one coherent and dominant nationalist discourse that omitted accounts of infighting and collaboration. From the 1970s on, a wave of scholarly works emerged that heavily drew on individual oral evidence, but it was mainly Rosemary Sayigh who pioneered a focus on women's narratives in the refugee camps in Lebanon. Today, a vast array of research attends to Palestinian popular and subaltern history, which presents invaluable insights into the Palestinian women's movement, women's narratives, and gendered memory, such as Dina Matar (2011), Laleh Khalili (2007; Humphries and Khalili 2007), Sherna Berger Gluck (1994), Ahmad Sa'di and Lila Abu-Lughod (2007), Fatma Kassem (2011) and Nur Masalha (2005).

It will be argued here that, while research works are important for recording the subaltern voices that challenge both Zionist hegemonic discourses and Palestinian elite narratives, informal and unrecorded ways of passing on oral history, for instance within families, remain powerful tools of resistance. This is particularly the case for women's histories ("herstories"), which, to a large extent, are kept alive through informal transfer, as they continue to be perceived as complicating male-dominated Palestinian nationalist narratives (Humphries and Khalili 2007). Naturally, such oral herstories, like written histories, are never free from factual error and personal biases. Many herstories that I collected contained elements of exaggeration, romanticizing, or nostalgia. Yet, despite such characteristics, which are in the nature of storytelling, it is argued here that they deserve special attention. In contrast to the majority of subaltern historical narratives in the existing research, the oral herstories that I encountered stood out, not only because they give a voice to Palestinian women's experiences, but also because they enable women to take the roles of storytellers, listeners, interpreters, and protagonists. In the context of women of the third *nakba* generation, the significance of informal herstories lies in the central role they play in engendering women's national, family, and frequently feminist identity.

The Central Role of Grandparents

The importance of historical narratives lies not only in what has been passed on, but also in what has not been passed on. Throughout my conversations with women of the third *nakba* generation, I sensed that that they were sensitive to the deprivation and dispossession of historical memory in particular ways. The reasons for their sensitivity are most likely rooted in the silence of their parents about their personal experiences of national and family history and the hegemonic Zionist educational system in which they were forced to partake. It is not surprising then that many women I spoke with stressed the importance of collecting and passing on their grandparents' memories.

Grandparents' histories play an important role for several reasons: first, in contrast to the women's parents' generation, who were suppressed by the military regime and coerced into being silent and refraining from any political action or talk, their grandparents actually did speak to them, did tell stories, and did answer their questions. Second, the women, who grew up under occupation, found a connection to their land and identity—a rooting—in these stories, as they could feel that they belonged to someplace through them. Essentially, real and imagined homes were constructed and passed on through these stories and with them their struggles for return (i.e., return to their villages). Third, from their grandparents' experiences of the *nakba*, and Palestine before the *nakba*, the women could create connections to a pre-1948 Palestinian identity, including one that was outside Israel. Finally, the women frequently attributed feminist qualities to their grandparents, as they were cast as the central actors, and frequently heroes and heroines, of their stories. Thus, not only a national, but also a feminist, subjectivity emerged from the women's narratives.

Passing on oral history, particularly family history and herstory, plays a crucial role for Palestinian women in both the struggle for national liberation and
women's liberation. Maintaining a collective Palestinian commemoration of
the *nakba* takes on various expressions in Israel today and is deemed particularly important by the generation of women who were born and raised in Israel.
The *nakba* occupies a central place in the Palestinian psyche inside and outside
the Green Line. Palestinian national identity took root long before 1948 (Masalha 2012) and the *nakba* has been a key site of collective memory and history
that "connects all Palestinians to a specific point in time that has become for
them an 'eternal present'" (Sa'di 2002, 177). The narratives that I collected in this
context also demonstrate that it is not only histories but also the accompanying
traumas of the violent rupture of the Palestinian people that can be passed on
and inherited over generations. Thus, oral history functions as an important
vehicle for victims of injustice and violence to articulate their experiences of
suffering and *sumud* (steadfastness) from one generation to another.

Notions of home are predominantly constructed through pre-1948 anecdotes
of home and family passed on from generation to generation. It took me by
surprise how many times the stories bespoke a close bond between women and
their grandparents. Usually, my interviewees would construct around at least
one grandparent their narratives of home past and present, and also their narratives of ways of how to resist the Israeli occupation of their homeland and homes.

Khulud, a student in Haifa in her twenties, told me how her family was
forced from the village of Bir'em years before she was born. Her grandfather
Wassim played a central role throughout our conversation or, as she put it,
"He is the hero in most of my stories about Bir'em." Wassim led the Biremite
initiative before the Israeli Supreme Court to claim the villagers' right to
return but also practiced the right by returning to the village frequently to
rebuild it and reside there. He passed away in 2012, shortly before the revival
of the youth summer camps in Bir'em. In order to commemorate the stories
of her grandfather's generation, Khulud took part in recording and collecting other stories of the Biremite elderly on tape and camera. I noticed that
throughout our conversations Khulud never used the word *nakba*, something
that I read is very common among the first *nakba* generation, who tend to refer
to the *nakba* with phrases such as "when they came" or "when they took us"
(see Kassem 2011, 82), as their memories and stories of the *nakba* never refer
to big historical episodes or processes but are very detailed and include very
specific events.

Nevertheless, I also encountered a few women who could not connect to
their grandparents' histories. In the matter of belonging, specifically, one
woman in her early twenties explained, "The biggest feeling is that I feel I don't

belong to anything: I'm not enough Palestinian, I'm not Christian enough, I'm not Israeli enough." Along similar lines, another feminist called Laila described her feelings as follows: "It's not just that I don't belong to Israel, the trouble is that I don't feel that I belong to the Palestinian people either... I mean the OPT [Occupied Territories]—I have almost never met anybody from there. I feel I'm somewhere between. I cannot say 'I'm Palestinian' like my grandfather can say that he is Palestinian. It's a generational issue."

Feminist Qualities Attached to Family Members

I encountered a large series of narratives among my research participants that attest to Palestinian women acting as powerful agents during the events of 1948. Many of my interviewees cast strong-willed female family members (mostly their grandmothers) in the manifold family histories of the *nakba* that they shared with me. These female actors had usually insisted on staying, returning, or even defending their home and homeland despite the threat of sexual violence. One of my interviewees, for example, began her own story by telling me the story of her grandmother. I was struck by not only how important this story was for the interviewee when talking about her own personal experiences, but also the themes of strength, resistance, humility, and humor in the portrayal of her grandmother as a "super woman":

> I was brought up not to feel like a victim. It's the story of my grandmother. Thanks to my grandmother, we are here today. My grandfather was afraid of what happened to us during the *nakba*, so he fled to Lebanon. My grandmother walked to Lebanon and brought him back. She always made sure that we knew that we had the right to be here, that we had a right to this place, our home. She would always refer to the Israelis as "these Europeans who came and gave us a headache." She hid rebels in her house.

Even though the majority of the self-identified feminists whom I interviewed claimed that some kind of feminist consciousness was required for an action to qualify as feminist, when it came to their own ancestors, they frequently argued that you do not have to identify as a feminist to practice feminism. Many described their mothers, grandmothers, aunts, and sometimes even fathers as "feminist role models," despite the fact that these people did not self-identify as feminists and were not aware of any kind of feminist ideology. Most commonly, practices of feminism were characterized as linked to practices of national resistance. At times, the two were equated or some acts of resistance were perceived as feminism despite the lack of any motivation that could be clearly identified as feminism. As one woman said, "In the Palestinian context, there are so many ways to express feminism, including resisting at home, resisting in your group, and refusing to accept oppression in daily practices."

Remarkably enough, all my interviewees attributed some kind of feminist identity and quality to family members (regardless of whether the person herself identified herself with feminism) and often described them as their personal feminist role models or as the women who had bequeathed feminism to them. In these narratives, feminism was loosely defined as speaking up and resisting various modes of oppression. Often, mothers and grandmothers were portrayed as feminist role models, particularly in the context in which many of them had resisted forced displacement by returning to historical Palestine with their families, taking on men's jobs, hiding resistance fighters, smuggling arms, or acting as decision makers when their husbands had failed to do so. A clear link was also made between feminism and claiming and practicing the right to return to one's home. Safah, for instance, a very successful feminist scholar in her fifties, described her mother's story as follows: "My mother is a feminist. She is my model of feminism. At the time of the *nakba*, my mother was completely alone, a fifteen-year-old little girl. She returned to Palestine on her own—isn't she a feminist? She came back from Lebanon . . . with three little kids. She just said, 'Screw power—I want to go home!' Is this not feminism?"

Yaminah, a feminist researcher, told me about the pain she felt from the recent loss of her grandmother, whom she grew up with. Like many other women, for her, being feminist was about breaking traditional gender roles and expectations. She also attributed the label "feminist" to her grandmother, as she was a super woman who raised nine children by herself. Overall, my interviewees described female relatives as feminist when they had taken on "men's jobs" while taking care of their children, when they managed to deal with extreme challenges by themselves, or when they resisted oppressive power, whereas male relatives frequently qualified for the label by tolerating women's wishes or taking on their share of the work in the household.

> I grew up with my grandmother, and all of my education always came from her; she was a very feminist lady, she raised nine children by herself. She was a widow when she was thirty-two years old and educated them and was the decision maker of the family. For me, that was something totally normal that a woman was taking on this position. My father was a feminist, too, he always took me to play soccer. I never thought that I was less for being a girl, but, when I was twenty-four, everybody looked at me strangely because I acted like a tomboy and there was no difference between me and other children,

including boys. . . . I simply didn't know the other side of it, and I was shocked to see the suffering of women who grew up differently from the way I grew up.

FEMINISM AND NATIONALISM

In his book *The Forgotten Palestinians* (2011), Ilan Pappé writes the following about the role of nationalism for Jewish and Palestinian women's rights activists during the late 1990s: "nationalism was still a potent force, which defined not only the collective but also individual and even gender activism. This predominance of nationalism caused a split within feminist activity in Israel. Jewish feminists saw a-nationalism, or even anti-nationalism, as crucial, but Palestinian women activists felt that, despite the centrality of the gender issue, they did not wish to give up their national framework and identification" (2011, 219). I find this presentation of Palestinian feminists' relationship to nationalism problematic on several levels. First, Israeli and Palestinian nationalisms and their significance for women's rights activists in Israel cannot be measured with the same yardstick. There are significant differences between Israeli and Palestinian nationalisms; one emanates from a highly militarized occupying settler colonial state while the other emanates from a stateless, dispossessed, and largely wiped-out and torn-apart colonized indigenous people. There is a striking and indubitable history of a power and privilege imbalance between the two nations at stake, one that needs to be taken into consideration during any discussion of their nationalisms.

Second, this disparity of power and the specific historical and political contexts of Jewish Israeli and Palestinian nationalism has led Jewish Israeli and Palestinian feminists to attribute a wide array of meanings to nationalism. Because of their historical and cultural migration background, Ashkenazi Jewish Israeli feminists have largely identified with and imported Western European and American feminist ideas. Within these specific settings, feminists perceive their ideology as incompatible with the ideology of nationalism (Kaplan 1997). This sentiment was reflected in my conversations with Ashkenazi feminists, who, as Pappé writes, largely identify as anti-nationalist (2011; 2019).

Throughout the history of the Arab region, however, the struggle for women's rights has always been closely connected to anticolonialist movements and nationalism. Women have been actively involved within these frameworks, which have often provided them with crucial agency. As Cynthia Enloe (1989) has pointed out, national consciousness has induced many women to feel confident enough to take part in public organizing and public debate because, more than other ideologies, nationalism has a vision that includes women. In the national liberation struggles, Arab women, including Palestinian women, have frequently gained a feminist consciousness through their political activism (Peteet 1991). For these reasons, comparing the relationship between nationalism and Palestinian feminists in Israel with that between nationalism and Jewish Israeli feminists not only ignores the specificity of the struggle of Palestinians as indigenous women but also separates them from the larger Palestinian nationalist discourse.

As a result, we need to pay attention to the specific terminology and concepts that women draw on when discussing nationalism. Throughout my fieldwork, Palestinian feminists made a clear distinction between nationalism and national identity. In fact, Pappé himself goes on to quote the prominent feminist leaders Nabila Espanioly and Aida Touma-Suliman, explaining their decision to create women's shelters specifically for Palestinian women as based on a desire "to return to separate frameworks in which we can develop and maintain a distinct *national Palestinian identity*" (2011, 220, emphasis added).

If discourse is any indication, I found that Palestinian feminists' relationship with nationalism is predominantly marked by acute tensions. While all the women clearly expressed and described a close emotional relationship they had with their Palestinian national identity, they just as clearly expressed a profound aversion to nationalism as an ideology, an organizing and mobilizing force of Palestinian nationalism as they experienced it. For many women, this dislike and rejection of nationalism was based on a deep-rooted personal disappointment with the various organized nationalist movements, parties, or other groups that they had supported during the First and Second Intifadas, which had refused to adjust to the women's calls for equality in terms of the restructuring, participation, and representation of women. One seemingly banal statement from a young feminist who ran for the leadership of a Palestinian nationalist society at her university turned out to be rather insightful about the inner dynamics between women and men: "They wouldn't let me run for this position because, guess what, I smoked as a woman and they wouldn't want to lose out on votes because of that. . . . It is still widely unacceptable for a woman to smoke and so they chose a man over me. This guy was a smoker, too! The fact that I worked my butt off the year before didn't matter. We are a fucked community. We don't respect women."

This frustration about continuing gender roles and women's marginalization within nationalist movements popped up in many of my conversations. It was also reflected in, and can be linked to, more general resentment toward the Palestinian political leadership, which many women described as currently being nothing but a "scam" or "tribal politics." Nevertheless, it is important to note that while some feminists boycott local elections as a result, others are keen on "leaving this channel open." Areej, a very successful and locally renowned feminist researcher and activist, for example, was deeply involved in national and local politics, specifically via the Balad party. While she was very much aware of the tension between feminism and the national party, she stressed the importance of her participation in both: "Nationalism is restricting, so it is difficult to combine it with feminism. So, I have different layers. I know this is the 'easy way' out but this works for me. I'm comfortable with this choice. 'In' and 'out' at the same time. Like the Israeli citizenship, we are 'in' and 'out' at the same time. I'm 'Balad' but I'm also feminist. When you say my name, people will think of both . . . 'feminist Areej' but also 'Balad-Areej.'"

The difficulty of being a member in both a nationalist and feminist group that Areej referred to here was also mentioned by other feminists. Central to the tension between feminist and nationalist politics was the fact that women felt that Palestinian nationalism was not gendered as a mere side effect but that its very functioning and ideological underpinnings were structured by the logic of gender. As with other nationalisms, Palestinian women continue to act as symbolic and physical markers of national boundaries. It has been shown that Palestinian women's bodies constitute a central site of the struggle between settler and colonized, as they embody Palestine not only in the eyes of the Israeli occupation but also in the Palestinian nationalist movement. While the latter frequently casts Palestinian men as the protectors and libera-tors of the nation, women are considered the caretakers and reproducers in need of men's protection.

Palestinian nationalism conjures up a gendered world in which women are principally mothers of the nation who are recruited for the nationalist project as reproducers (Peteet 1991, 184; Yuval-Davis 1997; Sharoni 1995; Massad 1995; Kanaaneh 2002, 65), which resonates with nationalisms around the world. In the Third World, the relationship between national and feminist movements is complex and multilayered. As Kumari Jayawardena's pioneering work *Feminism and Nationalism in the Third World* (1986) pointed out, feminist movements in the "non-West" very often emerged from within a nationalist movement that was based on an anticapitalist and anti-imperialist struggle. In Palestine, the women's movement as it emerged during the British Mandate did not stem from a sudden interest in feminist ideology and women's rights per se, but rather originated as a result of women's experience within the national move-ment (Jad 2018, 10; Fleischmann 2003).

The fetishization of fertility and the struggle over demographics have made Palestinian women specific targets of a nationalist rhetoric that deeply

politicizes their reproduction (Kanaaneh 2002, 65). Rhoda Kanaaneh's revealing research on birthing strategies among Palestinian women in the Galilee,
Birthing the Nation (2002), sheds light on how the nationalist framing of reproduction, even though it is not widely recognized as such, constitutes one
of the key components of the cosmology of family planning in the Galilee.
Kanaaneh's study came to mind when a male Bedouin interviewee of mine
finished our conversation by saying "I tell you, I'm sure we will win. And we
will win through numbers!"

But nationalism affects not only Palestinian women's reproduction. As
Palestinian nationalist ideology attributes paramount importance to paternity, mixed marriages or various forms of alternative family planning such
as adoption and artificial insemination are considered a loss for the nation if
women pursue them. What is more, the preference for boys continues as men
are deemed more important for national liberation because, unlike women,
they are perceived as strong enough to stand up to the Israeli state and its police,
bureaucracies, and individuals (Kanaaneh 2002, 72).

Naturally, for feminists who struggle for ownership of their bodies and the
abandonment of sexist oppression, patriarchal nationalist understandings of
womanhood and women's sexuality stand in sharp contrast to their interests,
basically depriving women of their right to their bodies and reinforcing traditional gender roles. While a significant number of feminists became involved
in various nationalist groups and movements, particularly during the Second
Intifada, they have become increasingly frustrated with the ongoing sexism
within these frameworks. Some of the women I spoke with questioned the
usefulness of nationalism in achieving national liberation and peace, as, for
example, did Nizreen, a lawyer from Haifa: "Five years ago, yes, nationalism
was definitely part of my identity. Today, I don't know. I feel that we are not able
to live together because our nationalisms are in the way. They keep us apart . . .
I'm happy with my national identity, culture, language, and whatnot, but I'm
not sure that nationalism is part of my identity. I would rather live in a state
where nationalism does not have a big role. In general, I prefer a multinational
model such as Canada or the US rather than Israel or France."

Another woman, Huda, described how, among nationalist gatherings, she
often felt as though a mask had been forced on her as she could not be both a
feminist and a supporter of national demonstrations:

> When I was fifteen, sixteen years old, I was very extreme. I was in
> the Communist Party. But the Communist Party—there were many
> contradictions. These people were very much "Arab patriots." I grew up with

this patriotism, which would sometimes go as far as hating the Jewish people. I was too young, too ignorant. Again, if the Arabs were to be attacked or under threat via discriminatory measures, of course, my nationalist identity would have its own expression and I would feel it strongly. You would see me at demonstrations against the government's discrimination against the Arab minority but, if you ask me, Would I want these demonstrations to be only for Arabs? I would tell you I want to go and demonstrate with the Jewish people as well. . . . For example, Land Day—one of the Commemoration Days that the Arab leaders here organize every year, I used to go when I was young [laughs]—of course—and I stopped going, and this year because of the discriminatory suggestions of Peres in the Knesset, the acceleration of racism against the Arab minorities, I thought, "Okay, I'm going. I'm taking the day off at my expense." Because it is considered a strike day for the Arabs. And, if it is a strike day and that means I'm just going to be sitting at home, I don't feel comfortable with that. I mean—what is a strike day? And it was very important for me to be there, but I felt like I didn't belong there. I just didn't belong there. It was one big . . . you are expected to talk in certain ways and you're being looked at as either patriotic or unpatriotic, and I can't play this game. It's not who I am. I took that action and that was enough. I'm saying this because I want to tell you that being sure that you are part of this collective identity is not always the way. To be in a place where you are perceived as one identity . . . you're only perceived as one identity. Like "Arab." And people go, "It's good, you're Arab, you're with us!" That's like putting a mask on your face. My commitment lies elsewhere: to empower the oppressed, no mattered why and who . . . what they are. If there were Jews and they were being discriminated against, then I would stick up for them; if there were Muslims that were being oppressed, I would support them. If they're Arab, if they're Christians, if they're Jews and they are less powerful and they are attacked and discriminated against, I'll be with them for sure. That's all I can say about my political commitment in that sense and I take this with me wherever I go.

The relationship between women's movements and nationalism in the Occupied Territories and that relationship within the borders of 1948 have significant differences. Within the Occupied Territories, a struggle for women's liberation emerged from within the national liberation struggle, but feminist movements here regard themselves as *part of* the national struggle. This relationship between women's and national movements is common in countries in the colonial south, as has been traced by Kumari Jayawardena (1986). In these contexts, women often argued that as long as men were not free citizens of their own national collectivity and state, there was no sense in struggling to be equal to them.

Within the 1948 territories, the situation is more complicated because Palestinian women, as Peteet has described them, "opine that gender equality must be an integral component of the current struggle for national liberation, that its achievement will not be an inevitable by-product, but a struggle on its own. The dilemma is to integrate it into a nationalist framework at this 'advanced defensive stage'" (1991, 97). The colonization of the indigenous population constituted a real rupture in the Palestinian women's movement that emerged during the British Mandate. As among some of their counterparts in the Occupied Territories, feminists here oppose a revolution in stages and emphasize in their official statements that national and women's liberation have to go hand-in-hand. I found, however, that it is not so much about the equal share of the postliberation resources but, as Ameer stated earlier in this chapter, about making the recipe for the liberation.

During my conversations, it became clear that Palestinian women's liberation is a struggle that is integral to a wider national struggle. Perhaps the integrity of the struggle is closely linked to the fact that most Palestinian feminists I spoke with in Israel did not desire a Palestinian state, but a "state for all of its citizens." For that reason, Palestinian feminists in Israel are not opposing the movement for national liberation but stand in definite opposition to many of its imaginings of what a future nation-state can look like. Nevertheless, expressions of national identity are of utmost importance to Palestinian women in Israel. This seeming contradiction, between the importance of national liberation and the rejection of nationalism, was captured precisely by a young feminist who said, "I want to be able to wave the Palestinian flag until we are liberated and then I'll be the first to burn it."

REJECTING FEMINISM

Although I interviewed a large number of Palestinian women who support the feminist project, it is important to note that I also encountered a significant number of women involved in women's rights activism who took a critical stance toward, or even rejected, feminism as both a terminology and an ideology. Concerning the former, the words *feminism* and *feminist* were always considered politically charged, and not seldom did women link it to radical egalitarian demands and Western conceptions of women's issues and rights. In that light, feminism was conceived as imported at best and imposed at worst. I noticed that feminism was not always clearly articulated, particularly among rural women, whom I frequently heard using *nisa'iyy* (that which relates to women) and *naswiyy* (feminist) interchangeably. Nevertheless, they always emphasized that there was a feminine way or a woman's way of doing things and that this was an important concern to them. While some women appropriated the term *feminism* to the Palestinian context, often arguing that feminism is part of their society regardless of the Western influence (whether it was referred to as such or not), and the British and Israeli occupation, other women dismissed feminism as something irrelevant to their lives, as they continued to associate feminism with Western influence and colonialism: "I always rebel when they say, 'You got this from Europe.' I didn't get this from Europe! My mother wears short hair, we used to wear miniskirts, it was common and not from Europe. In Ramallah, the women are so open-minded and they are not exposed to Israeli women or European culture" (Afra from Haifa).

Throughout my conversations with women's rights activists, it became clear that the majority of the women who rejected feminism had significant reasons other than its linkage to imperialism and colonialism. Their dismissal of feminism was frequently based on the fact that Palestinian feminism in Israel is dominated by a powerful group of individuals who are almost all from very educated, middle-class, secular backgrounds and whose discourses (and practices) of feminism, to them, show many similarities to elitist white Western liberal feminism.

As a result, a significant number of women criticized the ways in which Palestinian feminism in Israel currently lacks an awareness of intersectionality, reproduces power hierarchies, and strives to represent women who may not agree with its principles. A black Muslim women's rights activist and social worker named Violet, for instance, gave me a really hard time when I tried to arrange an interview with her. As soon as I mentioned the word feminism, she quickly jumped in with "If you want to speak to a feminist, you should not talk to me, really. I'm not a feminist. I can tell you straight away." The reason for her discomfort, as she explained later, was very clearly linked to her negative experiences with feminist groups from the north, who had dismissed her beliefs and politics as "nonfeminist" or "not feminist enough." Violet's experiences with women who she referred to as northern feminists testified to the marginalization of religious and black women's voices in Palestinian feminist discourses in Israel.

Other women said that they simply didn't need the term *feminism*, even though they conducted their lives very much along what could be perceived as feminist lines. I spoke to Hayat, for example, a female Bedouin soccer player who had been publicly celebrated as a "feminist Bedouin woman" in the Israeli media. She told me that she had never identified herself as feminist in public and actually rejected the term: "I find 'feminism' problematic. I don't think that football [i.e., soccer] should only be for women. I'm strong and I take control of my life. I think that I'm on eye level with men and I don't want to get married. People think that makes me 'a man,' but I don't think it makes me 'a man' or a 'feminist.'" In a completely different context, a Druze woman who had run for the local elections said, "I don't think feminism is needed. I just live my life according to what I think is the right way." Moreover, she explained to me that she basically avoided the term in order not to provoke any anger or distract from her political messages, I was also under the impression that she did not want to risk losing any votes from using the stigmatized terminology.

Zeinab, an (atheist) communist feminist who works for a religious feminist organization, also linked feminism to a specific rhetoric and approach taken by northern feminist groups, such as Isha L'Isha. In her experience, the radicalness of such groups often prevents important changes within society:

> It's a term. I don't define it according to the West but according to the conditions and contexts here. There has to be equality between her [a woman's] obligations and participation within the family as well as society in general. Our vision is to achieve a society in which women and men have the same status through religion. Many feminist organizations seem a bit tough ... like Isha L'Isha. Of course, you need to be strong, but you also need to integrate into society instead of being radical for the sake of being radical.

CONCLUSION

REVISITING THE FIELD: JALILAH'S WEDDING

My trip to Laqiya for my friend Jalilah's wedding in March 2015 also constituted my first return to the field since the end of my fieldwork about a year before. Only upon my arrival did I realize that the bride and her family chose me as a sort of maid of honor, assisting the bride from the time she woke up very early in the morning to get ready for the day until late in the night when she needed help taking off her makeup, a rather complicated gown, and hundreds of tiny hairpins. More important, my tasks included calming Jalilah down at all times of the day and running last-minute errands in the blazing heat such as picking up the bridal bouquet or shopping for the right underwear when hers failed to match the wedding dress. The latter I had to manage within the scope of a few hundred meters around a beauty salon in central Rahat, which for about half a day served as some kind of bridal headquarters. After a successful but arduous henna party that had entailed hours of preparation, followed by hours of dancing, Jalilah and I could easily read the tiredness from the rings under each other's eyes the next day. After concealing the rings with layers of makeup throughout another half a day at the bridal headquarters, we were finally sitting next to each other for the main wedding ceremony; Jalilah, all dressed in white, waited in her parents' living room for the groom and his procession to pick her up and take her to his parents' village.

Despite Jalilah's exhaustion (her dress looked extremely uncomfortable to wear in the heat) and the occasional annoyance in her eyes about the groom's delay, I could tell that she was above all things terribly nervous, grabbing my hand every couple of minutes and asking me for the time. To me, it felt as though our time together had come to some kind of full circle as it was in this room where I conducted my very first interviews with Jalilah's mother in the spring of 2012, followed by numerous conversations with other relatives and friends. Back then, Jalilah and her groom were nowhere near an official relationship, as their cautious contact was strictly limited to secret text messages, sneaky gazes, and the occasional whispered and brief conversation on the shared university campus, and they were both always accompanied by at least one other trusted friend.

Surrounded by about forty familiar faces of women, practically all of whom I had met and spoken with within the framework of my research, I felt as if I was in the midst of friends who, unlike me, appeared to be not at all tense about the idea of the groom invading this intimate gathering, but, instead, were completely preoccupied with taking advantage of the opportunity to catch up on each other's lives. I suppressed a grin when I noticed that every now and then a pair of striped tracksuit trousers peeked through one of the women's long dark dresses as they crossed their legs to sink more comfortably into the massive leather sofas while chatting vividly, laughing, and sipping sodas out of plastic cups. Despite the relaxed casualness with which most women treated Jalilah's wedding (perhaps because there were simply too many weddings to attend to still get overly excited about them?), to me, it was anything but ordinary. Perhaps naively, I had considered my fieldwork completed and intended to enjoy Jalilah's wedding as just a wedding, refraining from any research-related thinking. Things were nowhere near that easy, however, and I realized that my field had no clear boundaries, especially as my relationships with many of the women had continued to thrive throughout the year after my departure. While coming back to Laqiya and seeing one of my closest friends get married in a ceremony that I had never experienced before was thrilling, knowing almost all the details of the unusual story that led to her wedding very much intensified my excitement.

Behind the curtain of a traditional Bedouin wedding that ticked all the boxes of the plan, we were, in fact, celebrating a love marriage that, initially, had not been considered acceptable at all. It had been gingerly negotiated by Jalilah over years, as her groom was a member of a smaller Bedouin tribe and, as such, from a social status considered to be too low for a potential marriage candidate for Jalilah. For years, the groom had worked, in parallel to his university studies, in order to earn the financial assets required to propose to a woman of Jalilah's status, and then there were the lengthy and strenuous tribal bargaining between the families. Nevertheless, the couple had managed to sustain their relationship and the wish to marry each other even during periods of hopelessness and frustration. All the while, I admired how Jalilah had never doubted her relationship or the possibility of marriage.

Even though Jalilah's wedding not only symbolized the success and an end of their struggle but also the beginning of a marriage, I was struck by the invaluable opportunity to witness the power of intimate politics. In spite of the outward normalcy of an ordinary and apparently traditional Bedouin wedding scene, the festivities represented a fundamental disruption of the plan, as Jalilah not only married a man from a family originally regarded as inappropriate but, more remarkably for a Bedouin woman from the Naqab, the man whom she loved and chose to spend her life with. The wedding and the endeavor leading up to it underscore how intimate politics are implicated in the everyday, how they require a complex, lengthy, and unrelenting effort within the confines of everyday contingencies, if they strive to change the plan, and how they entail both visible and discrete elements. Even though their achievements frequently remain celebrated tacitly and obscured from view, by circumventing and disrupting the plan, intimate politics can bring about radical change in Palestinian women's lives.

RETHINKING INTIMATE POLITICS

This book has attempted to canvass and render visible some of the tangible intimate politics of Palestinian women in Israel that have largely remained obscured from view, bypassed by existing scholarship, silenced by the women themselves, and marginalized within official political discourses. It offered an investigation of these intimate politics in a framework that has sought to dismantle contemporary Zionist strategies to control Palestinian women's intimate lives in an effort to complete its settler colonial project. To that end, this research has sought to join the ranks of scholarship that challenges common understandings of intimate politics as a corollary of the struggle between colonizer and colonized but, in lieu thereof, considers them as the "everyday grounds of contestation" (Stoler 2001, 894). By interrogating important links between women's politics of the body, sex, and love, intimate politics do not constitute a supplementary point of entry but provide a critical vantage point for grasping the current workings of Zionist settler colonialism and its possible future realignments as it is forced to adapt to the new realities lived by a generation of Palestinian women who were born and raised within the State of Israel.

This book began by proposing the plan as a more fruitful way than the commonly used notion of two layers of oppression to conceptualize the context in which Palestinian women's lives in Israel are situated. The first chapter, "Embodied Citizen Strangers," outlined how settler colonial citizenship acts as a key mechanism of *exclusionary inclusion* through which the Zionist state advances its logic of elimination and self-indigenization, for instance, through strategies of assimilation. At the heart of the plan for indigenous women designed by the state lies the expectation of them to disappear while, at the same time, remain identifiable through readable bodies. The analysis of citizenship as a gendered and racialized corporeal experience demonstrates how Palestinian women's bodies, conceptualized as both object and agent, constitute a key site of the struggle and between settler and colonized. Particularly as indigenous women's bodies become directly representative of land, they are subject to invasion and occupation while the patriarchal regimes inherent in both settler and indigenous society use their bodies as markers of identity and power. This results in intersecting forms of control of and violence against Palestinian women's bodies. By illuminating some of the ways in which the Zionist targeting of Palestinian women's bodies is a very much ongoing process, the findings presented here support the claims made by Patrick Wolfe, who conceptualizes settler colonial invasion as a structure rather than an event (Wolfe 1994, 96), and thereby dispel the myth of an equal citizenship.

I have attempted to highlight some the important ways in which Palestinian women's bodies are Othered and marked by difference in everyday life in order to clarify which bodies are in and which are out of place in Israel according to Zionist logic. Zionist constructs of Palestinian citizens as inner enemies, the good Arab, and Arab-Israeli women were discussed that serve this purpose. By drawing on some of the women's quotidian experiences, the first chapter revealed that the difference constructed on their bodies is constantly (de-) stabilized and (re-)negotiated as the boundaries between settler and colonized are continuously unsettled and complicated. In the process, however, ruptures allow opportunities to emerge for Palestinian women, particularly in light of the frequent failures of Israelis to read the Other successfully. As a result, passing as the Other has become one of the strategies that Palestinian women have adopted in order to defy the plan for them to not belong or access certain privileges reserved for Jewish Israelis.

The plan was considered the product of a complex interplay of interlocking systems of domination, to which patriarchy is intrinsic, such as settler colonialism, classicism, racism, and ableism. Thus the chapter built on its forerunner's investigation of the Zionist state by deconstructing what has frequently been referred to as patriarchal Palestinian society. By taking a more nuanced look at Palestinian society, the second chapter drew a complex and coherent picture that includes the experiences of women who have remained by and large excluded from existing discourses and accounts of Palestinian women such as black Palestinian women, women with disabilities, Bedouin women, and LGBTQI women. While the plan appears as individually tailored to the diversity of experiences of Palestinian women, chapter 2 focused on important collective structures of patriarchal oppression and expectations that women share across different social memberships.

The ways in which Palestinian women defy the plan through their bodies were interrogated and revealed some of the powerful stories and experiences of women who refused for their bodies to be read and dominated by others. The politics of menstruation, women's tattoos, and dress choices offered insights into how Palestinian women defy social norms and taboos through their bodies in both public and provocative as well as subtle and discreet ways. Intimate politics here are about how the body is used by women as an important means and medium for (re-)defining borders (border skirmishing) between the self, the Other, society, and nation. Women frequently use their bodies to tell their own stories, which include elements of family history, national belonging, and (feminist and religious) identity. This does not mean that women's bodies are constantly exposed to speak—the ability to cover and hide the body from external gazes remains an important right for women. Moreover, as settler colonialism is a spatial project, women's bodies are used to access spaces that are reserved for the somatic (Jewish) norm. Thus, Palestinian women destabilize hegemonic power that is inscribed on their bodies and the spaces that they are allowed to access through reclaiming their bodies and using them to challenge boundaries and to transgress space. While women are regularly confronted with aversion from Palestinian society, they also refuse to be co-opted by Israeli modernist discourses that aim to use the opportunity to present them as assimilated colonial subjects.

An apparent contradiction was explored: On the one hand, there has been a movement of women to increase communication about sex within Palestinian society. Talk about sex mainly takes place within the framework of sexual education programs led by various feminist organizations and includes topics like sexual violence and health but also sex advice for couples. The initiatives, the women activists emphasize, are all the more important in light of Israel's modern sexuality that neglects the sexual education of Palestinians through educational segregation while simultaneously the state fails to provide adequate protection to Palestinian women from sexual violence. Even though public discussions about these issues increase, personal sexual experiences, including experiences of sex, the loss of virginity, sexual harassment, and abuse are kept strictly silent even among the most outspoken women's rights activists and feminists. The main reason for this reticence, it was claimed, is the interplay of patriarchal settler colonial and traditional regimes that make the price to pay for speaking openly about their sex lives simply too high for Palestinian women, especially for those who cannot count on the support of their families in case of social scandals.

Control over Palestinian women's sexuality remains of critical importance to the completion of Israel's settler colonial project for two main purposes: Zionism's interest in winning the demographic race between the Jewish and Arab population in Israel and the preservation of the identity categories of (self-indigenized) Jew and Arab. The Israeli construction of Palestinian women as simultaneously sexually hyperactive and sexually oppressed feeds into these categories a logic, according to which Palestinian women are offered the opportunity to be sexually liberated only through Israeli modern sexuality. While sexual liberalism is propagated in certain Jewish Israeli left-wing discourses, serious relationships between Palestinian women and Jewish men remain largely untolerated by mainstream society. Also, the myth of the Arab male rapist and the hysteria over the possible sexual assault of Jewish women by Arab men, like the colonial rape scares in various other colonial contexts, remains crucial for preventing mixed relationships and legitimizing important racist laws while securing the gender order within settler society itself.

Despite the difficulties that they face, Palestinian women maneuver around the sexually oppressive structures and lead fulfilled sex lives by frequently keeping them secret, drawing on alternative practices like performing virginity, or having sex with ex-partners or Jewish men. For example, crucial opportunities for mixed sexual affairs emerge through daily contact between Palestinian women of the third *nakba* generation and Jewish men. Notably, the meanings the women ascribe to these affairs are not as brief episodes of pleasure, but they have political and feminist connotations because of the threat they pose to Zionist notions of racial purity. In contrast to their often provocative and sarcastic rhetoric about their affairs they used with me as an external researcher, they generally kept their personal sexual experiences secret even from close friends while they continued living the sex lives that they desire as autonomous sexual agents, free from both Palestinian conservative control and Israeli modernist discourses, thereby destabilizing the plan for their sex lives made by both.

Zionist state control over and direct encroachment in Palestinian intimate relationships and family life remains crucial for the preservation of the Jewishness of the state. Formal and informal methods of surveillance and regulation include, among others, the withholding of citizenship for partners, the prevention of family unification, the overlapping of religious and civil courts in matters of family law, and the difficulty for Palestinians to access alternative ways of family formation, such as adoption. Both Palestinian and Israeli society adhere to traditional social order when it comes to serious intimate relations and family life, as they prefer a model of sexual normalcy that implies hetero-sexuality and sticking to one's own religious, class, racial, and ethnic member-ship. The book explored the stories of women who have—out of love—resisted such control in order to form alternative families, be in mixed relationships and marriages, remain single, or get divorced. Their decisions were primarily based on what price the women had to pay for them, which was contingent on their social status, financial well-being, and family support.

Palestinian women's narratives of feminist selves revealed the emergence of a new national subjectivity according to which national and women's liberation are perceived as inextricably linked. While constructions of feminist identity were often linked to notions of naturalness and the idea of being born a feminist, this sentiment was exclusively spread among middle- and upper-class women who ac-tively participated in and contributed to organized feminist discourses. Women who remained marginalized from such discourses (and the organizations that bring them forth)—such as religious, black, and poorer women—frequently criticized or rejected feminism as a result of their exclusion or misrepresentation. Notably, all my interviewees rejected nationalism as they felt—as women—they remained excluded, patronized, or marginalized within Palestinian nationalist frameworks. Nevertheless, they stressed time and again the importance that they ascribed to their national identity and the meanings they attached to being Pal-estinian. Being Palestinian was commonly linked to being free, self-determined women. Especially younger women emphasized the importance of their grand-parents as feminist role models who, throughout their stories, illustrated and embodied a national subjectivity that insists on gender equality as an integral component of the struggle for Palestinian national liberation.

How does canvassing Palestinian women's intimate politics help to under-stand their daily lived realities in Israel? Do they give us any new insights into the workings of a settler colonial regime, how it changes and adapts over time? In turn, is there anything to learn from Palestinian women's experiences in Israel about the nature of intimate politics in other settler colonial contexts? Are intimate politics that political? Can they count as a form of resistance? These are just a few questions that were posed in this book; questions that raise broader debates about whether resistance and political action have to be expressed overtly, whether they have to be organized, and so forth. Despite their relevance, these discussions go beyond the constraints of this book.

Nevertheless, I would like to address a few of them: It is likely that the greatest significance of my research lies in its insights into the role of intimate politics in the workings and transgression of Zionist settler colonialism. As has been argued throughout this book, Palestinian women's intimate practices that defy the plan should be seen as political for several reasons: First, daily intimate politics constitute a contested ground not only for settler colonialism but also for indigenous people. "At the moment, we are just surviving. You cannot 'only survive,' you need to live," one woman said to me once. The plans and wishes that people hold in regard to their intimate needs, relations, and desires, particularly the people whom they love, are what, in the end, life is all about. Second, while not all acts that defy the plan are specifically intended by women to resist patriarchal or settler colonial structures, they serve the purpose of Palestinian women's self-determination and, thereby, undermine the legitimacy of the plan. Even if they unsettle normative practices by only a small measure, they can be transformative, as they contribute to opening up new possibilities for themselves and other women. Unlike overt, political dissent, not all intimate acts of defiance are expressed publicly or verbally but frequently entail a lengthy, strenuous process and are kept quiet or secret in order to be sustainable. This book has argued that nonverbal defiance is not necessarily less political. Silencing intimate acts of defiance does not contribute to upholding binary constructions of personal and political, private and public. Rather, silence can be an important means for women to sustain their politics and strengthen their strategies and keep their actions from being prevented, interrupted, or co-opted by Israeli modernist, assimilationist, or homonationalist discourses, on the one hand or Palestinian nationalist discourses on the other. Third, considering the deep incursions of Israeli state and society into Palestinian women's day-to-day intimate lives, nothing is completely personal or completely political. This is made patently clear by the fact that the Israeli police can—and do—enter Palestinian family homes in the middle of the night to search for enemies of the state. The fact that some acts of defiance are too subtle to be surveyed or policed does not mean that they do not exist. Particularly in its struggle to secure its own modernization (Kanaaneh 2002, 252), Zionist strategies are under constant pressure to realign themselves. Through discourses such as modern sexuality, pinkwashing, or sexual liberalism and others, they increasingly focus on intimate matters of Palestinians.

In spite of manifold variations and inconsistencies in the intimate politics discussed here, certain systematicities can be discerned: More than feminism (or any other ideology, for that matter), there is a Palestinian national subjectivity that is frequently articulated and that functions as a driving force in many women's intimate politics. This subjectivity is evoked in women's narratives and practices and carves out an imagining of Palestinian women as liberated and free-acting agents with the right to write and rewrite their own plans on all levels. Nevertheless, Palestinian women's intimate politics have limits that are undeniable and should be pointed out too: For most women, the plan continues to dictate their lives because the price of potential punishment for Palestinian women (and often for their loved ones too) who defy it remains too high to risk. This is particularly and most atrociously reflected in the continuously high number of Palestinian women and girls who have become victims of femicides and sexual violence in Israel.

There is certainly room and need for further research on the topic. For instance, it would be revealing to compare Palestinian women's experiences in Israel with those in other settler colonial contexts and look into possible similarities and differences between their intimate politics. What is really *sui generis* about Israeli settler colonialism and what aspects dismantle deep-seated claims of Israeli exceptionalism? Perhaps indigenous women in other parts of the world are able to express their intimate politics more overtly or less so under settler colonial regimes? Further research that does not situate silence against action but, instead, looks into the use of silence as well as the action of nonlabeling of intimate politics by women would certainly be instructive. Especially from a feminist perspective, it is vital to pay attention to who refuses to label their intimate politics as feminist and, if so, why: who do we—feminists—continue to exclude?

It is likely that the Zionist project of self-indigenizing will become increasingly difficult because of the frailty of the generic categories of settler and colonized. Settler colonialism is not some kind of omnipotent force but is flawed with rifts and ruptures that Palestinian citizens are aware of and strategically use to their advantage. Therefore, it is vital not to neglect the lived quotidian reality in which Jewish Israelis and Palestinians come into regular and intimate contact in Israel, every time they go to work, school, or the university, when they go shopping but also when they go out, hook up, or get tattooed. Here, intimate politics offer an opportunity for a more comprehensive account of current developments within a generation of Palestinian citizens who master the Israeli language and customs and who do not hesitate to use their competence to pursue their personal and collective interests. While, as yet, the Palestinian feminist movement in Israel fails to speak on behalf of many women, perhaps, one day, an augmented women's discourse might emerge, one that is more inclusive of the experiences of women other than those from the upper echelons of Palestinian society—one that will acknowledge and give credit to the powerful and poignant struggles of those who, thus far, were left with no choice but to act alone.

GLOSSARY

ARABIC

'aanis	"spinster," derogatory term used for (older) unmarried woman
abaya	thin overcoat worn by women
'abeed	derogatory term used for black Bedouins
al'ard qabl al'ird	"land before honor"
a'rāb	"original Bedouins"
'ashirah	Bedouin tribe
'asl	"nobility," "origin," "ancestry" (Bedouin dialect)
'aswad	"black"
'azab	"unmarried man," "bachelor"
'azbaa	(young) unmarried woman
badal	exchange marriage
bint	(virgin) girl
deq	Arabic and Kurdish traditional face tattooing
fellaheen	agricultural workers, farmers
gaba'il	Bedouin confederation
hamula	"clan"
haram	"forbidden" or "sinful" according to Muslim tradition
hijab	headscarf worn by Muslim women
ightisab	rape
'ird	honor
isqat siyassy	downfall

jilbab	long loose-fit garment worn by Muslim women
kaffiye	traditional scarf
leylat al-dokhola	wedding night
mandeel	headscarf worn by Bedouin women
mukhtar	religious or village leader
muṭalaqa	divorcée
nakba	literally "catastrophe," the forceful expulsion and displacement of at least 750,000 Palestinians from their homeland in 1948
naswiyy	feminist
nisa'iyy	feminine
qasar	"unmarried woman," "minor" (woman)
'ruba	Bedouin sub-tribe
saf	group of Bedouin tribes
samra	"black" (used by black Bedouins to refer to themselves)
sharaf	honor
shari'a	Islamic religious law
sumran	landowning Bedouins

HEBREW

avodah ivrit	Hebrew labor
bney ha-miutim	members of the minorities
Eretz Israel	the Land of Israel
ezraḥut	citizenship
frumka	literally "devout" in Yiddish, a black garment that covers the entire body worn by Haredi women
goyim	"Gentiles" or "non-Jews," it has a demeaning connotation
halaḥah	Jewish religious law
Haredi	Jewish Orthodox, sometimes colloquially referred to as "ultra-Orthodox" in English
hasbara	literally "explanation"; commonly known in Israel as strategic and selective explanations for (usually political) actions whether or not they are justified
kibush ha-adamah	conquest of the land
leum	nationality
Magav	Colloquial name for the Israel Border Police
Mahash	colloquial name for the Police Investigation Unit of the Israeli Ministry of Justice

migzar ha-aravi	"the Arab sector"
mikvah	Jewish ritual bath
niddah	"menstruating woman"
olim	new immigrants
shal	a face veil worn by Haredi women
tohar ha-neshek	the purity of arms
Yishuv	the Jewish community in Palestine before the creation of the State of Israel

BIBLIOGRAPHY

Abboud, R., ed. 2010. *Waqfet Banat—Personal Narrative*. Haifa: Aswat—
Palestinian Gay Women.

Abdo, N. 2011. *Women in Israel: Race, Gender and Citizenship*. London: Zed.

———. 2014. *Captive Revolution: Palestinian Women's Anti-colonial Struggle within the Israeli Prison System*. London: Pluto.

Abu-Baker, K. 2002. "'Career Women' or 'Working Women'? Change versus Stability for Young Palestinian Women in Israel." *Journal of Israeli History* 21, nos. 1–2: 85–109.

Abulhawa, S. 2013. "Confronting Anti-black Racism in the Arab World," *Al Jazeera*, July 7, https://www.aljazeera.com/opinions/2013/7/7/confronting -anti-black-racism-in-the-arab-world.

Abu-Lughod, L. 2016. *Veiled Sentiments: Honor and Poetry in a Bedouin Society*. Oakland: University of California Press.

Abu-Rabia, R. 2011. "Redefining Polygamy among the Palestinian Bedouins in Israel: Colonialism, Patriarchy, and Resistance." *Journal of Gender, Social Policy and the Law* 19, no. 2: 459–92.

Ahmed, L. 1992. *Women and Gender in Israel: Historical Roots of a Modern Debate*. New Haven, CT: Yale University Press.

Ahmed, S. 2000. *Strange Encounters: Embodied Others in Post-coloniality*. New York: Routledge.

Ahmed, S., and J. Stacey, eds. 2001. *Thinking through the Skin*. New York: Routledge.

Alcoff, L. M. 2006. *Visible Identities, Race, Gender and the Self*. Oxford: Oxford University Press.

Al-Haj, M. 1987. *Social Change and Family Processes—Arab Communities in Shefar-a'm*. Boulder, CO: Westview.

AlQaisiya, W., G. Hilal, and H. Maikey. 2016. "Dismantling the Image of the Palestinian Homosexual: Exploring the Role of alQaws." In *Decolonizing Sexualities: Transnational Perspectives, Critical Interventions,* edited by S. Bakshi, S. Jivraj, and S. Posocco, 125–140, Oxford, UK: Counterpress.

Anderson, K. 2000. *A Recognition of Being: Reconstructing Native Womanhood.* Toronto: Sumach.

Angier, N. 1999. *Woman: An Intimate Geography.* New York: Random House.

Anthias, F., and N. Yuval-Davis. 1993. *Racialized Boundaries: Race, Nation, Gender, Color and Class and the Anti-racist Struggle.* New York: Routledge.

Aretxaga, B. 2003. "Maddening States." *Annual Review of Anthropology* 32: 393–410.

Bailkin, J. 2005. "Making Faces: Tattooed Women and Colonial Regimes." *History Workshop Journal* 59, no 1: 33–56.

Barak-Brandes, S. 2011. "Internalizing the Taboo: Israeli Women Respond to Commercials for Feminine Hygiene Products." *Observatorio* 5, no. 4: 49–68.

Bartky, S. L. 1997. "Foucault, Femininity and the Modernization of Patriarchal Power." In *Writing on the Body: Female Embodiment and Feminist Theory,* edited by S. Conboy, N. Medina, and S. Stanbury, 129–54. New York: Columbia University Press.

Bell, S. 1999. "Tattooed: A Participant Observer's Exploration of Meaning." *Journal of American Culture* 22, no. 2: 53–58.

Biasio, E. 1998. *Beduinen im Negev: Vom Zelt ins Haus.* Zurich: Verlag Neue Zürcher Zeitung.

Bobel, C., and S. Kwan, eds. 2011. *Embodied Resistance: Challenging the Norms, Breaking the Rules.* Nashville, TN: Vanderbilt University Press.

Bourdieu, P. 1986. "The Forms of Capital." In *Handbook of Theory and Research for the Sociology of Education,* edited by J. G. Richardson, 241–60. Westport, CT: Greenwood.

Braunberger, C. 2000. "Revolting Bodies: The Monster Beauty of Tattooed Women." *NWSA Journal* 12, no. 2: 1–23.

Brownson, E. 2019. *Palestinian Women and Muslim Family Law in the Mandate Period.* Syracuse, NY: Syracuse University Press.

Brumberg, J. J. 1997. *The Body Project: An Intimate History of American Girls.* New York: Random House.

Brush, P. 1998. "Metaphors of Inscription: Discipline, Plasticity and the Rhetoric of Choice." *Feminist Review* 58: 22–43.

Butler, J. 1990. *Gender Trouble.* New York: Routledge.

———. 2004. *Undoing Gender.* New York: Routledge.

Chatterjee, P. 1993. *The Nation and Its Fragments: Colonial and Postcolonial Histories.* Princeton, NJ: Princeton University Press.

Chief Economist Department, Israeli Ministry of Finance. 2015. "Israeli Labor Market—First Quarter 2015," 9.

Cohen, H. 2010. *Good Arabs—the Israeli Security Agencies and the Israeli Arabs, 1948–1967*. Berkeley: University of California Press.

Collins, P. H. 2000. *Black Feminist Thought*. New York: Routledge.

Connell, R. 2009. *Gender*. 2nd ed. Cambridge, MA: Polity.

Coulthard, G. S. 2007. "Subjects of Empire: Indigenous Peoples and the 'Politics of Recognition' in Canada." *Contemporary Political Theory* 6, no. 4: 437–60.

Csordas, T. J. 1994. *Embodiment and Experience: The Existential Ground of Culture and Self*. Cambridge: Cambridge University Press.

Dahan-Khalev, H., and E. Le Febvre. 2012. *Palestinian Activism in Israel: A Bedouin Woman Leader in a Changing Middle East*. New York: Palgrave Macmillan.

Daoud, S. A. O. 2009. *Palestinian Women and Politics in Israel*. Gainesville: University Press of Florida.

———. 2012. "Palestinian Working Women in Israel: National Oppression and Social Restraints." *Journal of Middle East Women's Studies* 8, no. 2: 78–101.

Darwish, M. 1982. "A Lover from Palestine." In *The Palestinian Wedding: A Bilingual Anthology of Contemporary Palestinian Resistance Poetry*. Compiled and translated by A. M. Elmessiri. Washington, DC: Three Continents.

Davis, K. 1988. *Power under the Microscope: Toward a Grounded Theory of Gender Relations in Medical Encounters*. Dordrecht, Neth.: Foris.

de Lepervance, M. 1989. "Breeders for Australia: A National Identity for Women?" *Australian Journal of Social Issues* 24, no. 3: 163–82.

DeMello, M. 2000. *Bodies of Inscription: A Cultural History of the Modern Tattoo Community*. Durham, NC: Duke University Press.

Derrida, J. 1976. *Of Grammatology*. Translated by G. C. Spivak. Baltimore: Johns Hopkins University Press.

———. 1978. *Writing and Difference*. Translated by A. Bass. London: Routledge and Kegan Paul.

De Troyer, C., A. Herbert, J. A. Johnson, and A. Korte, eds. 2003. *Wholly Woman Holy Blood: A Feminist Critique of Purity and Impurity*. London: Trinity Press International.

Douglas, M. 1966. *Purity and Danger: An Analysis of Concepts of Pollution and Taboo*. London: Routledge and Kegan Paul.

Dowty, A. "Is Israel Democratic? Substance and Semantics in the 'Ethnic Democracy' Debate." *Israel Studies* 4, no. 2: 1–15.

Edut, O., ed. 2004. *Body Outlaws: Rewriting the Rules of Beauty and Body Image*. 3rd ed. Berkeley, CA: Seal.

El Feki, S. 2013. *Sex and the Citadel: Intimate Life in a Changing Arab World*. London: Chatto and Windus.

Enloe, C. 1989. *Bananas, Beaches and Bases: Making Feminist Sense of International Relations*. London: Pandora.

———. 2000. *Maneuvers: The International Politics of Militarizing Women's Lives.* Berkeley: University of California Press.

Entwistle, J. 2000. *The Fashioned Body: Fashion, Dress and Social Theory.* Cambridge, UK: Polity.

Evans, R. 1982. "Don't You Remember Black Alice Sam Holt? Aboriginal Women in Queensland History." *Hecate* 8, no. 2: 6–21.

Fanon, F. 1967. *Black Skin, White Masks.* New York: Grove.

Firestone, S. 1970. *The Dialectic of Sex: The Case for Feminist Revolution.* New York: Farrar, Straus and Giroux.

Fleischmann, E. L. 2003. *The Nation and Its "New" Women: The Palestinian Women's Movement 1920–1949.* Berkley: University of California Press.

Foucault, M. 1984. "Nietzsche, Genealogy, History." In *The Foucault Reader,* edited by P. Rabinow, 76–99. New York: Random House.

———. 1990. *The History of Sexuality Volume 1: An Introduction.* 3 Volumes. New York: Vintage.

———. 1995. *Discipline and Punish: The Birth of the Prison.* 2nd Vintage ed. London: Vintage.

Gatens, M. 1996. *Imaginary Bodies: Ethics, Power, and Corporeality.* Oxford: Routledge.

Georgis, D. 2013. *The Better Story: Queer Affects from the Middle East.* New York: State University of New York Press.

Ghanem, A., N. Rouhana, and O. Yiftachel. 1998. "Questioning 'Ethnic Democracy': A Response to Sammy Smooha." *Israel Studies* 3, no. 2: 253–67.

Gilbert, M. R. 1994. "The Politics of Location: Doing Feminist Research at 'Home'." *The Professional Geographer* 46, no. 1: 90–96.

Gimlin, D. L. 2002. *Body Work: Beauty and Self-Image in American Culture.* Berkeley: University of California Press.

Ginsburg, F., and R. Rapp. 1991. "The Politics of Reproduction." *Annual Review of Anthropology* 20: 311–43.

Gluck, S. B. 1994. *An American Feminist in Palestine: The Intifada Years.* Philadelphia: Temple University Press.

Graham-Brown, S. 1990. *The Palestinian Situation.* Geneva: World Alliance of Young Men's Christian Association.

Grosz, E. 1994. *Volatile Bodies: Toward a Corporeal Feminism.* Bloomington: Indiana University Press.

Haraway, D. 1988. "Situated Knowledges: The Science Question in Feminism and the Privilege of Partial Perspective." *Feminist Studies* 14, no. 3: 575–99.

Harding, S. 1991. *Whose Science? Whose Knowledge?* New York: Cornell University Press.

Hassan, M. 2002. "The Politics of Honor: Patriarchy, the State and the Murder of Women in the Name of Family Honor." *Journal of Israeli History* 21, nos. 1–2: 1–37.

———. 2005. "Growing Up Female and Palestinian in Israel." In *Israeli Women's Studies: A Reader*, edited by E. Fuchs, 181–89. New Brunswick, NJ: Rutgers University Press.

Hasso, F. S. 2000. "Modernity and Gender in Arab Accounts of the 1948 and 1967 Defeats." *International Journal of Middle East Studies* 32, no. 4: 491–510.

Hawari, Y., S. Plonski, and E. Weizmann. 2018. "Introduction: Settlers and Citizens: A Critical View of Israeli Society." In Hawari, Y., S. Plonski, and E. Weizmann, eds. Settler and Citizen: A Critical View of Israeli Society. *Settler Colonial Studies* 9, no. 1: 1–5.

hooks, b. 2004. "Feminism: A Transformational Politics." In *Feminisms and Womanisms: A Women's Studies Reader*, edited by A. Prince and S. Silva-Wayne, 109–14. Toronto: Women's Press.

Humphries, I., and L. Khalili. 2007. "Gender and Nakba Memory." In Sa'adi and Abu-Lughod, 207–27.

Jabareen, H. 2004. "Comments on the Unreasonableness of the Attorney General's 'Reasonable Discrimination Policy.'" *Adalah's Newsletter* 1: 1–9.

Jacobs, M. D. 2009. *White Mother to a Dark Race: Settler Colonialism, Maternalism, and the Removal of Indigenous Children in the American West and Australia 1880–1940*. Lincoln: University of Nebraska Press.

Jad, I. 2018. *Palestinian Women's Activism: Nationalism, Secularism, Islamism*. Syracuse, NY: Syracuse University Press.

Jayawardena, K. 1986. *Feminism and Nationalism in the Third World*. London: Zed.

Junka, L. 2006. "The Politics of Gaza Beach: At the Edge of the Two Intifada." *Third Text* 20, nos. 3–4: 417–28.

Kahf, M. 1999. *Western Representations of the Muslim Woman*. Austin: University of Texas Press.

Kahn, S. M. 2000. *Reproducing Jews: A Cultural Account of Assisted Conception in Israel*. Durham, N.C: Duke University Press.

Kanaaneh, R. 2002. *Birthing the Nation: Strategies of Palestinian Women in Israel*. Berkeley: University of California Press.

———. 2003. "Embattled Identities: Palestinian Soldiers in the Israeli Military." *Journal of Palestine Studies* 32, no. 3: 5–20.

Kanaaneh, R., and I. Nusair 2010. *Displaced at Home: Ethnicity and Gender among Palestinians in Israel*. New York: State University of New York Press.

Kandiyoti, D. 1988. "Bargaining with Patriarchy." *Gender and Society* 2, no. 3: 274–90.

———. 1991. *Women, Islam, and the State*. New York: Macmillan.

Kaplan, G. 1997. "Feminism and Nationalism: The European Case." In *Feminist Nationalism*, edited by L. West, 3–40. New York: Routledge.

Kassem, F. 2011. *Palestinian Women: Narrative Histories and Gendered Memory*. London: Zed.

Katz, S. H. 1996. "*Adam* and *Adama,* '*Ird* and *Ard*: En-gendering Political Conflict and Identity in Early Jewish and Palestinian Nationalisms." In *Gendering the Middle East: Emerging Perspective,* edited by D. Kandiyoti, 85–107. London: IB Taurus.

———. 2003. *Women and Gender in Early Jewish and Palestinian Nationalism.* Gainesville: University of Press of Florida.

Khalili, L. 2007. *Heroes and Martyrs of Palestine: The Politics of National Commemoration,* Cambridge: Cambridge University Press.

———. 2010. "Gendered Practices of Counterinsurgency." *Review of International Studies* 37, no. 4: 1471–91.

———. 2015. "The Politics of Pleasure: Promenading on the Corniche and Beachgoing." *Environment and Planning D: Society and Space* 34, no. 4: 583–600.

King, J., D. Neon, A. Wolde-Tsadick, and J. Habib. 2009. *Employment of Arab Women Aged 18–64.* Jerusalem: Myers-JDC-Brookdale Institute (Hebrew). http://brookdale.jdc.org.il/?CategoryID=192&ArticleID=39.

Kissling, E. A. 2006. *Capitalizing the Curse: The Business of Menstruation.* Boulder, CO: Lynne Rienner.

Knight, C. 1991. *Blood Relations: Menstruation and the Origins of Culture.* New Haven, CT: Yale University Press.

Kressel, G. 1992. *Descent through Males: An Anthropological Investigation into the Patterns Underlying Social Hierarchy, Kinship, and Marriage among Former Bedouin in the Ramla-Lod Area (Israel).* Mediterranean Language and Culture Monograph Series, vol. 8. Wiesbaden, Ger.: Otto Harrassowitz.

Kretzer, D. 1990. *The Legal Status of the Arabs in Israel.* Boulder, CO: Westview.

Kristeva, J. 1982. *Powers of Horror: An Essay on Abjection.* New York: Columbia University Press.

Laws, S. 1990. *Issues of Blood: The Politics of Menstruation.* London: Macmillan.

Leddy, T. 1995. "Everyday Surface Aesthetic Qualities: 'Neat,' 'Messy,' 'Clean,' 'Dirty.'" *Journal of Aesthetics and Art Criticism* 53, no. 3: 259–68.

Lefebvre, H. 1991. *The Production of Space.* Malden, MA: Blackwell.

Lowe, L. (1991) *Critical Terrains: French and British Orientalism.* Ithaca, NY: Cornell University Press.

Mahdavi, P. 2009. *Iran's Sexual Revolution: Passionate Uprisings.* Stanford, CA: Stanford University Press.

Marx, E. 1967. *Bedouin of the Negev.* Manchester, UK: Manchester University Press.

Masalha, N., ed. 2005. *Catastrophe Remembered: Palestine, Israel and the Internal Refugees,* London: Zed.

———. 2012. *The Palestine Nakba: Decolonizing History, Narrating the Subaltern, Reclaiming Memory.* London: Zed.

Massad, J. 1995. "Conceiving the Masculine: Gender and Palestinian Nationalism." *Middle East Journal* 49, no. 3: 467–83.

———. 2007. *Desiring Arabs*. Chicago: University of Chicago Press.

Matar, D. 2011. *What It Means to Be Palestinian*. London: I. B. Tauris.

McCall, L. 2005. "The Complexity of Intersectionality." *Signs* 30, no. 3: 1771–1800.

McClintock, A. 1995. *Imperial Leather: Race, Gender, and Sexuality in the Colonial Context*. New York: Routledge.

Mead, M. 1949. *Male and Female*. New York: Morrow.

Mifflin, M. 2001. *Bodies of Subversion: A Secret History of Women and Tattoo*. 3rd ed. New York: powerHouse.

Mills, C. W. 1997. *The Racial Contract*. Ithaca, NY: Cornell University Press.

Moghadam, V., ed. 1994. *Gender and National Identity: Women and Politics in Muslim Societies*. London: Zed.

Molavi, S. C. 2014. *Stateless Citizenship: The Palestinian-Arab Citizens of Israel*. Chicago: Haymarket.

Monture-Angus, P. 1995. *Thunder in My Soul: A Mohawk Woman Speaks*. Halifax, NS: Fernwood.

Mor, Z., E. Grayeb, and A. Beany. 2016. "Arab Men Who Have Sex with Men in Israel: Knowledge, Attitudes, and Sexual Practices." *HIV Medicine* 17, no. 4: 298–304.

Morgensen, S. L. 2011. *Spaces between Us: Queer Settler Colonialism and Indigenous Decolonization*. Minneapolis: University of Minnesota Press.

———. 2012. "Theorizing Gender, Sexuality and Settler Colonialism: An Introduction." *Settler Colonial Studies* 2, no. 2: 2–22.

Morris, B. 2004. *The Birth of the Palestinian Refugee Problem*. Cambridge: Cambridge University Press.

Muhammad, A. S., L. Abu-Mukh Zoabi, M. Shehadeh, S. Miaari, F. Moadi, and L. Fahoum. 2012. "Reality of Women in Israel." *Mada al-Carmel*.

Mullaney, J. 2006. *Everyone Is Not Doing It: Abstinence and Personal Identity*. Chicago: University of Chicago Press.

Najmabadi, A. 2005. *Women with Moustaches and Men without Beards: Gender and Sexual Anxieties of Iranian Modernity*. Berkeley: University of California Press.

O'Brien, M. 1981. *The Politics of Reproduction*. London: Routledge and Kegan Paul.

O'Keefe, T. 2006. "Menstrual Blood as Weapon of Resistance." *International Feminist Journal of Politics* 8, no. 4: 535–56.

O'Reilly, K. 2005. *Ethnographic Methods*. Abingdon-on Thames, UK: Routledge.

Oz, S. 2008. "Teaching Sex Education in the Arab Sector in Israel: An Approach for Working with a Traditional Population." *Journal of Sex and Marital Therapy* 22, no. 1: 54–62.

Ozyegin, G. 2015. *New Desires, New Selves: Sex, Love and Piety among Turkish Youth*. New York: New York University Press.

Pappé, I. 2006. *The Ethnic Cleansing of Palestine*. Oxford, UK: Oneworld.

———. 2011. *The Forgotten Palestinians*. New Haven, CT: Yale University Press.

Parla, A. 2001. "The 'Honor' of the State: Virginity Examinations in Turkey." *Feminist Studies* 27, no. 1: 65–88.

Pateman, C. 1988. *The Sexual Contract*. Stanford, CA: Stanford University Press.

Peirce, L. 2010. "Domesticating Sexuality: Harem Culture in Ottoman Imperial Law." In *Harem Histories: Envisioning Places and Living Spaces*, edited by M. Booth. Durham, NC: Duke University Press: 104–35.

Peteet, J. 1991. *Gender in Crisis: Women and the Palestinian Resistance Movement*. New York: Columbia University Press.

———. 2017. *Space and Mobility in Palestine*. Bloomington: Indiana University Press.

Peterson, S. V. 1994. "Gendered Nationalism." *Peace Review* 6, no. 1: 77–83.

Pitts, V. 2003. *In the Flesh: The Cultural Politics of Body Modifications*. New York: Palgrave Macmillan.

Pursely, S. 2012. "Daughters of the Right Path: Family Law, Homosocial Publics, and the Ethic of Intimacy in the Works of Shi'I Revivalist Bin Al-Huda." *Journal of Middle East Women's Studies* 8, no. 2: 51–77.

Puwar, N. 2004. *Space Invaders: Race, Gender and Bodies Out of Place*. Oxford, UK: Berg.

Rabinowitz, D. 2001. "The Palestinian Citizens of Israel, the Concept of Trapped Minority and the Discourse of Transnationalism in Anthropology." *Ethnic and Racial Studies* 24, no. 1: 64–85.

Rabinowitz, D., and K. Abu-Baker. 2005. *Coffins on Our Shoulders: The Experience of the Palestinian Citizens of Israel*. Berkeley: University of California Press.

Ratner, A. 1996. *The Effect of Legal and Extra-legal Variables on Sentencing among Jews and Arabs in Israel*. Haifa, Isr.: University of Haifa Press.

Ray, C. 2013. "Interracial Sex and the Making of Empire." In *A Companion to Diaspora and Transnationalism*, edited by A. Quayson and G. Daswani, 190–211. London: Blackwell.

Richter-Devroe, S. 2018. *Women's Political Activism in Palestine: Peacebuilding, Resistance, and Survival*. Urbana: University of Illinois Press.

Robinson, S. 2013. *Citizen Strangers: Palestinians and the Birth of Israel's Liberal Settler State*. Stanford, CA: Stanford University Press.

Rosenberg, R. 2002. "On the Collective Criminalization of Political Protestors." *Adalah's Review* 3: 9–25.

Rosenfeld, H. 1968. "Change, Barriers to Change, and Contradictions in the Arab Village Family." *American Anthropologist* 70, no. 4: 732–52.

Rosenfeld, H., and M. Al-Haj. 1987. *Social Change and Family Processes: Arab Communities in Israel*. Boulder, CO: Westview.

Rouhana, N., and A. Ghanem. 1998. "The Crisis of Minorities in Ethnic States: The Case of Palestinian Citizens in Israel." *International Journal of Middle East Studies* 30, no. 3: 321–46.

Sa'ar, A. 2004. "Many Ways of Becoming a Woman: The Case of Unmarried Israeli-Palestinian 'Girls.'" *Ethnology* 43, no. 1: 1–18.

———. 2007. "Contradictory Location: Assessing the Position of Palestinian Women Citizens of Israel." *Journal of Middle East Women's Studies* 3, no. 3: 47–74.

Sa'di, A. 2002. "Catastrophe, Memory and Identity: Al-Nakbah as a Component of Palestinian Identity." *Israel Studies* 7, no. 2: 175–98.

Sa'di, A., and L. Abu-Lughod, eds. 2007. *Nakba: Palestine, 1948, and the Claims of Memory*. New York: Columbia University Press.

Salamanca, J. O., M. Qato, K. Rabie, and S. Samour, eds. 2012. "Past Is Present: Settler Colonialism in Palestine." *Settler Colonial Studies* 2, no. 1: 1–8.

Salih, R. 2017. "Bodies That Walk, Bodies That Talk, Bodies That Love: Palestinian Women Refugees, Affectivity, and the Politics of the Ordinary." *Antipode* 49, no. 3: 742–60.

Sayigh, R. 1979. *Palestinians: From Peasants to Revolutionaries*. London: Zed.

———. 1987. "Femmes palestiniennes: une histoire en quête d'historiens." *Revue d'études palestiniennes* 23 (Spring): 13–33.

———. 2007. "Nakba Stories: Between Being and Knowing." In Sa'di and Abu-Lughod. *Nakba: Palestine, 1948, and the Claims of Memory*. New York: Columbia University Press, 135–58.

Schildkrout, E. 2004. "Inscribing the Body." *Annual Review of Anthropology* 33: 319–44.

Secor, A. 2002. "The Veil and Urban Space in Istanbul: Women's Dress, Mobility and Islamic Knowledge." *Gender, Place and Culture* 9, no. 1: 5–22.

Sehlikoglu, S. 2016. "Exercising in Comfort: Islamicate Culture of Mahremiyet in Everyday Istanbul." *Journal of Middle East Women's Studies* 12, no. 2: 143–65.

Sereny, G. 1977. *Into that Darkness: From Mercy Killing to Mass Murder*. London: Picador.

Shafir, G., and Y. Peled. 2002. *Being Israeli: The Dynamics of Multiple Citizenship*. Cambridge: Cambridge University Press.

Shahar, I. 2015. *Legal Pluralism in the Holy City*. New York: Routledge.

Shalabi, M. 2010. "The Sexual Politics of Palestinian Women in Israel." In *Displaced at Home: Ethnicity and Gender among Palestinians in Israel*, edited by R. A. Kanaaneh and I. Nusair, 153–68. New York: State University of New York Press.

Shalhoub-Kevorkian, N. 2004. "Militarization and Policing: Police Reactions to Violence against Palestinian Women in Israel." *Social Identities* 10, no. 2: 171–94.

———. 2012. "The Grammar of Rights in Colonial Contexts: The Case of Palestinian Women in Israel." *Middle East Law and Government* 4, no. 1: 106–51.

———. 2015. *Security Theology, Surveillance, and the Politics of Fear*. Cambridge: Cambridge University Press.

Shalhoub-Kevorkian, N, S. Ihmoud, and S. Dahir-Nashif. 2014. "Sexual Violence, Women's Bodies, and Israeli Settler Colonialism." *Jadaliyya*, November 17.

http://www.jadaliyya.com/pages/index/19992/sexual-violence-women's
-bodies-and-israeli-settler.

Sharabi, H. 1988. *Neopatriarchy: A Theory of Distorted Change in Arab Society.*
Oxford: Oxford University Press.

Sharoni, S. 1995. *Gender and the Israeli-Palestinian Conflict: The Politics of Women's
Resistance.* New York: Syracuse University Press.

Shilling, C. 1993. *The Body and Social Theory.* 2nd ed. Thousand Oaks, CA: Sage.

Shlaim, A. 1999. "The Debate about 1948." In *The Israel/Palestine Question,* edited
by Ilan Pappé, 139–60. London: Routledge.

Shuttle, P., and P. Redgrove. 2005. *The Wise Wound: Menstruation and Everywoman.*
London: Marion Boyers, London: Paladin.

Slyomovics, S. 1998. *The Object of Memory: Arab and Jew Narrate the Palestinian
Village,* Philadelphia: University of Pennsylvania Press.

———. 2007. "The Rape of Qula, a Destroyed Palestinian Village." In Sa'di and
Abu-Lughod, 27–51.

Smith, A. 2003. "Not an Indian Tradition: The Sexual Colonization of Native
Peoples." *Hypathia* 18, no. 3: 70–85.

Smooha, S. 1997. "Ethnic Democracy: Israel as an Archetype." *Israel Studies* 2, no.
2: 198–224.

Spivak, G. C. 1988. "Can the Subaltern Speak?" In *Marxism and the Interpretation of
Culture,* edited by C. Nelson and L. Grossberg, 271–313. London: Macmillan.

———. 1992. "Women in Difference: Mahasweta 'Devi's Douloti the Bountiful.'"
In *Nationalisms and Sexualities,* edited by A. Parker, M. Russo, D. Sommer, and
P. Yeager, 96–120. New York: Routledge.

Stasiulis, D., and N. Yuval-Davis. 1995. *Unsettling Settler Societies: Articulations of
Gender, Race, Ethnicity, and Class.* London: Sage.

Stoler, A. 1989. "Making Empire Respectable: The Politics of Race and Sexual
Morality in 20th-Century Colonial Cultures." *American Ethnologist* 16, no. 4:
634–60.

———. 1995. *Race and the Education of Desire.* Durham, NC: Duke University
Press.

———. 2001. "Matters of Intimacy as Matters of State: A Response." *Journal of
American History* 88, no. 3: 893–97.

———. 2002. *Carnal Knowledge and Imperial Power: Race and the Intimate in
Colonial Rule.* Berkeley: University of California Press.

———. 2006. *Haunted by Empire: Geographies of Intimacy in North American
History.* Durham, NC: Duke University Press.

———. 2008. "Imperial Debris: Reflections on Ruins and Ruination." *Cultural
Anthropology* 23, no. 2: 191–219.

Swedenburg, T. 1995. *Memories of Revolt: The 1936–1939 Rebellion and the Palestinian
National Past.* Minneapolis: University of Minnesota Press.

Sweetman, P. 1999. "Anchoring the (Postmodern) Self? Body Modification, Fashion, and Identity." *Body and Society* 5, no. 2: 51–76.

Tavris, C. 1992. *The Mismeasure of Women: Why Women Are Not the Better Sex, the Inferior Sex, or the Opposite Sex*. New York: Simon and Schuster.

Tekiner, R. 1988. "The 'Who Is a Jew' Controversy in Israel: A Product of Political Zionism." In *Anti-Zionism: Analytical Reflections*, edited by R. Tekiner, S. Abed-Rabbo, and N. Mezvisnky. Brattleboro, VT: Amana.

Thompson, B. Y. 2015. *Covered in Ink: Tattoos, Women, and the Politics of the Body*. New York: New York University Press.

Tilley, V. 2005. *The One-State Solution*. Ann Arbor: University of Michigan Press.

Turner, T. 1994. "Bodies and Anti-bodies: Flesh and Fetish in Contemporary Social Theory." In *Embodiment and Experience: The Existential Ground of Culture and Self*, edited by T. Csordas, 27–47. Cambridge: Cambridge University Press.

———. 1995. "Social Body and Embodied Subject: Bodiliness, Subjectivity, and Sociality among the Kayapo." *Cultural Anthropology* 10, no. 2: 143–54.

Ussher, J. 2006. *Managing the Monstrous Feminine: Regulating the Reproductive Body*. New York: Routledge.

Van Dinter, M. H. 2005. *The World of Tattoo: An Illustrated History*. Amsterdam: KIT.

Veracini, L. 2010a. "Imagined Geographies of Settler Colonialism." In *Making Settler Colonial Space*, edited by T. B. Mar and P. Edmonds, 179–97. London: Palgrave Macmillan.

———. 2010b. *Settler Colonialism: A Theoretical Overview*. London: Palgrave Macmillan.

———. 2011. "Introducing Settler Colonial Studies." *Settler Colonial Studies* 1, no. 1: 1–12.

Vostral, S. L. 2008. *Under Wraps: A History of Menstrual Hygiene Technology*. Lanham, MD: Lexington.

Walby, S. 1990. *Theorizing Patriarchy*. New York: Blackwell.

Warnock, K. 1990. *Land before Honor: Palestinian Women in the Occupied Territories*. Houndmills, UK: Macmillan.

Weitz, R. 2001. "Women and Their Hair: Seeking Power through Resistance and Accommodation." *Gender and Society* 15, no. 5: 667–86.

White, J. 2005. "Marks of Transgression: The Tattooing of Europeans in the Pacific Islands." In *Tattoo: Bodies, Art and Exchange in the Pacific and the West*, edited by T. Nicholas, A. Cole, and B. Douglas, 44–69. Durham, NC: Duke University Press.

Wolfe, P. 1994. "Nation and MiscegeNation: Discursive Continuity in the Post-Mabo Era." *Social Analysis* 36: 93–253.

———. 2002. "Race and Racialization: Some Thoughts." *Postcolonial Studies* 5, no. 1: 51–62.

———. 2005. "Race and Citizenship." *Organization of American Historians (OAH) Magazine of History* 18, no. 5: 66–71.

———. 2006. "Settler Colonialism and the Elimination of the Native." *Journal of Genocide Research* 8, no. 4: 387–409.

Working Group on the Status of Palestinian Women Citizens of Israel. 2016. *List of Issues Related to the Status of Palestinian Women Citizens of Israel.* https:// tbinternet.ohchr.org/Treaties/CEDAW/Shared%20Documents/ISR/INT _CEDAW_ICS_ISR_24248_E.pdf.

Yegenolgu, M. 1998 *Colonial Fantasies: Toward A Feminist Reading of Orientalism.* Cambridge: Cambridge University Press.

Yiftachel, O. 1997. "Israeli Society and Jewish-Palestinian Reconciliation: Ethnocracy and Its Territorial Contradictions." *Middle East Journal* 51, no. 4: 505–19.

———. 2006. *Ethnocracy: Land and Identity Politics in Israel/Palestine.* Philadelphia: University of Pennsylvania Press.

Young, I. M. 1997. "Menstrual Meditations." In *One Female Body Experience: Throwing like a Girl and Other Essays in Feminist Philosophy and Social Theory,* edited by I. M. Young, 79–122. Bloomington: Indiana University Press.

Young, L. 1996. *Fear of the Dark: Race, Gender and Sexuality in the Cinema.* New York: Routledge.

Yuval-Davis, N. 1997. *Gender and Nation.* London: Sage.

Zengin, A., and S. Sehlikoglu. 2015. "Introduction: Why Revisit Intimacy?" *Cambridge Journal of Anthropology* 33, no. 2: 20–25.

———. 2016. "Everyday Intimacies of the Middle East." In Zengin, A., and S. Sehlikoglu, eds. Special Issue: Everyday Intimacies of the Middle East, *Journal of Middle East Women's Studies* 12, no. 2: 139–42.

Zoabi, H. 2009. "Palestinian Women in the Israeli Labor Market." *Jadal* 4, Haifa: Mada al-Carmel Arab Center for Applied Social Research.

INDEX

Note: Page numbers in *italics* indicate a figure.

Abdo, Nahla, 10, 16, 99, 176
Abed, Asra'a Zidan, 41
abjection, 101
Abu-Baker, Khawla, 15
Abu Hanna, Talleen, 75–76
Abulhawa, Susan, 90
Abu-Rabia, Rawia, 83
adoption, 164–66, 172n1
Ahmed, Sara, 40, 46, 49
al'ard qabl al'ird (land before honor), 4, 37, 133. See also *'ird* (honor)
Al-Haj, Majid, 68
al-Naqab, xiii, 11, 22, 27, 70, 76, 77, 78, 80, 83, 85, 88, 120, 151n2, 193
Al-Qaws for Sexual and Gender Diversity in Palestinian Society, 73
anal sex, 138, 145
Anderson, Kim, 26
Anthias, Floya, 61
antibodies, 106
antimiscegenation, 160, 161
a'rāb (landowning Bedouins), 117; and intermarriage, 82, 88–89; organization of, 77; and racist language, 86–87
"Arab-Israeli" concept, 14, 51–55
Arab Ladies Club, 178
Arab Women's Association (AWA), 178, 179
Arab Women's Executive Committee (AWE), 178

Arab Women's Union (PAWU), 178
artificial insemination, 165, 168
Ashkenazi Jews, 10, 13, 46, 90, 112, 164, 182, 204
'asl (ancestry), concept of, 80–81
assimilation, 14, 56
Aswat—Palestinian Gay Women in Haifa, 73, 75
avodah ivrit (Hebrew labor), 6
AWA. See Arab Women's Association (AWA)
AWE. See Arab Women's Executive Committee (AWE)

badal (exchange marriage), 68, 91n3
Baker, Khawla Abu, 69
beauty standards, 89–90, 108–9
Beauvoir, Simone de, 102
Bedouins: *a'rāb* (landowning Bedouins), 77, 86–87, 88–89, 117; black, 77, 82, 86–90; categories of, 77; *fellaheen* (landless "peasants"), 77, 82, 88; as Palestinian subgroup, 11, 47; research methodology among, 24
Bedouin women: and *'asl* (ancestry), 80–81; dress of, 120–21; inadequate education for, 66; and intermarriage, 70; limited occupations for, 69; limited opportunities for, 66; and marriage, 81–84, 88–89;

237

KIM JEZABEL ZINNGREBE is Deputy Program Director of the BA in History at the University of London Worldwide, where she teaches Modern European and Middle Eastern History. She is currently based in Frankfurt, Germany, where she also works as a birth doula for queer and migrant families.